DIANE ALISA

A Love Letter to Suburbia

How to Restore the American Village

First published by The Olive Conservatory 2024

First edition

ISBN (paperback): 979-8-9919183-2-9
ISBN (hardcover): 979-8-9919183-3-6
ISBN (digital): 979-8-9919183-4-3

Editing by Audrey Barth
Advisor: Spencer Tuft

This book was professionally typeset on Reedsy.
Find out more at reedsy.com

For my children

—*my reason for writing this book,*
and for the world I dream they will inherit.

Contents

Acknowledgments

With deep gratitude to my village—

To my incredible husband, whose sacrifices of time and talent made this journey possible.

To Mom, the very first to read these words and believe in them.

To Audrey, whose unwavering dedication and countless hours brought clarity and shine to every page.

To Katie, for caring for my children in my hour of need.

To John and Tiffany, whose thoughtful feedback was essential in shaping this book. Your support means more than words can express.

Prologue

"It's a fine life!"

Disney managed to make child labor look glamorous with its release of *The Newsies* in 1992[1]. Although its initial box office debut was lackluster, it progressively became a cult classic as it caught hold of the American imagination. It is truly an American story about grit, determination, and triumph—the miraculous victory of working-class children who banded together against crony newspaper companies and employers who wished to take full advantage of them without proper pay.

These working children were scrappy and lively. Despite their apparent poverty, most modern Americans would consider them well-dressed. So distant from us, we see the foreign eccentricities of a time when adults pedaled out children to work. 'Despicable' is the word most would use to describe it today. Still, we can't help but coo at old photos of little girls in stockings with buckled shoes and little boys sporting berets and suspenders while trampling through crowded streets, selling newspapers for lousy pennies, some being as young as six years old.

Children were an integral part of everyday society. They took hold of city streets, sidewalks, stoops, balconies, and alleyways. There were always new things to explore, new people to meet, and new trouble to get into— a conglomeration of adult mimicry, child-like interests, and, best of all, freedom. Imagine children scavenging for trinkets, peddling goods, and

1

buying fresh produce from local shops. These children organized the world around them. They created social systems and unwritten rules with other children, protecting their properties and profits. They walked to school in droves. Much of their money went to their families for survival. Still, they managed to salvage enough funds for some personal consumption. They inhabited candy shops, amusement parks, vaudeville halls, affordable eateries, and pushcart vendors. The streets were their playgrounds, and the neighborhood shopkeeper was their moral check.

They also dealt with specific challenges like extreme weather, food scarcity, poor working conditions, and unfamiliar deadly illnesses. *The New England Journal of Public Policy* cites that a percentage of these children were homeless. The fixation on these issues is why 'Newsie culture' is often considered dangerous and absurd.

Despite these hardships, the child homeless population is much greater today, and this era deserves more nuance than most people give it credit for.[2] David Nasaw, author of *Children of the City: At Work and at Play*, interviewed some former working children and asked what they thought of their childhood. They expressed hardship but mostly recounted the fun, mischief, friends, and hope they had growing up on American streets.[3] This narrative contradicts the usual political view that these working children were simply victims of despair and abuse.

The story of American Newsies offers a compelling lesson: these children were exemplars of resilience and ingenuity. Despite working within an imperfect system, they thrived thanks to the unique opportunities and supportive environment around them. Their presence in American life was so commonplace, they became a political force of their own. Can you imagine modern children achieving such a feat? Their experiences cultivated qualities—such as resourcefulness, responsibility, and self-reliance—that many children today find challenging to develop. The Newsies' success, despite their youth, backed by their community and families, highlights how their environment molded them into capable and purposeful individuals.

The "American Dream"

Like "Newsie culture," many Americans long for a bygone era depicted in Norman Rockwell's paintings. Whether we experienced his era or not, there is something idealistic, hopeful, and truly *American* about his work. It draws us in and keeps us thinking about ol' America—perhaps with haggard sadness.

Consider some of his greatest works: a mischievous group of half-naked boys cling to their clothing as they dart from a no-swim zone; two teens sit beside an intrigued war veteran, ready to go to a school dance, while the bartender admires the girl's corsage; a child surveying, rather overtly, a love-struck couple entwined on a train; or a large family gathered around a grand turkey dinner. Rockwell's distinct and charming ability to represent community, patriotism, multi-generational families, vibrant children, and prosperity keeps us coming back again and again. It's an America that inspired the world and drew in exceptional people from all nations.

The Newsies and Rockwell capture the essence of the "American Dream"—a culture brimming with family, community, and a deep sense of morality. Discounting the Declaration of Independence as the first and most notable declaration of equality and freedom, "All men are created equal, that they are endowed by their Creator," the popularization of the phrase "American Dream" comes from a book called *Epic America* by author James Truslow Adams in 1931, where he stated:

> *It is not a dream of motor cars and high wages merely, but a dream of social order in which each man and each woman shall be able to attain to the fullest stature of which they are innately capable, and be recognized by others for what they are, regardless of the fortuitous*

circumstances of their birth… It has been a dream of being able to grow to the fullest development as man and woman, unhampered by the arrears that had slowly been erected by older civilizations, unrepressed by social orders that had developed for the benefit of classes rather than for the simple human being of any and every class. And that dream has been realized more fully in actual life here than anywhere else, though very imperfectly even among ourselves.

Adam's dream of America is a meritocracy in which every person can grow to their fullest potential—a place where people are free from the oppressive nature of aristocratic vices and systems that predetermine their worth and life status.[4]

Adam's version of America often seems at odds with her current state. According to a 2023 poll from *Pew Research*, nearly 63% of Americans feel the U.S. is in a moral, emotional, physical, and economic crisis.[5]

Since its inception, the "American Dream" has endured many reinterpretations, but none have permeated American culture more than the 1950s suburban ideal. In the 1950s, the "American Dream" was living in a quiet, peaceful suburban neighborhood with a wife and children, taking a 9-to-5 job with a pension, and playing baseball with your kids on the weekends. The suburban experiment epitomized the "American Dream," promising a life of comfort, security, and upward mobility.

This interpretation has largely remained since its outset—at least, acquiring a suburban home is still part of the equation, with Pew Research finding a 42% increase in desire for suburban living since 2018.[6] However, the "American Dream" took a severe shift in attitude during the Great Recession of 2008. *The New York Intelligencer* argues that it was around this time, Americans stopped believing in the American dream, "What's not to like? Plenty, as it turns out. The mood in America is arguably as dark as it has ever been in the modern era."[7] While the American Dream once evoked images of suburban bliss and familial stability, today, many Americans find themselves grappling with a sense of disillusionment and uncertainty. This is further emphasized by a survey conducted by the *Public Religion Research Institute* that found that nearly half of Americans no longer believe that the "American Dream" holds true today.[8] This faith crisis is rooted in many factors, including economic instability, social inequality, and deepening differences between urban and suburban communities.

Individuals may be inclined to blame political leaders, technological advancements that seem beyond our abilities to handle, or the ideological propagation of once-trusted institutions.

From my observations, I have determined that deep infrastructural problems have instigated and perpetuated the crisis of the "American Dream." Since suburbia began in the 1950s, it has caused cataclysmic cultural consequences in a relatively short amount of time. As we delve deeper into the consequences of suburbia as we know it today, it becomes clear that it has failed to deliver on its lofty promises of safety and peace. The Newsies and Norman Rockwell did not grow up in a system of American suburbs, but they represent the type of America worth admiring. It is my hope that by addressing infrastructural failures, Americans will recover faith in the original "American Dream" and recapture the essence of "The Newsies" and Norman Rockwell's paintings.

What Is the Problem?

As a small introduction to myself, I've only recently entered the urbanist realm, co-founding an organization with my husband called End Car Dependency in Utah. While many examples in this book are from Utah, they illustrate infrastructural issues and principles that apply across the United States.

The issues caused by poor urban design have grated on me for a long time, even though I couldn't quite identify the cause. My frustration finally found its voice when I stumbled across a YouTube video by author Jason Slaughter on his channel *Not Just Bikes*. His ten-minute video on suburbia, titled "Why We Won't Raise Our Kids in Suburbia," led me down a rabbit hole of research and realizations.[9] I felt my perspective transform, and I was compelled to share this new direction with everyone I encountered. While on this journey of discovery, I saw how merely reshaping our environment alleviates many of the burdens American citizens face today and replaces the monotony of our lives with vitality and flourishing culture.

When I've discussed that almost every political, social, and economic issue ties back to the conception of car dependence, some have relayed to me that the problems we face are trivial. By arguing that Americans live in the most prosperous era in history, they dismiss our visible suffering, labeling us as simply 'spoiled rotten.' This view is deeply painful for me and those of us genuinely suffering under the current system—our voices unheard. It's striking that many who champion the status quo have faced their own hardships yet persist in believing that 'all is well' as if conditioned to accept their circumstances. To them, I say, sure, American materialism is breathtaking to behold, but if a well-intended parent thought the only thing their child needed was *things*, they would predictably stunt them. Children need more than material comforts; they require consistent guidance, emotional warmth, and opportunities for exploration and learning to thrive. America is like an overindulged child, spoon-fed by overbearing government forces and corporate parents that neglect genuine care and essential needs. Americans are suffering; without decisive action, this suffering will only deepen.

As we discuss solutions to help Americans flourish again, I argue that experimental suburban infrastructure has unraveled America's cultural excellence in a dazzlingly short amount of time. In doing so, the localization, self-sustainability, and vitality of communities crumbled. This system prioritizes R1 zoning, separating commercial areas from single-family housing.

This change in habitat has tragically crippled the middle class, induced physical health complications, hindered healthy family development, and, with that, brought about a national mental health crisis.

Suburban infrastructure, filled with car-dependent, sprawled, and low-density housing, is a degenerative system. Given enough time, it fails and brings misery to both its inhabitants and those barred from entry. This is because suburban infrastructure nationally and acutely shackles the free market, creates unavoidable class separation, falsely romanticizes low-density, parasitically contributes to the uglification of states, and enables the death of small businesses.

The advent of technology has also exacerbated this urban problem by expanding our social networks to an incomprehensible extent. Without an environment that innately fosters localization and community, individuals and families turn to the vast and empty virtual world for connection but end up feeling more isolated than before. Since adopting the suburban experiment, falsely epitomized as the "American Dream," we have forgotten American systems that once supported strong communities.

When it really comes down to why I am doing this, having my first son shook me to the core. I couldn't bear the thought of raising my children in this environment and vowed to do everything I could to create a better world for them and for myself. Many of the struggles Americans face stem from infrastructural corruption rather than moral failure, and I believe in the inherent goodness of the American people. This faith in Americans has fueled my conviction that change will come.

With deep respect for the brilliant individuals who first identified and tackled these infrastructure issues, this book aims to build upon their efforts and provide further insights and solutions.

I

From Asphalt to Awakening: Rethinking Suburbia's Promise

1

Dear Suburbia, it wasn't supposed to be this way.

We collectively harbor a quiet guilt for suspecting something might be amiss in American life. We seemingly have it all, yet there's a palpable emptiness. This dissatisfaction is coupled with a nagging feeling of selfishness for wanting *more*. What more could we be given? It has become my mission to give the American public the language to describe this unease. There *is* something grave missing from American life. The essential landscapes and conditions that support lasting health and happiness have been withheld from us. We lack a clean earth, community, multi-generational family life, locality, purpose, meaningful recreation, religion, quality food, healthy children and parents, and work that helps us feel fulfilled. These things are possible when America creates *environments* that cultivate these values. How a society builds its cities is the scaffolding to a wholesome culture and meaningful life.

To my fellow urban enthusiasts reading, adding more bus stops, improving walkability, or implementing more bike lanes is not enough. Americans must undergo a profound paradigm shift in how we live. We must understand the catastrophic effects of an infrastructure that only values cars or single-family houses and start uplifting an infrastructure that values *people.*

What America lacks now are villages: functional places where communities support families and city structures abundantly distribute wealth through free market values. In tandem, villages will return political and economic power to the American people, create beautiful and peaceful spaces to live in, and enable greater well-being for the average American—most importantly, for children.

There are two competing blueprints for how people build societies: The first is the modern-day "Car-only" or "Suburban Infrastructure," and the second is the most historically relevant—"Pedestrian-first." In this book, I refer to pedestrian-first societies as cities or villages (a much less dense cousin).

Pedestrian-first societies are the healthiest and most common building standard among developed nations.[10] Human ingenuity designs these environments to be convenient and easy to navigate, offering a range of transportation options: walking, animal and buggy, cycling, cars, trains, buses, or trams. Commercial and residential properties are combined in this environment, which we now refer to as "mixed-use." This system fosters a vibrant community, leading to numerous benefits. Combining commercial and residential properties promotes wealth accumulation as people work and live side-by-side. They rely heavily on local crops for trade and consumption. With walkability, significant consideration is taken to make public spaces appealing.

These societies are not only beautiful and peaceful but also functional. They are generally safer for people of all ages, including tiny children. Many of these cities exist worldwide as revered tourist attractions for their awe-inspiring aesthetic and sense of place, but pedestrian-first cities are nothing new. How these villages developed has stood the test of time. They span back to any renowned developing nation as far as history allows:

Rome, Italy; Athens, Greece; Quebec City, Canada; Copenhagen, Denmark; Jerusalem, Israel; Kyoto, Japan.

In contrast, car-only infrastructure—a problematic zoning framework that prioritizes cars and suburban sprawl—is linked to nearly every major cultural, political, and economic issue in modern America. Once a person understands its natural consequences, it cannot be unseen or ignored. American suburbia is essentially an embryo, just 70 years old, in the context of human societies. Despite its recent conception, it has, like a parasite, progressively made Americans very ill. It will ultimately conquer the American body in its tyrannical lifecycle.

I have noticed many conspiratorial conversations suggesting that anyone trying to shift America away from being solely car-centric is part of a Socialist or New World Order movement. These ideas are partly because America has pushed its pedestrian-first cities into extinction, giving individuals no frame of reference for positive examples.

Conspirators need to recognize that even 'suburban' America has a rich history of pedestrian-first cities that were both functional and world-famous. Suburbanites often dismiss my thoughts by saying, "Oh, so you're interested in European villages," implying that building functional villages or cities is unique to Europe and not part of America's identity. Although generations of demolition have hidden most of our previous cities to make way for automobiles, much of America's vast potential for connection without vehicles is only temporarily lost. Constructing functional places is just as much a part of America's identity as it is of Europe's. Despite popular opinion, those who are trying to make America less car-centric are not being *progressive* but rather *restorative*, reclaiming the operative American landscape that was once common.

Despite Carl Benz's invention of the car in 1885, these cities continued to be built in America and thrived as ever. The invention of the vehicle itself is not the issue. Rather, the car is merely one of many tools available to the public in a pedestrian-first infrastructure.

Being a car-independent nation is not the same as being car-free. It's about creating an abundant environment where people can live without a car; if done well, they might even prefer not to have one at all. When cities abandon harmful zoning laws and design streets for people, societies thrive, and driving becomes less appealing—even for car owners.

To the average American, car independence seems like a crazy concept. The justifiable response to asking Americans to walk more is fear—removing cars from our current framework would be catastrophic. Nobody wants to bike 40 minutes to the grocery store. The public is further jaded when activists fiercely push public transportation onto a city or town that hasn't been designed to accommodate it.

In a city planning meeting I once attended near my hometown, the city council proposed implementing a bus transportation network in a very car-centric area. A limited train system had been established only five years earlier, serving much of the county and connecting it to the metropolitan areas. A heated resident stood up to oppose the new plan: "I see the train pass by all day, and nobody is on it! We don't want the buses!" The environment was not prepared for another extensive transportation option, and they instinctively knew it. Still, they attributed the issue to the 'lousy' bus system rather than the suburban infrastructure.

The American public also worries that conniving government authorities are trying to "steal away their cars." PragerU released a video called "The War on Cars," arguing, "The reason why people love cars? Personal freedom. Which is why regulators can't stand them."[11] They misunderstand that the American people are, in fact, slaves to the infrastructure and the corporate car industry. The irony is that the real conspirators are the historical figures who instigated our dependency on car travel. If gas prices become inaccessible or government authorities manage to destroy American cars, Americans are doomed. The more fear individuals have that their 'freedom' is under threat, the more they play right into the hands of insatiable corporations that benefit from this structure. Americans are fighting the wrong battle. They should be contending to transform American suburbs into self-reliant villages so prosperous they no longer rely on corporate or government entities.

To understand how we arrived at this point, it's essential to look at the history of cars and their accessibility to middle-class citizens. Despite modern belief, the rising popularity of cars was not entirely welcome. As cars began filling the streets, both reckless and drunk driving started to kill or injure residents. According to the Smithsonian, by 1925, automobile accidents accounted for two-thirds of all deaths in cities with populations over 25,000.[12] The streets, which used to be places of safety, social interaction, and business, were invaded by dangerous and chaotic vehicles. Citizens joined together to politically remove cars from the city entirely and promote extensive public transportation.[13]

Anxious about diminishing popularity, the car industry lobbied for a new law in the late 1920s. According to author Peter D. Norton in his book *Fighting Traffic: The Dawn of the Motor Age in the American City*, the car industry, eager to shift blame away from drivers and protect its public image, campaigned for the concept of jaywalking as we know it today.[14]

This law placed shame and dues on the disobedient pedestrian rather than the dangerous cars. This radically shifted the cultural view of cars versus people, squashing any objections to vehicles. Automobiles became king of the streets, not the people who were the rightful owners. Streets were stripped of public use, and people could no longer walk where they pleased, with little to no alternatives. Perhaps difficult for the modern American to understand, this was only the beginning of an absorbing loss to the people of the time and for generations to come.

Fast-forward to the 1950s: zoning laws, originally established in 1917 to prevent pollutant industrial factories near residential areas, had since evolved. This evolution included the creation of R1 zoning, a reactionary measure to the Supreme Court ruling *Buchanan v. Warley*, which addressed racial housing segregation.[15] R1 zoning was implemented to establish exclusive single-family housing areas, further entrenching segregation and restricting the free market.

After WWII, war veterans returned from combat. In a near-traumatic response, the country longed for peace. Not everyone could escape the city and live on a farm, but they could move to a new development called "the suburbs." Herbert Hoover's New Deal Federal administrator, Rexford G. Tugwell, said, "My idea is to go just outside centers of population, pick up cheap land, build a whole community, and entice people into it. Then go back into the cities and tear down whole slums and make parks for them."[16] The American suburbs, colloquially known as R1 zoning, were born and quickly became popular as millions of families moved there. Due to the new zoning separation of commercial and residential areas, every suburbanite had to own at least one family car, causing the automobile industry to boom like never before.

Unfortunately, this wasn't entirely due to consumer desire. In 1949, the states sued the motor and oil manufacturers in a monopolization conspiracy. In *United States v. National City Lines*, major motor and oil companies were found guilty of using front companies to acquire public transportation businesses and destroy their tracks. This left the public with more space for cars and open roads but stripped them of alternative transportation options.

The lawsuit, "charged defendants with having knowingly and continuously engaged in an unlawful combination and conspiracy to secure control of a substantial number of the companies that provide public transportation service in various cities, towns, and counties of the several states, and to eliminate and exclude all competition in the sale of motor busses, petroleum products, tires, and tubes to such transportation companies then owned or controlled by National City Lines, Inc., or Pacific City Lines, Inc."[17]

After being caught dismantling transportation options, the car and oil industries were not required to restore the thousands of streetcars lost. The damage was done. At breakneck speeds, Americans were zoned out of the option to commute to work or run errands without a car. Only a minority of the American public was bothered by this; most were enamored with the glamour of the vehicle, a symbol of status and freedom.

Now, instead of walking to a neighbor's bakery for fresh bread, Americans could drive to Dunkin' Donuts or the supermarket for Wonder Bread! Minimum parking laws were established to accommodate the monumental rise in motor vehicles, leading to guesswork about which buildings deserved more parking than others.

Traffic became unbearable in the blink of an eye due to increasing density and unprepared roads. In 1954, a propaganda film called *Give Yourself the Green Light* was released. It aimed to improve the general public's attitude toward road development in the United States, as cities and highways were becoming increasingly congested with cars.[18] With most public transportation gone and neighborhoods relying on cars to get around, the American public had to adapt without hesitation. In 1956, the *Federal-Aid Highway Act* provided the authority and funding to tear down cities to make way for more roads.[19] It failed to relieve traffic in any significant way.

Meanwhile, countless historic buildings, homes, churches, and schools across America were demolished to make way for more asphalt. Valued architecture, created with painstaking effort and magnificence, was lost. Entire neighborhoods that had once been functional and safe were split in two by noisy, fast-moving freeways; unable to sustain themselves, they transformed into slums. The scars from this irreparable loss remain to this day.[20]

As renowned urbanist Jane Jacobs discussed in *The Death and Life of Great American Cities*, housing projects with no mixed zoning were quickly built to compensate for displaced people in high-density cities like New York. This simultaneously discouraged mixed-income development. Low-income communities were shuffled into dull, dense areas plagued by cars from distant suburban traffic. Mom-and-pop shops were barred from entry, stifling prosperity, interest, and community engagement. Without the opportunity to start their own businesses or meaningfully invest in their neighborhoods, communities deteriorated, and families moved away when offered better financial opportunities.

Miraculously, some urban neighborhoods had the communal strength to maintain old zoning laws and reject new street designs with deep loathing. They did not face these issues and became rare and highly sought after. With the combined efforts of diverse businesses, individuals, and incomes, people continued to rule the streets. Their children explored freely, commerce thrived, and any trouble caused by rowdy teenagers or drunks was quickly squashed by local observers.[21]

The untouched city neighborhoods were very alluring. As a result, poor residents were pushed out to make room for a wealthier class of people. These areas rarely thrived, as the people who knew how to make them great were gone. Without involved community members, children in these areas could no longer safely roam the streets. As a form of consolation, empty fields of grass or children's parks were added. Since the parks were primarily designed for children and not for the average local, mothers seldom used them during certain times of the day. Uninhabited and bland, these areas often became hotspots for violent crime among unsupervised teenagers.

Suburbanites, a middle-class group that did not face the same problems, began to falsely correlate high density with crime. They were not crime-riddled like the so-called 'degenerate' city; they considered themselves a moral group, separate from the dreaded curse of high density and free to drive anywhere in their shiny new cars. The future seemed bright for them and their children. Unlike city-dwellers, whose children lacked greenery and streets to explore, suburban children could play outside until dusk, surrounded by rural America and perfectly manicured lawns. While historic and vibrant parts of America were being demolished, displacing families into bleak poverty, suburbanites enjoyed fresh air, new roads, malls, and a family-centered community. They were blissfully unaware of the problems and discriminated protectively against any non-homogeneity to maintain order.

The "American Dream" wasn't simply about egalitarian opportunity anymore; it was about living in the suburbs with a family and a job with a pension. Hollywood began producing content to reflect and capitalize on this new lifestyle, with shows like *I Love Lucy*, *The Andy Griffith Show*, and *Leave It to Beaver*. These shows captured the hearts of the American people with wholesome family propaganda, humor, and galvanized validation that this was the ideal place to raise their children. The suburban housewife became a central figure in this vision. After WWII, women, exhausted from bearing the burden of the American economy, embraced a purely maternal role, staying home and engaging with their like-minded neighbors. For the first time in history, the modern "suburban housewife" was born. At this moment, America, so caught up in corporate conspiracy and suburban gleam, forgot what it was like to live in a world where they could not exist without a car.

So much has been lost since the 1950s suburban movement, but the greatest loss is the impact on the American family. As we explore the pitfalls of car-centric infrastructure and discover principles to address them, the ultimate goal is to restore social and functional communities where families can once again thrive.

2

Dear Suburbia, it's not safe anymore.

This section is the most technical section in the book, but I do believe it is absolutely necessary to understand the key principles discussed later on.

Ever since I started driving, I have been haunted by the thought that I may be responsible for irreversible harm to another, especially a child, driving on American roads. I think about the fender bender I caused coming off the freeway and the whiplash I inflicted on the man in front of me with frequent sorrow. It could have been so much worse for both of us. Injury, disability, jail, death, or a lifetime of guilt are real possibilities for my lack of skill or distractibility. I have been told this is the risk I must take if I am to drive a car. Yet, driving isn't just a risk in suburbia—it's a mandate. The question isn't *if* you'll take that risk, but *when*.

I debated where to put this chapter because vehicle safety may be the least compelling argument an urbanist can make to a suburbanite. For them, if it comes between "freedom" and the risk of driving a car, they'll take the "freedom" every time. However, if America is to reprioritize its people, then *real* safety, peace, and choice for all must be reembedded within the infrastructure. Our roads are unsafe for everyone. Heartbreakingly, the National Safety Council states that, between pedestrian deaths and preventable vehicle deaths, over 46,000 people died in 2022.[22] Car deaths are only increasing. Not only do the tragedies of pedestrian and car deaths affect the direct victims and their families, but they also impact entire communities. A mother of two toddlers doesn't intend to hit a cycling student on her way to the grocery store. An aging grandfather, desperately clinging to his fading autonomy, doesn't mean to kill himself and two children on their way to school. A young and inexperienced teenager, distracted by peers, doesn't set out to skid in the snow and injure a family of five. These accidents are real examples of the tragic consequences of our current car-centric infrastructure.

The gut response to these common scenarios is usually, "Irresponsible drivers should be kicked off the road!" or, "The biker should've worn reflective gear." While there is some truth to these reactions, they overlook the fact that a combination of infrastructural failings repeatedly facilitates these situations. Even if someone admits to themselves, "I'm not that great of a driver, and I don't feel safe on the road..." what choice do they have? Most Americans face a framework that offers virtually no other transportation options, including their own two feet. Which ordinary person will be the next to face the lifelong nightmare of injuring a child on the road simply because America has failed to provide viable transportation alternatives?

Still, if an individual loses their license or chooses not to have one, they are indirectly ostracized from society. Instead, they must constantly rely on other forms of transportation, such as generous carpooling neighbors or inadequate public transit. If they are desperate enough, they may even drive illegally to survive.

So, how can pedestrian-first villages provide Americans with safer choices and save thousands of lives every year? While the goal is to reduce car dependence, designing infrastructure that accommodates and integrates vehicles effectively is essential. The impact of different types of roads on communities is significant—some enhance community life, while others destroy it. By grasping how modern car infrastructure contributes to these issues, communities can better resolve them. There are three key types of roads to consider: streets, roads, and stroads.

Streets and Roads

Streets are for people. They accommodate low-speed car travel, allowing cars to pass by an area slowly and steadily. A street is designed for a speed threshold of 15-25 mph or less. Its narrow width or variability is engineered to organically slow down drivers without needing speed limit signs or traffic enforcement. This design fosters safe and peaceful walkability. Consequently, streets are the most economically prosperous form of road design. With low speeds, communities can incorporate interesting and beautiful visual complexity into the environment without endangering drivers or pedestrians. However, streets are only feasible if car congestion is minimal and a town is localized with strategically implemented mixed-use zoning.[23]

The road was born from the safety and engineering standards of the 1950s. This design removes visual or physical obstacles to allow cars to travel from point A to point B as quickly as possible. Roads are most effective on the outskirts of society, with a speed design of 55 mph and up. Their wide, low-impact design forgives small mistakes that would otherwise result in immediate death at high speeds. Roads should not be placed near pedestrians or businesses, as they are dangerous, unlovely, and loud.[24]

Properly placed, these two road designs enhance the safety and charm of a village. They are the preferred type of connectors because they eschew car congestion, diminish or remove the hum of traffic, enable engaging spaces, promote small businesses, and provide safety and walkability, all while allowing speedy, uninterrupted travel. The street protects and prioritizes people, and the road protects drivers.

The Issue of Stroads

The third example is a new term coined by engineer Charles Marohn: a stroad. A stroad is exactly what it sounds like—a hybrid of a street and a road.[25] A street supports foot traffic for businesses or homes, while a road is designed for expedited travel. Stroads attempt to do both.

A stroad is the most popular type of road design in the United States. It is located near people and provides high-speed access to businesses in commercial areas, with speeds ranging from 25 to 55 mph. Stroads are often littered with stoplights to manage the high volume of drivers in metropolitan areas. They typically have many lanes, which leads to an over-reliance on stoplights rather than traffic-streaming roundabouts.

Stroads are ineffective at everything from moving cars to protecting pedestrians to enabling businesses. Despite their fast pace, they impede traffic flow. According to Charles Marohn, while traveling on a 30 mph stroad, he calculated that, due to the bloated number of stoplights, his average speed would have been under 10 miles per hour if he had never stopped.[26] That's a lot of high-speed starting and stopping with little gain. It would be incredibly frustrating if the United States Department of Transportation (USDOT) started putting speed bumps on the freeway! Yet Americans begrudgingly deal with stroads and feel delighted when granted a few green lights in a row, even though it's a deceptive victory.

The two alternatives to stroads provide routes where drivers can travel at a steady, uninterrupted pace, at speeds of either 10–25 mph or 55+ mph. Not only are both options faster for the driver, but it also feels better not to be stopped every thirty seconds. Why must individuals be forced to drive a $40,000 car yet endure the speed of a horse and buggy in every central domain in America? It feels exasperating. Knowing what I know now, it's more vexing than ever to be stopped at a light on a stroad, and it should be for everyone when they discover their inefficiencies.

Safer for Whom?

To understand the full scope of road safety issues, we need to look beyond driver behavior and examine the engineering behind our roads. While reckless driving contributes to road accidents, poor engineering practices are the root of many problems. The major issues with how roads are engineered in America stem from the 'standard of safety,' a widely accepted guideline from the 1950s originally designed for freeways. This standard has been applied to every type of new road-making, regardless of the space, with strict regulations. The 'standard of safety' is oxymoronic because many of its core values stem from the car industry's latent values established in the 1920s: the car is more important than anything. When car travel's efficiency and convenience are prioritized over pedestrians' safety and well-being, it begs the question: 'Safer for whom?'

One principle should be clear: cities should never place car infrastructure at lethal speeds near people. The speed of a stroad is much too dangerous for both drivers and pedestrians. While street and road designs are generally straightforward, stroads are preposterous to navigate and perilous to bike or walk by. Biking infrastructure is often merely painted, and sometimes, cities neglect to include sidewalks altogether. Multi-lanes, right turn lanes, slip lanes, left turn lanes, left turns on a yield red, left turns out of businesses (which become progressively more dangerous with added lanes), hawk crossings, zebra crossings for pedestrians, and endless stoplights—all contribute to this hazardous environment.

The idea perpetuated by modern road 'safety' is that drivers need to be unobstructed in every capacity: perfectly straight lanes, vegetation cut down for clear zones, unreasonably wide roads, etc. This type of design is suitable for high speeds because it makes the environment very forgiving for distracted drivers. However, when this "standard" is applied to road-making near people, as engineer Charles Marohn explains in his book *Confessions of a Recovering Engineer*, removing visual obstacles from a driver's path does not make things safer; it artificially bolsters the driver's belief that there is nothing to watch out for. This is how pedestrians and drivers end up getting killed.[27]

The complexity and diversity of an environment naturally prompt drivers to slow down around pedestrians. Features like trees, people, winding roads, narrow lanes, raised crosswalks, attractive architecture, art, businesses, and outdoor activities all signal the need for cautious driving. They communicate, "Beware! There are hazards in this area. Pay attention and drive more slowly." This prompts drivers to recognize that they are maneuvering a dangerous vehicle through a sensitive environment. However, when roads are widened or obstacles are removed under the guise of "improving safety," drivers and pedestrians receive conflicting messages. In response, engineers often install artificial speed limit signs to force drivers into compliance.

Driving on American roads requires constant discipline, and Americans do not live up to the challenge in some way or another. Historic downtown Center Street in Provo, Utah, aims to be pedestrian-friendly with its mom-and-pop shops, but its road design undermines this purpose. The speed limit is set at 15 mph to protect pedestrians. However, the road's width is intended for faster travel, making the speed limit seem arbitrary and fake. As a result, drivers frequently ignore the posted speed, getting up to 30 to 40 mph, even when passing by Provo's police department. Drivers instinctively sense the true purpose of the road, not the one dictated to them on the sign. The temptation to abandon the speed limit is too strong without proper street design. Provo Center Street further tried to improve drivers' behavior by adding two raised crosswalks. This startled oncoming drivers, unaware that their bumpers were about to get dinged, and only slightly reduced speeding. Provo Center Street's mismatched design makes it dangerous for everyone.

The dominance of cars in an infrastructure that exclusively favors them creates a sense of entitlement among drivers, who often believe getting to their destination is more urgent or important than the schedules of anyone outside their car. I witnessed this firsthand when I saw a biker attempting to cross an unmarked residential street that led into a busy road. The truck driver clearly saw the biker, but he barreled ahead anyway; the biker skidded to a stop to avoid crashing into the front tires. It was a close call. While written laws may favor the biker's right of way, the road design conveys a different story.

Take, for example, a situation where a car is given the green light to proceed while also being instructed to "yield to left turns." Meanwhile, a college student walks on a zebra crossing in the perpendicular lane. Although both the car and the student have green lights, the driver must wait for the student to cross. However, if the driver is bold or frantic enough, they might zip past the student before the crossing is complete. The driver is expected to wait, but the green light can create a compelling urge to "slip by."

> *Dear Sarah,*
>
> *While crossing the street with our baby, I was almost hit by a car trying to make a quick right turn. The guy didn't even look my direction when he neared the intersection! He barely noticed us before slamming on his brakes. I instinctively smacked the car with my hand. I'm just relieved we made it home safely.*

These types of deaths are not uncommon in this environment. According to the Governors Highway Safety Association, in 2022, 7,500 pedestrians were killed by cars. Shockingly, pedestrian deaths have risen a troubling 77% between 2010 and 2021.[28] Both pedestrians and drivers are constantly fed mixed messages about who has the right of way. Unfortunately, it only takes one lapse in judgment to cause a tragedy.

In 2021, at Edgemont Elementary School in Provo, Utah, a child was hit on a crosswalk during the morning rush. The road usually has a speed limit of 35 mph, but its width suggests a design speed of at least 40 mph. Although the speed limit is reduced to 20 mph during school hours, the road's lack of visual complexity and inconsistent speed limit create a misleading environment for drivers. The combination of distracted driving, failure to adhere to the lower speed limit, the urgency to navigate morning traffic, and the oversimplified road design contributed to the accident. As a result, the child suffered a traumatic brain injury while simply walking to school.

A couple of months later, a driver struck another child at the same crosswalk. The city attempted to address the issue by installing a lighted crosswalk, but statistically, such superficial changes are unlikely to significantly alter driver behavior. The person who shared this story with me is a crosswalker who dresses in costume daily to increase visibility for herself and the children she helps cross the street. These incidents were tragedies for everyone involved, including the drivers, who now carry the heavy burden of having caused so much grief. Additionally, the responsibility for safety has increasingly shifted to pedestrians, who must go above and beyond to protect themselves in the face of inadequate road design.

These drivers could easily be any one of us, burdened with the reality of causing irreparable harm. With no choice but to navigate a vehicle daily, can you imagine being the one who unforeseeably takes the life of a teen or young father? Or, perhaps, disables them for life? Americans must exercise strict discipline in operating a 2-ton vehicle every day, regardless of their maturity level, engagement on the road, or life situation.

The road safety issue stems from a system that produces an overabundance of cars, which rely on an ever-growing network of stroads rather than simpler road designs. While irresponsible drivers do bear some blame, infrastructural failings and a lack of transportation choices significantly contribute to the high number of fatalities and injuries on our roads. Villages offer well-designed streets and freeways with various transportation options that prioritize both drivers and pedestrians. Engineering band-aids are insufficient to solve this problem. Instead, we must reevaluate how we build our societies and create environments that go beyond the indisputable need for personal vehicles. Ultimately, this will require a significant shift in mindset and priorities. The benefits of creating safer, more livable communities for everyone are well worth the effort.

3

Dear Suburbia, I'm tired of waiting in traffic.

At the beginning of my urbanist journey, I wrote a blog entry named "There Is No Escape" about the dreadful traffic infestation that suburban zoning causes and its consequences. I later realized that it was my most-viewed article, which reflects a deep yearning to escape chaotic traffic environments.[29]

It's been this way for a long time. "We're running out of roads... We didn't dream big enough!" is one of the first lines in the 1954 propaganda film *Give Yourself the Green Light.* The premise is to inspire 1950s America to restore existing underdeveloped roads and add more highways for suburbanites to get to high-density areas. It was supposed to rid people of vehicle bottlenecking in the cities and highways. Road restoration improved convergence and transportation between farmers and delivery trucks. Extensive networks of roads are essential for transporting goods, as many rural businesses depend on car transportation. Adding more roads or widening existing ones to counteract rising congestion may have seemed like a plausible solution. However, suburban zoning facilitates endless traffic, no matter "how big you dream." Commutes through rush hour traffic are drudgery for those who deal with it daily and infuriating for those who encounter it unaware.

Essentially, if a developer creates a suburban subdivision with thousands of homes that have no access to commercial businesses other than by car—meaning residents cannot complete even the most menial tasks without one—that often results in roughly double the number of cars on the road (as most modern suburban households require two vehicles to function). If congestion becomes unbearable, as it inevitably does, cities tear down everything in sight to make the road wider. As the population increases and developers create another suburban subdivision with a thousand homes, the cycle starts again. This induced demand for suburban infrastructure means that, no matter how often engineers add another lane, communities will likely experience worse rush hour traffic than a few years before. The infrastructure can never catch up, and it never will until most of the United States is covered in asphalt.

Many urbanists point to Texas as a prime example to support this supposition. Texas accommodates the Katy Freeway (I-10), one of the largest freeways in the United States, with 26 lanes of traffic. In 2011, Texas invested 2.2 billion dollars into widening I-10 to reduce intense congestion. Not only was this unthinkably expensive for Texas taxpayers, but according to *City Observatory*, it *lengthened* travel time by 30%. Texas plans to widen the Katy Freeway again to accommodate the growing suburban population.[30]

Suburban residents initially expel a sigh of disgruntled relief when states expand a congested highway—particularly when chaotic construction zones inconvenience them on habitual routes. However, they rarely memorialize the destruction and personal devastation frequently occurring when a road expands. States will sacrifice businesses, churches, schools, historical buildings, and residential homes to make space.

I learned this firsthand during a city council meeting I attended in Lehi, Utah, to oppose the construction of a high-density subdivision between two vehicle-congested towns. As a close resident, I was already aware of the heavy traffic that began as early as 2:30 p.m. A dashing young man in a well-pressed suit stood up to sweet-talk the council into voting for 2,000 high-density units. With another ghastly prerogative, he also argued against adhering to the "one tree per unit" law, claiming it would be 'too difficult.' The entire area was planned to be residential only, with just a single, infrequent bus to the train station. With no mixed zoning or walkability, around 4,000 cars were expected to flood the freeway and metropolitan area. The road systems were far from ready to handle such a load.

I was heartbroken to hear the responses of the frantic citizens who had come to fight the decision. One man, who had lived there for fifty years, was furious that his town was losing its peaceful rural status: "Don't we get a say?" Others denounced the high-density development itself, claiming, "We don't want it! We don't want the crime!" Most people were appalled at the anticipated traffic increase. "It's already so bad. You can't do this to our city until we solve our problems. This will destroy us." As the line filed out of the room with complaints, a man meekly approached the council. He said, "They have plans to widen the freeway because of the oncoming traffic. The house in front of mine will be torn down, and the freeway will be at my front door. I don't have money to move, and I wish you would consider this when you vote for the plans… thank you." Despite everything said, the council unanimously voted for the plans that had been in the works for five years.

This example is just one of many in which residents believe their quiet suburban or rural town is immune to population influx and poorly implemented road development. Induced demand doesn't just add traffic to oncoming freeways; it also begins infringing upon suburban neighborhoods' centers. Developers and city engineers often believe that promoting this chaotic expansion supports economic growth, but in reality, it victimizes towns. Those currently unaffected have yet to experience this phenomenon and wrap themselves in a false sense of security.

Lehi residents may believe that increasing density is the root of their havoc. They understandably feel out of control as more people file in. However, the real issue isn't the density itself; it's the combination of density with car dependence that creates car traffic, pollution, and chaos. When cities are properly designed, density can bring many advantages without the raucous trail of cars behind it.

After discussing what I had witnessed with someone from Wisconsin, they responded, "What's happening in Utah will never happen in my home state. The two are totally different." They were convinced Wisconsin's lower population would shield them from such problems. The reality is that Utah looked like Wisconsin only 30 years ago, with abundant rural land and tranquility. Unless Wisconsin implements radically different zoning laws, its residents will likely face similar challenges as their population grows and development patterns mirror those of other states.

Car infrastructure is unsustainable, and it tears into communities as it expands. After the same city council meeting, a woman confided in me, "I lived in Washington, but I moved five times to escape because the car traffic was getting so bad. That's when I decided to come here." She lamented that she might have to move again, as the car traffic was about to double in her community, and she could do nothing about it.

Ironically, the lack of car traffic and noise is why suburbia is so popular among Americans. It's one of its greatest appeals. The sprawling, low-density layout reduces fast-paced and excessive car traffic because only a few people, other than residents or visitors, drive through neighborhoods. Though children rarely do this now, parents feel more at ease with supervised play on the streets, knowing there is less risk of getting run over. Suburbia provides the peace and 'safety' people crave so desperately. By barricading commercial businesses through R1 zoning, they temporarily avoid the dangerous roads and the reverberating raucous of speeding vehicles.

The problem is that if density becomes too intense for an area, peace begins to crumble with newly enlarged high-speed stroads, which then morph into high-speed highways. This first affects the outskirts of suburbia, which are unlucky enough to be closer to the highway, but then it begins to inflict similar problems on the central areas. Demand increases as more young families yearn to take a piece of suburbia. Roads become intolerably close to houses, so the wealthy move deeper into suburbia to avoid the hum of cars and the unsightly asphalt. Roads originally suitable for the town must widen to accommodate more affluent residents who still need to leave for work or errands. Neighborhoods that never dreamed they would ever be bothered by car traffic suddenly lose their view to a brick sound wall protecting them from the freeway. It can be tragic for residents who have lived in an area all their lives to suddenly find themselves bombarded by hundreds of racing cars.

It is this irritant that first sparked my interest in proper urbanism. My rural hometown, Saratoga Springs, underwent a dramatic transformation in a remarkably short time. In the span of my college years, it became unrecognizable to me; the beautiful farmland I had once cherished was gone. The roads, once again unprepared for the extensive traffic expansion, had become clogged with cars. While visiting my parents, I was astonished to discover I could hear what sounded like a semi-highway from their house. The influx of people had lengthened rush hour traffic so extensively that my visiting commute on the worst days doubled by at least half an hour compared to just a few years earlier.

The catastrophic morning rush prompted the HOA to add speed bumps to my street, discouraging impatient drivers from speeding through my child-filled neighborhood at 50 mph. As developers built thousands of suburban houses with no apparent plan for how residents would get in or out, I became deeply concerned about my town's future. Currently, only two congested avenues lead out of the city to I-15, while another suburban city rapidly rises behind it. The remaining streets flow through residential neighborhoods, creating a bottleneck.

To this day, I'm unsure what solutions are being proposed for the furious residents waiting for traffic to clear. I can only assume that the plan is to expand every possible outlet into wide highways, including the once-beautiful, tree-lined back road intended solely for residents. Despite the lack of space and funds, suburban development will continue. Still, according to Saratoga Springs city planners, road expansion will remain unresolved or unaddressed for another nine years. There has even been talk of creating a freeway across Utah Lake, which would be one of the state's most expensive and unsightly projects yet. It might be worth it if it spared the citizens from traffic; it won't.

Those unfamiliar with car dependence usually cheer on adding another lane to clogged roads. However, this will never be the solution. People must change development tactics to avoid traffic infesting all commercial and middle-class residential areas. The only way to solve this issue is to design communities that naturally reduce car reliance, allowing people to live and work in peaceful, beautiful areas. When cities center their planning around freeway systems, the roads can't keep up with the resulting car traffic, and they never will.

4

Dear Suburbia, I don't want to be under corporate control.

Growing up in America, most never question having a Walmart downtown and consider it a modern luxury. Under tighter scrutiny, it soon becomes clear that these mega-box stores are much more sinister than meets the eye. Car-only infrastructure disassembles the keystones of mom-and-pop shops, imprisoning communities into corporate dependency. The 'Land of the Free' is unknowingly being enslaved by corporatism, a form of dictatorial fascism that pairs itself perfectly with governmental tyranny.

Economic localization is imperative for granting political power to city districts. At the same time, commercial corporatism broadly pushes power away from the American people and toward the elite class. As Americans progressively lose economic and political power, they obsessively turn to national politics to solve local issues, further exacerbating their powerlessness. America must begin building villages and cities where people live and work in the same place to avoid this conundrum.

Current zoning laws and road designs instigate the death of the middle class by hiding under the facade of a 'free market' society. Yes, businesses technically operate in a free market system, but our current market is not impartial. Today, just because a company exists does not mean it is due to consumer desire. An economically diverse society, where local businesses are plentiful and thriving, disperses power among the American people. Instead, franchisees and box stores act like an invasive species, infesting areas with zeal and eventually becoming totalitarian. Americans can see these effects all over the United States.

Once a suburban downtown area hits a certain density threshold, franchises breed like weeds: a McDonald's, a Target, a Chick-fil-A, a Starbucks, a Walmart, a Big O Tires, a Home Depot, a Comfort Suites, a Dollar Tree, a Costco... and the list goes on. For the average American, driving downtown is an eerie experience. We are surrounded by stores and restaurants that are... exactly the same. It doesn't matter which state these shops are in; they are omnipresent.

How can we prevent every downtown from becoming identical to another? Is capitalism to blame? I once begrudgingly thought so and saw no other way around it. The truth is, the problem isn't the free market. The issue lies in how the free market is undermined by corrupt zoning laws that disproportionately favor big box stores, effectively stifling competition and allowing these large corporations to dominate and homogenize downtown areas. Other laws and regulations also hinder small businesses, like the dismissal of the Robinson-Patman Act, which is used to prevent price discrimination between large chains and small businesses.[31] This law ensures that large retailers cannot undercut smaller competitors by offering lower prices to some buyers and not others. While such laws help small businesses compete, restoring local control to cities would make these regulations unnecessary. Ultimately, this corporate dominance is an infrastructural disaster. The free market can only thrive under proper frameworks that prevent monopolies and ensure fair competition.

You may wonder, "What's wrong with franchises coming into a community and taking over? Should this even bother us if it benefits the consumer and economy?" I can't count the number of times someone has told me, "Walmart has cheaper goods and more of them than the local grocery store. I'd rather drive further to shop there." Some believe that the affordability of box stores and franchises justifies any issues they may cause. As will be discussed, the costs of a car-centric world might be more expensive than one assumes. The advantages of a vibrant local town with small shops far exceed the costs for its residents.

There are many reasons why Americans should reject corporate franchises or box stores: they make American individuals and cities poorer, steal meaningful jobs and businesses from local communities, promote unhealthy lifestyles and processed food, breed dull and stifling town character, haphazardly destroy the environment for profit, and, with enough power, eventually become politically tyrannical.

Small businesses are the heart of the "American Dream." They endow individuals with the economic ability to meaningfully contribute to a town's needs. Their intrinsic charm creates many avenues for communities to give back to each other magnificently. When a city designs spaces correctly and allows organic growth, it establishes a strong culture and small businesses become community hubs. They are places of interest that provide beauty, prosperity, local identity, safety for children, quality goods, and protection from crime. Due to their innate sociality, they produce districts with invested political power. Lastly, family businesses can better pass their dreams on to their posterity for generations.[32]

Local businesses form the foundation of thriving communities by collaborating and supporting each other, creating a vibrant, interconnected economy. They understand each other's needs and fight for the peace and sanctity of their communities. They find political strength in eschewing harmful developments or regulations that hinder their community's progress. They also discourage crime because much of the neighborhood is involved in their local economy. Shop owners become the eyes on the street to protect property and get a sense of incoming crowds. They keep traveling children in line if they are causing a raucous, and discourage suspicious behavior.

As just one example, one of my favorite ice cream shops in Utah is Brooker's Founding Flavors Ice Cream. It's a small business created by Brian Brooker, a man who gave up his career in law to pursue a deep passion for ice cream.[33] His shop is themed after the founding fathers and provides an open window into the ice cream-making process. Sometimes, people can see him churning out ice cream for entertainment and education.

Brooker supports local dairy farmers by exclusively using locally sourced milk, strengthening the local economy. The ice cream is dazzlingly unique, with 18% cream instead of the standard 11%. Brooker's Founding Flavors exemplifies how localized small businesses can collaborate to create strong economic ties amongst each other, foster originality, and provide exceptional service and enjoyment to their residents.

The reason why we don't have a strong ecosystem of small businesses is that most of our society has virtually no walkability. Localized walkability is the only way for small businesses to survive. Strong Towns, Rachel Quednau writes that small businesses need proximity and convenience to be economically productive; they rely on the ease, safety, and simplicity of a street's walkability.[34] Locals must be able to easily access the businesses by walking, biking, or public transit. When artificial forces dismantle the substructures that sustain mom-and-pop shops, they have no power to compete.

Here is how suburban zoning and car-centric infrastructure interfere with small businesses. Suppose zoning regulations force a local grocer to be located next to a multi-billion dollar Walmart in a commercial area. In that case, it is nearly impossible for the grocery store to survive unless the public is determined to renounce Walmart. The local grocer is smaller, costlier (partially due to exploitative corporate practices), and less stocked than Walmart. It will inevitably be extinguished by Walmart's arrival, and it doesn't end there. Walmart will probably take over other businesses, such as dress shops, butcheries, bakeries, pharmacies, cosmetic stores, and candy shops. One entity bulldozes what could have been accomplished through a combined community effort. Instead of a father running his own deli—where he could connect with the community, offer organized charitable services, serve as the neighborhood watchdog, experiment with new sandwiches, and mentor his children in the family business—he is now reduced to being just a lowly cashier at the new box store.

Stacey Mitchell, the co-director of the Institute for Local Self-Reliance, points out that even the seemingly most benign franchises can harm a weakened community. She discovered that multiple Dollar Trees were infiltrating poorer and rural areas, with projected new developments expected to quadruple across the U.S. According to her observations, it only takes 15-30% of revenue from a Dollar Tree to collapse a local grocer, even if the community still buys 70-85% of their products at the grocery store.[35] As small businesses weaken in particular areas, predatory behavior from franchises intensifies, stripping individuals of their ability to contribute to communal economic prosperity. This leaves some communities with the extreme and inadequate option of shopping at a Dollar Tree for groceries.

The Stroad and the Box Store

Road designs also favor big-box stores over other businesses, even in diverse commercial areas. If a person has to drive on a multi-lane and dangerous stroad, they might as well make the extra mile worth the journey. Modern road designs encourage drivers to be one-track-minded when it comes to doing errands. Walmart, being deceptively cheaper and more expansive, becomes the default choice; drivers settle into its familiar parking lot, get what they need, and get out. People do not casually loiter near these places to explore new shopping options because the parking lot is a barren wasteland. The miles of asphalt and lack of trees make it inhospitable. This environment offers no beauty to appreciate or reason to prolong one's visit. The entire setup says, "Grab your things and leave." This playing field offers no room for smaller businesses to capitalize on their unique strengths.

Humans are habitual creatures and yearn for familiarity. Stroads make it challenging for drivers to recognize the value of mom-and-pop shops, as these local businesses are unfamiliar and can easily be overlooked in this fast-paced blur of chain stores and billboards. Busy drivers are unlikely to stop by a shop they've never visited and feel they don't need. Mom-and-pop shops are less advertised; they don't have national commercials circulating on TV, and they typically have smaller parking lots. Even if a place becomes more popular, a smaller or difficult-to-access parking lot can deter drivers. The danger and complexity of a stroad often make these places more inconvenient to reach. So even if an unknown store somehow piques a driver's interest, the obstacles a stroad presents are an additional hurdle to navigate.

Hey friends,

I'm so sorry you spent twenty minutes trying to find parking near this local cafe I love. Unfortunately, they don't have much parking, and I happened to take the last spot.

Let's visualize a typical scenario on a stroad. A group of friends hops into a car to grab a bite to eat downtown. They pass a Burger King, walk in, eat, and then jump back in their car because the parking lot is loud and bleak. Alternatively, they might skip the dining experience and rush through the drive-through. They then head to a more interesting or peaceful place by car.

A new burger joint opened just a block before Burger King, but they have never noticed it. Its signage isn't as bright or familiar, the parking lot is much smaller, and they must make a dangerous left turn against oncoming traffic to access it. This scenario illustrates how a small business can lose traction, even when these friends would have been more interested in other sandwiches.

Alternatively, let's visualize a properly localized town. Small businesses dominate and are interwoven into the community through walking or public transit. The group of friends can pass the new burger shop at a human pace. They might be intrigued by the shop's design and ambiance. Trees overhang the outside dining area, keeping it cool. The lack of car raucous means there is very little sound pollution. The shop is popular, and the local gossip confirms they make the best sandwiches in town. There is no need for large-scale parking lots, and all dangerous obstacles are eliminated. Even if they don't want to stop and eat, it's easy for them to briefly consider the shop by the front door or peek inside to check the menu. The ease of accessibility allows the shop to thrive rather than struggle for survival on a busy stroad. In this mixed-use scenario, the community's preference for local businesses over franchises like Burger King would likely prevent such chains from entering the area.

In the first scenario, Burger King's dominance is secured by its recognizable brand and convenient accessibility by car, leaving the new burger joint struggling to survive amid corporate giants. Small businesses wither away in an environment that favors the familiar and franchised, crushing entrepreneurial dreams and ambitions. The small burger joint never had a chance to prove its worth to the community.

Conversely, when corporate behemoths like Burger King are absent, a culture emerges where local businesses can thrive, fostering a vibrant economy and a connected community. The success of the burger joint becomes a victory for the community that chooses to invest in its future. Walkability will always enable the local shops to participate in the free market and fairly compete.

Culture

Oh, how Americans are weary of living in an apocalyptic landscape where every town feels dead and indistinguishable! The prevalence of franchised stores strips towns of their unique character. Brooker's, one of the few successful mom-and-pop shops in this car-centric environment, is expanding across Utah. Though I love Brooker's, this expansion is facilitated by zoning laws that favor franchises over local businesses. If zoning supported local businesses, Brooker's would face stiffer competition and might struggle to grow, as communities would prefer their own unique ice cream shops. This is advantageous to the culture and economy. A flourishing network of small businesses would infuse each community with its own distinct charm across the U.S. In an idealized version of America, one town might offer intricate libraries, twinkling lights, and lively festivals, while a neighboring city would provide a completely different experience with art exhibits, fountain-centered courtyards, and vibrant multi-use parks. Unique localization allows each place to offer distinct eateries, sights, and activities that others may lack. This is how states function as a living body, with each town contributing to a vibrant and diverse society through shared wealth. Sadly, this is not our reality; we have millions of suburban tract neighborhoods and downtowns filled with the same boring franchises and tired layouts.

This lack of culture creates a social hierarchy where the wealthy enjoy vibrant and beautiful environments, and the rest of us endure stifling and unhealthy spaces.[36] We are gaslighted into believing we should be content with our so-called "prosperity". This disparity drives many to escapism, flocking to destinations like Disney World or Venice, which offers rare, beautiful walkability. The steep cost of living in such desirable, well-designed places is a result of their scarcity and high demand. Only a privileged few get to experience them. The wealthy elite are increasingly moving to more walkable and ecologically balanced areas, such as new developments in Miami, while the rest of society endures the daily grind of rush hour traffic. However, this disparity doesn't have to be the norm. By developing functional urban environments in diverse areas, we can make these enriching experiences more accessible and affordable for everyone.

If every city in the U.S. embraced diversified walkability and supported local businesses, the middle class would thrive, revitalizing the heart of American society. Well-designed neighborhoods would create strong barriers against the dominance of chain stores, fostering culturally rich communities. The abundance of local competition would lead to a society where everyone could be enchanted by each town's unique character and charm. You wouldn't need to travel the world to find beauty and worth; imagine if your own backyard was considered a coveted destination. By transforming our cities into bustling ecosystems of communal creativity, we can forge a future where the "American Dream" is not just a concept but a lived reality for all.

Politicization and Government Dependence

This corporate dominance goes further than economic suffocation. I naively never believed that corporate franchises would become political entities that monopolize an area. Beyond these franchises destroying local economies, wealthy investors with political agendas control these big box stores, pushing propaganda onto the public under the guise of choice and the "free market." Collusion between franchises, media networks, pharmaceutical companies, and government officials restricts accessibility, forcing consumers to conform to an enforced political agenda. This influence affects people across the political spectrum.

For example, Target's 2023 Pride Month display of an LGBTQ+ children's section marked its departure from political neutrality, highlighting the growing trend of corporate franchises engaging in political activism. The general public felt so betrayed on both sides of the aisle that millions of Americans boycotted Target. The left felt aghast that Target rescinded the clothing line, and the right couldn't believe they had done it in the first place. Target's stock prices plummeted, and the boycott went on for months.[37]

Target isn't the only company participating in political shenanigans. Chick-fil-A has been involved in several political and social issues over the years, particularly related to LGBTQ+ rights.[38] Corporate companies have been dipping their toes in political propaganda for some time. Still, plenty of Americans can currently boycott Target, even if it's inconvenient. Americans are at the mercy of major franchises' political posturing. If the trend away from small businesses continues and franchises dominate American cities, the public will lose the ability to choose where to shop.

The lack of walkability in many areas also contributes to the rise of online monopolies like Amazon. Consumers may prefer the convenience of having goods delivered to their doorsteps rather than driving to soulless industrial parking lots, where they feel more like consumer slaves than community members. Amazon is a major player in diminishing the role of local businesses and contributing to the homogenization of shopping experiences.

The destruction of choice leaves the American public very vulnerable to tyranny. The COVID-19 pandemic is an excellent example of how corporate politicization can spiral out of control. After its grand entrance, public opinion on the dangers of the COVID strain split drastically. Americans held differing views on the enforcement of mask-wearing in public spaces. Despite the flood of conflicting information in the media. Corporations didn't give Americans much of a choice in following mandates. In the name of morality, all major corporate mercenaries declared that individuals could not enter or purchase in their stores unless they wore a mask.

For many, these stores were the only accessible options for essential goods; those who disagreed still begrudgingly bought groceries, and those who rejected the premise entirely still needed to feed their families. In a disturbing tandem, governments closed small or local businesses while keeping box grocery stores open for the public. This corrupt decision further crippled local economies while governments stuffed the pockets of unphased billionaires. This left individuals feeling powerless, as corporate control dictated the terms under which they could obtain necessities.

Corporations with no interest in local perspectives took a strong political stance in favor of pandemic regulations, leading to chaos in stores for those who refused to wear masks. Incidents of harassment and even violence occurred toward those who rejected covering their faces. These industrial downtowns are dangerous places for political conflict because they gather strangers who have no vested interest in their neighbors, making them susceptible to violent behavior when tensions rise.

Franchises can withstand surprisingly severe public backlash because Wall Street backs them with billions of dollars in stock holdings. For instance, although Target faced intense public criticism, it had the power to endure until the controversy passed. Unlike corporate stores, small businesses cannot afford to engage in major political movements because any sig-nificant income loss could drive them out of business. Out of necessity, communities with a strong presence of local small businesses often maintain political neutrality. This encourages a healthy economic environment where everybody is more likely to enjoy undisturbed consumer power.

If towns returned to self-sustained localization, in which more than half of a town contributes to its economy, governments could not have shut down local businesses because they would have been core to community survival. This bottom-to-top approach would leave decisions up to local governments and individuals, enabling communities to determine what is best for them.

The influence of media corporations and influencers, disconnected from local realities, has led to inaccurate portrayals of our neighbors' beliefs and actions, further promoting the glamorization of detached individualism and encouraging greater reliance on government and consumerism.

Doomsday and Resilience

Today, suburbanites are terrified of what would happen if something like that occurred again, but more severely. Could they get formula for their babies, bread for their children, or gas for their cars? The American people are immensely vulnerable right now if catastrophe strikes. Some Americans instinctively believe they should become preppers to combat this vulnerability. Instead, they should fight for environments that uplift local farmers, allowing rural commerce to circulate wheat and fresh produce to them—not Walmart, which controls the market internationally and their ability to eat.

Americans live in such a dysfunctional environment that they believe if a national crisis were to occur, the best course of action would be to move to the woods, stock up on food, and acquire firearms to fend off pillagers. Not only is this approach ineffective in the long term, but it is also unrealistic for the average modern American. I know I speak for many when I say I would be utterly helpless foraging for food, as I lack the skills and supplies to sustain myself, let alone my small children. For years, I clung to the desperate hope that my only option would be to find an extended family member who hunts as a hobby—assuming I could even reach him in a world gone mad. But the harsh reality is that relying on hunting, fishing, or foraging for survival is a dangerous fantasy. These activities are far too unpredictable and unreliable, especially when faced with a crisis where resources are scarce and competition is fierce. The wilderness can't possibly provide for the masses, and there's no guarantee that wild game will be available when it's needed most.

In times of crisis, self-reliance might seem like the ultimate safeguard, but even the most prepared individuals are not immune to the consequences of societal collapse. Many homesteaders pride themselves on their self-sufficiency, believing they have all the necessary resources and skills to survive. One might say, "I have everything I need. Those other people clearly didn't prepare for this." While there's some truth to the idea that people like homesteaders have cultivated a lifestyle that supports self-reliance, this independence will not necessarily protect them in extreme situations. If Americans were to reach a point of widespread desperation for food, nothing would stop them from invading these spaces en masse. This potential for chaos is frightening. Those compelled to live in high-density housing are acutely aware of their vulnerability, while those on homesteads may have a false sense of security.

Our political and economic powerlessness creates an 'I am an island' attitude that has seeped into the American psyche. Americans live in environments where they fearfully depend on volatile box grocery stores and contribute almost nothing to their suburban communities. Simply put, if it came down to food and all other systems failed us, it would be a bloodbath.

One of the most beautiful attributes of a pedestrian-first society is that local communities and individuals become politically and economically self-reliant. Villages of the past, such as Matera, Italy, have endured for centuries despite droughts, wars, or periods of poverty, thanks to infrastructure that stands the test of time. As Lewis Mumford notes in his book *The City in History: Its Origins, Its Transformations, and Its Prospects*,

> *Such communities, through their small scale and intimate social organization, often maintained a more resilient and adaptable form of life. They were less dependent on external resources and more capable of self-sufficiency, which allowed them to withstand periods of drought, economic downturn, and even warfare. The very structure of these villages, with their compact form, communal resources, and*

shared responsibilities, contributed to their longevity and stability across centuries.[39]

The best way to weather the storms of life is to rely on strong-knit local communities that consistently work through challenges together. Individuals don't have to abandon society and attempt to do everything on their own, which isn't feasible. By fostering local self-reliance, we can build communities that are prepared for crises and flourish in everyday life. In such communities, people can more effectively provide jobs, produce food for one another, and contribute trades and services. These communities promote collaboration, innovation, and mutual support, allowing individuals to feel empowered and connected. Deepening localization helps resist crony capitalism and limit federal government overreach, enhancing political strength. People in mixed-use environments are more likely to engage in constructive dialogue and find common ground, leading to greater civility and cooperation. This collaborative approach ensures that communities remain resilient and optimistic in the face of adversity. In this way, we move toward a society that values cooperation over isolation, ensuring a sustainable and prosperous future, whether one is a prepper or not.

Reclaiming Local Power

If something as political as COVID happened once, it could happen again with even greater enforcement and consequences. Do we want to grant corporations unrestrained power to determine when we can eat, all under the guise of political virtue?

The American public faces a crucial decision: reject the Trojan administration of billion-dollar corporations that steal local businesses, dictate consumer behavior, and enforce political whims, or embrace a future of self-reliant communities. By prioritizing pedestrian-first urban planning and supporting small businesses, we can dismantle corporate dependency, strengthen social bonds, and enhance the quality of life for everyone.

48

Restoring mixed-use infrastructure, promoting walkable and bikeable cities, and offering diverse transportation options will empower us to reclaim control over our communities, protect them from external political influences, and ensure a resilient and thriving society.

5

Dear Suburbia, America looks… different.

For a long time, I considered Utah one of the most hideous states in the nation and blamed it on the dry climate. "I'm not a desert girl," was my typical response. I lived in thirteen states before settling in Utah as a tween. I have remained here for many reasons, but at one point, I was determined to move to the East Coast so that I could surround myself with more greenery. Over the years, I was surprised to hear people comment on Utah's beauty—whether it was the magnificent mountains, colorful canyons, or varied rock formations. Gradually, I realized I had taken these things for granted and began to concede their points. Yet, I couldn't shake the frustration I felt about my surroundings. Eventually, I understood that it wasn't Utah's natural landscapes that I despised; it was the way we built homes, businesses, and roads. Utah cities are an unworthy partner and a distracting eyesore from the truly unique Utah landscape. I now appreciate the exquisite mountains behind me—but only if I squint past everything else.

After this epiphany, it dawned on me that almost all cities in the United States were built the same way and that I wouldn't find solace by simply moving elsewhere. Even if I could, the potential for any place to be disrupted by car infrastructure seemed imminent.

Just as a virus invades and damages cells, car infrastructure degrades a city's environment and erases its beauty. I imagine those who dismiss beautification for what they perceive as virtuous "capitalism" likely reside in serene and beautiful places, far removed from the dreary Dollar Tree. However, more Americans are perpetually living in indigently ugly and noisy areas that drain the soul.

Beauty holds a prominent position among human pleasures. According to an essay by Drexel University, *Understanding the Pursuit of Happiness in Ten Major Cities*, of all the factors that contribute to a great city, the strongest correlation to satisfaction was a beautiful environment. A resident's desire for attractive environments is self-evident; it promotes great gratification and emotional well-being.[40]

Simply beautifying a disadvantaged community can transform it and improve residents' quality of life. Adding features like architectural designs, greenery, and water features can elevate projects from neglected areas. For example, as cited by the YouTube channel *The Aesthetic City*, Le Plessis-Robinson, a town in the suburbs of Paris, transformed itself into a desirable, safe, and economic hub by redesigning the exterior of its neglected housing projects with traditional architectural styles.[41] If an unknowing individual were to walk through that town today, they might naively believe it had looked that way for centuries. Beautification invites businesses and enhances prosperity for even the most impoverished residents in the area.

Americans yearning for daily tranquility and beauty must shift away from car infrastructure and toward localized walkability. Walkability lies at the heart of fostering architectural and ecological beauty, while car infrastructure exacerbates urban decay, spreads asphalt, eradicates vegetation, promotes subpar housing, and bombards landscapes with corporate advertising.

Suburbia is Only Quaint

As we delve into the uglification imposed by car infrastructure, we must acknowledge what people usually laud as a beautiful sanctuary from bustling downtowns: suburbia.

When people say, "Well, my neighborhood is beautiful," I cheekily respond, "In comparison to Walmart, yeah." All jokes aside, while suburbia isn't completely without charm, suburban neighborhoods often receive undue praise for their supposed beauty simply because they're less chaotic and dismal than commercial districts. This praise is merely a testament to the absence of traffic infestation rather than any inherent appeal. More often than not, suburbs are dominated by rows of bland houses that age poorly, get dirty easily, and contribute little to the community's visual appeal.

The truth is that America holds far greater potential for aesthetic allure than what many suburban neighborhoods offer. A brief scroll through Pinterest or Instagram—popular platforms dedicated to sharing lifestyle ideas—reveals the stark contrast between our idealized visions of beauty and the reality of suburban living. These tract homes rarely meet our expectations, let alone serve as a backdrop for engagement photos. Seriously though... would you take your wedding photos in most American suburbs? Probably not.

It's confusing to witness even affluent Americans investing in newly built neighborhoods or homes that skimp on quality materials, such as brick, stone, wood, or stained glass. Rather than buy homes with architectural character, they pay a mint for cookie-cutter McMansions with stucco facades or vinyl siding. Take, for instance, the upcoming suburban tract homes across Utah, all donning the same millennial farmhouse gray style. These fad-driven homes, constructed with cheaper materials, quickly lose their luster, leaving behind a colorless, dystopian landscape. This contrasts sharply with buildings made of quality materials, like the beloved New

York brownstones, which are architecturally profound, built to endure, and so rare in American life that they are designated within costly historic preservation districts.[42]

Beyond architectural shortcomings, suburbia's inefficient use of space and stringent regulations squander valuable farmland and trees that could have been repurposed for local economies, future housing, or aesthetic pleasure.

The reality is that it doesn't matter whether residents appreciate the potentially dull aesthetic of their neighborhoods. Suburbia is frequently lauded as beautiful by its residents because its oppressive infrastructure serves as a temporary refuge from encroaching concrete industrialization in other parts of the state while simultaneously being one of its primary causes. As we further discuss suburban infrastructure's effects on downtown landscapes, it's essential to recognize that while people may see suburbia as a beautiful sanctuary from urban chaos, its true impact is seen in how it contributes to the deterioration of everything around it.

Advertisement

High density paired with excessive car traffic leads to billboarding along freeways and stroads. The Las Vegas area exemplifies how this combination results in an overwhelming visual clutter of advertisements. What's the real value in seeing a billboard featuring a plaguey-looking man with antiquated lettering that says, "Alcohol: It's cheaper than therapy!"?[43] Not only are drivers continually subjected to such tacky billboards, but they're also encouraged to engage in self-destructive behavior. Moreover, it's impossible to shield children from these unsightly messages constantly thrust into their view. Hideous and sometimes discourteous billboards are placed every few hundred yards, harassing drivers with consumer advertisements on their way to and from work. Whether the messaging ranges from benign to boorish, it's soul-withering—death by a thousand cuts. The best way to eliminate these eyesores is to reduce car usage by developing more appealing environments elsewhere. If fewer people used cars, billboards would become obsolete.

It's the Same

Not only are there billboards everywhere, but corporate dependency has made all areas of the United States look the same. Cars travel at lightning speed compared to people walking, so businesses use billboards to grab drivers' attention rather than beautifying downtown areas to boost profit. Consequently, this corporate reliance leads to cookie-cutter towns overwhelmed by billboards. Meanwhile, it prevents residents from investing in their own communities. A community cannot creatively build a unique sense of place if there is nothing unique about it.

Businesses must vie for a car's attention on a much grander and brighter scale than if a person were walking by, especially when competing against popular franchises. This can sometimes be so drastic that it's nearly impossible for someone walking to identify a store in a commercial area without a car. During a leisurely stroll through downtown Orem, I encountered a perplexing urban layout. On one side loomed a sprawling parking lot, while on the other stood a row of stores housed within a long, box-like warehouse. Walking along the sidewalk shaded by a 4-foot ledge, I struggled to distinguish each business. The lack of clear signage forced me to step into the parking lot and strain to read the large, colorful labels adorning the stucco walls. It became evident that these businesses prioritized catering to car-bound customers, assuming everyone would arrive by car and easily spot their conspicuous signage.

Commercial billboarding must be favored to beg drivers to enter their space. This is why Orem State Street in Utah was labeled the "Ugliest Street in America."[44] If you drive down State Street, you are bombarded with a seven- to nine-lane asphalt stroad featuring hundreds of large-scale, colorful, and ugly advertisements, all desperately urging drivers to pull into their space.

This concept is also reminiscent of Googie architecture, where businesses resort to flamboyant designs or signage to grab attention in an otherwise bland environment.[45] Take McDonald's as an example: the iconic yellow "M" on a red rectangle is instantly recognizable to drivers, evoking an image of the flashy building. While not aesthetically pleasing, it effectively serves its purpose, especially for drivers in need of a quick meal.

The billboards themselves also replace the natural landscape. If a developer builds a new Domino's and a beautiful oak stands in the way of a driver's view, they believe the tree must be chopped down and replaced with a towering red and blue pizza box. This behavior would be entirely unnecessary for a pedestrian, as the tree would provide shade, and the business would be clearly visible from a human scale.

Parking Lots

Another aspect of car dependency that denies us beauty is parking lots. Parking lots are ugly, barren spaces that suck the life out of our cities, making them less vibrant and more dangerous. This is especially evident given America's overabundance of parking spaces. According to *The Hill*, parking lots cover 22% of American cities, with places like San Bernardino, California, allocating a staggering 49% of its area to parking lots. Parking lots are ugly, barren, and dirty.[46] They consume space with hundreds of acres of asphalt, stripping cities of their character. While suburbanites may want parking availability in commercial areas, it's telling that they avoid asphalt lots near their communities whenever they can. Parking lots are not places to gather but places to flee.

Parking lots are so forsaken that we've created loitering laws for them; lingering in these places is considered so bizarre that it's perceived as criminal. Their lack of appeal makes them hazardous, especially during the darker times of the day. According to LotGuard USA, parking lots rank third on the list of locations where crimes are committed in the U.S.[47] As a woman, I have been advised all my life to carry a defense tool when running errands alone, as these errands inevitably lead me to a parking lot.

Proper urban planning eliminates these fearful situations by avoiding the creation of spaces where no one wants to be. Well-planned areas naturally foster environments where people are consistently present, which deters errant behavior. These spaces accommodate regular residents and are attractive enough to encourage people to spend time in them throughout the day.

Instead, America builds millions of sightless black holes with no alternative. These parking lots are ripe for mischievous behavior because nobody wants to stay in them longer than it takes to put their groceries in the car. This situation is both absurd and profoundly unfortunate, and it's unnecessary to delve into specific instances of horrific crimes in parking lots across America; their prevalence is all too familiar.

Hiding parking isn't straightforward or practical either; it's not just about flat areas near stores. Cities build towering parking structures to cope with increasing density, leaving metropolitan areas surrounded by unsightly parking towers. Underground parking is also pricey and complex compared to surface lots, making it impractical for beautification efforts. Given the expense and complexity of various parking solutions, the only sustainable resolution to decrease parking is to inhibit the induced demand for personal cars.

Even if parking lots weren't expensive or crime-riddled, these empty and unattractive spaces steal valuable space, productivity, and joy from the American people.

Safety and Beauty

The approach engineers take to ensure safety in a car-oriented society often results in environments that are both damaging and visually unappealing. In the thought-provoking book *Confessions of a Recovering Engineer*, author and engineer Charles Marohn records an interesting conversation with a prominent local woman about the future road designs in her developing town; her front street is the first topic of discussion. It's a frustrating and circular conversation for the woman, who sincerely questions how the proposed changes would make her front street safer. He, the engineer, views her with patronizing sympathy and becomes impatient with her evident lack of 'education.' Despite her disapproval, he chalks it up to ignorance, and the developers continue with the plans. These are the changes that were made:

To enable 'safety' in an environment where her little children once played on the narrow street in front of her house, the engineers added two more lanes of asphalt for high-speed traffic, installed a previously unnecessary speed limit sign, built a monstrous overpass adjacent to her front door, and cut down 25 feet of handsome trees in her front yard to create a clear zone for reckless drivers. Additionally, more traffic signs and lights are expected to clutter the area as traffic increases. Her home, once a sanctuary of peace and charm—a place where her children could freely play in the shade, and she could safely walk to productive places—was now destined to become a mess of asphalt, a sea of cars, and an unsightly overpass. Her house value decreased as she was unexpectedly placed in a traffic-heavy part of town. Charles never convinced her that it was for her benefit.

Towns should be encouraged to grow economically. However, a town's progress is crucial, and Americans should prioritize people and local businesses over machines. Due to our inability to create spaces that are not utterly dependent on car transportation, it has become common for entire communities to be situated or compelled to face treeless, insipid, and unsightly busy roads as a town becomes more populated. They lose property value, beauty, and a proper place of refuge for their families. These value systems paradoxically create unsafe and unattractive environments for both drivers and pedestrians.[48]

Why True Safety Matters

Safety is crucial in creating beautiful cities, which is why I've devoted so much attention to the dangers of stroads. When a setting is safe and peaceful, people will naturally gather there; thus, developers are incentivized to create mixed-use ecosystems that are appealing and human-scale. Mom-and-pop shops, which rely on foot traffic, are significantly more successful in contributing to a city's beautification compared to car-dependent franchises.

According to urbanist Belinda Yuen, when villages prioritize safety and convenience for pedestrians and cyclists, they're more likely to explore charming streets and appealing shops.[49] Successful small businesses understand this dynamic and enhance their storefronts with flowers, greenery, architecture, or interesting art to attract customers. As a result, buildings are less likely to appear cheap or unkempt because residents feel compelled to make their public spaces more delightful—it is their home, after all.

As villages transition from stroads to streets, visual complexity returns to the environment, encouraging developers to foster natural greenery and sophisticated architecture. The emphasis on walkability reduces car congestion, thereby preventing disproportionate asphalt expansion and enhancing overall attractiveness.

The safety of streets over stroads also turns car-centric spaces into pedestrian-only spaces. In Charles Montgomery's book, *Happy City: Transforming Our Lives Through Urban Design,* this can be seen in places such as shopping courtyards, parks, or exclusive pathways for cyclists and pedestrians.[50] This metamorphosis encourages developers and communities to use different methods to enhance character in popular places, such as trees, shrubs, planter boxes, cobblestones, brick walkways, splash pads, fountains, lights, community artworks, or statues. I have seen this in Japan, where the community established a lucrative local marketplace. The crowd gathered under hundreds of brightly colored umbrellas for shade and embellishment. These types of locations speak to the heart of human desire. They have a sense of place—a unique look and feeling that speaks volumes about the residing community. They create immense satisfaction and expand the human experience.

Beautification is a national mindset, and in countries that prioritize it, every destination offers something novel or distinctive. However, due to our car-centric mindset in America, such places are scarce, often becoming overcrowded with tourists or too expensive to be easily accessible. Countries that prioritize beautification are not only economically profitable but also globally popular. For instance, in Switzerland, car-free villages like Zermatt protect the neighboring Matterhorn from pollution and offer not only peaceful surroundings but also incredible views, making them highly sought-after tourist destinations.[51]

Though going car-free is not necessary to create captivating environments, the human soul craves such places because they mimic the striking complexity of nature through an assembly of color, vegetation, and peace. Dreary and bored Americans seek these places but rarely find them outside of the online world. Additionally, authentic international travel to destinations that excel in beautification is expensive and time-consuming.

Yet, despite the appeal of globally celebrated beautiful places, Americans favor stroads, which profoundly obstruct our ability to create and maintain appealing environments. Even if a city attempts to beautify itself with modest flower pots on Main Street or similar efforts, the presence of stroads renders these areas hazardous and noisy for anyone outside of a car, ultimately having little impact on encouraging people to walk near them.

Car infrastructure, particularly in the form of stroads, often disrupts a town's most cherished resources. For example, Amsterdam's picturesque waterways, like the Emperor Canal, are designed for the enjoyment of both residents and tourists.[52] The Dutch highly value these rivers as precious assets worthy of protection and preservation at any cost. They prioritize constructing beautiful buildings along the riverside with easy walkability, effectively restricting car traffic from encroaching upon these areas. This design philosophy is in stark contrast to that of Provo, Utah, where the approach to the river is vastly different. The Provo River, which cuts through downtown Provo, is barely memorialized. They did consider developing a small park next to it, with residential housing on the other side. However, even in the deepest point of the park, individuals may be unable to escape the sound of racing cars as both a freeway and several stroads surround it. Much of the river runs through the commercial district, flanked by bustling and noisy main roads adjacent to low-cost, high-density housing, parking lots, fast-food outlets, and industrial parks.

Ironically, a path is still carved next to it for walking or biking individuals. Unfortunately, most of the trip is interrupted by blaring traffic, trashy and frighteningly thin underground road bridges, overpasses, parking lots, and unsightly stucco businesses. What a waste of a wonderful resource, all in the name of car travel and 'capitalism.' In reality, the utilization of the Provo River was just terrible planning in a world that wishes everything to be built around an unfeeling engine and not the people in it.

For years, I lived by the river without knowing it existed. When I finally discovered it, I was ecstatic and longed for it to be a place of tranquility. However, when I visited, I found myself in a constant state of stress. It wasn't until I learned about the area's poor urban planning that I understood why the river had remained unknown to me and why it wasn't a place of peace.

Provo fell victim to car-centricity and, in the process, failed to properly utilize the beautiful river for its residents. The lack of peaceable walkability disincentivizes developers or businesses from making anything on a human scale because there are no humans out and about. There are only cars, and this is the principal reason why stroads are so successful in amassing hideously dull surroundings.

Suburbia's induced demand

Urban planners and enlightened engineers have discovered the truth: suburbia's car dependence enables the average stroad to tear down almost everything beautiful about a city under the guise of 'safety.' Stroads create dull and oversimplified environments, squashing creativity and preventing communities from establishing a unique and pleasant sense of place. They make the world unsafe for both drivers and pedestrians. Without foot traffic, developers and business owners react with Googie architecture and billboarding to incessantly advertise to the American driver. This discourages walking, harms small businesses, makes every place in America look the same, and promotes the never-ending and unattractive acres of asphalt used for empty parking lots.

So long as dull suburbia continues to pump out houses that are inevitably car-dependent to survive, we will continue to industrialize and uglify the United States. We will lose the immense satisfaction of living in unique and enchanting environments. The most appealing and beautiful places are found in pedestrian-first areas because they value people over everything else. Pedestrian-first societies build around the river to enjoy it, not tear through it. In echoing the sentiments of 'America the Beautiful,' let's ensure our country actually looks that way.

6

Dear Suburbia, I really want a home.

Housing crises are a suburban infrastructure's bread and butter. When the housing market spiked in 2020, most local Utahns assumed it would be temporary. "Utah has always had cheap housing; don't worry about it, let it pass." Except it didn't pass—it was only getting worse for Utah residents. Though my husband had a stable, middle-class job for six years while attending school part-time, we suddenly couldn't afford anything after he graduated. While on the hunt for a cheap place to rent, I found a 700-square-foot, one-bedroom house split into a duplex. It was far from ideal—half of the square footage came from the basement, which acted more like a crawl space, and both the basement and the shared laundry room were only accessible if you stepped outside and walked around the house. The kitchen was so small that the fridge sat in the living room. The silver lining was that it had a blessed yard for my very zealous baby. Despite its ridiculous layout, it was the most promising place I could find within my budget, and I was eager to save for a home. However, I was shocked to discover that over a hundred people had inquired about it, including young adults from out of state. Bizarrely, the competition was too stiff, and we were not chosen.

Suburban infrastructure is at the heart of a cascade of societal challenges: housing crises, gentrification, homelessness, and a surge in crime. My home state, Utah, and other states are only beginning to witness this phenomenon. Many fail to realize how suburban development actively contributes to these crises. Suburban zoning regulations worsen housing affordability by maintaining a static housing market that fails to adapt to changing economic conditions.[53] Either a town is growing, or it's dying. Current zoning laws are so restrictive that once suburban developments reach their housing capacity, they begin to instigate death and poverty in the area. For simplicity's sake, there are two main reasons why car centricity leads to these outcomes.

First, the spread-out design of suburbs and their reliance on cars drain resources and strain infrastructure.[54] Zoning laws that favor single-family homes on specific lot sizes are so rigid they leave no room for new housing development. This limitation on available space reduces the supply of homes, which in turn drives up their prices. As neighborhoods grow and spread closer to economic centers, they exhaust the available space for housing, limiting further expansion or development. Since everything is developed around a limited freeway system, cities cannot expand into self-sustaining entities or provide adequate housing for their residents. These car-dependent communities create excessive traffic, especially when cities try to build denser housing. The cost of expanding roads and infrastructure to accommodate growing car usage quickly depletes public funds. This unsustainable cycle traps communities in a web of congestion, skyrocketing costs, and dwindling opportunities for growth.

Second, this lack of housing development is exacerbated by the fact that people despise car infestation and do whatever they can to avoid living near high-traffic areas. In *Suburban Nation: The Rise of Sprawl and the Decline of the American Dream*, the authors explain how residents oppose higher-density housing because, in a car-dependent framework, it brings chaotic road and commercial development near them.[55] As populations grow, there is resistance among residents to housing options other than single-family homes and townhomes. Again, this resistance reduces the supply of available homes and hinders development progress. When efforts to keep low density inevitably fail, as people need places to live, wealthy residents move to exclusive communities farther from urban centers, buying larger lots to avoid the chaos of car-centric density and maintain a peaceful place to live. Even the wealthy, despite their resources, become prisoners of a system that pushes them further from productive society as they seek to avoid what they consider the worst aspects of urban growth.

What most Americans don't understand is that they are trying to escape the glut of cars and industrialism, not people. Higher density in well-designed, walkable villages does not have the same negative impact. Unlike car-centric suburbs, villages handle increasing density gracefully, expanding like a bushel of flowers with strong local pistils, each town naturally growing outward as needed. In stark contrast, the unsustainable expansion of suburbs is much like a flower cut and placed in a vase, ultimately destined to wilt and perish.

The Housing Crisis and Gentrification

As supply dwindles and prices skyrocket, gentrification rears its ugly head, with wealthier people moving into low-income neighborhoods, driving up property values and ultimately forcing out the original residents. In *Cities of Tomorrow*, Peter Hall outlines how historical zoning and planning decisions have contributed to these crises, as the middle class, who now have nowhere to live, turn to places like housing projects, expensive fixer-uppers, undesirable apartments, and mobile homes.[56] These options are not ideal, but at least they are closer to a reasonable price point, allowing these unfortunate individuals to eventually save for a 'real' home.

Gentrification can be seen on a national scale. During the COVID-19 pandemic, there was a great migration across the U.S., with each state having different economies and densities. Residents who could no longer comfortably afford a home in their state traveled to others with comparatively cheaper houses. While a $400,000 home is affordable for a Californian, it is a significant expense for a Utahn. Similarly, while a $150,000 home might be a reasonable investment for a first-time buyer in South Carolina, it's essentially theft to a migrating New Yorker. This nationwide migration pushed housing prices out of reach for many and contributed to the displacement of low-income residents, moving them closer to homelessness.

The Flaws in Policy Approaches

Homelessness is a growing issue across the United States. Just a few years ago, panhandling was rare in Orem, Utah, but it has become a daily occurrence. People are eager to blame government regulations, mistakenly believing that aligning with the correct political party would resolve the housing crisis. Living in Utah, I'd often hear people compare our homelessness challenges to California's. They would say, "At least we don't live in California; their politics are behind their homelessness." I mistakenly believed that Utah's vastly different political climate would mitigate the problem of citizens living on the streets. I've come to realize that this is not true.

The conviction that having the correct policies in place would solve the homeless problem is understandable. I am painfully aware of how modern policies can exacerbate the housing issue. For instance, in 2023, unbeknownst to my husband and me, the Utah government introduced a grant to assist first-time home buyers. The grant offered a $20,000 loan with a 7% interest return on down payments for new constructions only.[57] We decided to bite the bullet and enter the housing market. After selecting a townhome we liked, the dealer sheepishly clarified, "Actually—those were last week's prices." The prices for all the homes in the subdivision had been raised by at least twenty grand. Even without the price gouge, the loan was scarcely a drop in the bucket. In an already hot market, we could no longer afford the home and walked regretfully out of the meeting. The

Utah government implemented a corrupt policy that divided the market, ensuring many first-time home buyers couldn't afford a home anymore.

This is a personal example of how political tactics meant to address the housing affordability crisis have inadvertently exacerbated it. Across the country, initiatives to provide affordable housing are often concentrated in the least desirable areas, particularly for low-income demographics. These policies unintentionally create densely packed slums that struggle to thrive. Although these measures seek to address the national housing crisis, they fail to tackle the core issue: inadequate infrastructure. We need a holistic approach to city building that emphasizes the creation of desirable, well-designed villages rather than merely adding more housing. When communities are thoughtfully designed, people from all economic backgrounds can coexist peacefully without the challenges that arise from concentrated low-income areas because more housing is available.

Packing vulnerable populations into undesirable areas inevitably leads to poor outcomes, such as increased gang formation, crime, squatting, and panhandling.[58] Citizens often blame rising crime on population growth or their city council, overlooking flaws in the zoning framework. Suburbanites may try to remove themselves from these problems through rigorous zoning laws, but they eventually face deteriorating infrastructure. In some regions of California, parks, and streets once meant for children have become overrun with homeless encampments and discarded needles. Over time, suburbia and its surrounding areas may deteriorate, with streets that once symbolized prosperity reflecting the harsh realities of a broken system.

Efforts to solve homelessness through policy have repeatedly failed.[59] California exemplifies this misfire. The state enforces hundreds of anti-homelessness laws, such as the "sit-lie" ordinance, which prohibits the homeless from sitting on benches or being in public spaces during certain hours.[60] This law merely displaces homeless individuals rather than resolving the issue. From 2018 to 2021, California spent nearly $10 billion on homelessness services. Yet, most of the half a million people who accessed these services remained without permanent housing.[61] A study by the Los Angeles Homeless Services Authority (LAHSA) found that 75% of individuals on the streets in Los Angeles County had a home in that same county before they lost it.[62] They lost their homes due to California's astronomical housing prices under the suburban framework. To put it simply, in order not to be homeless, people need access to affordable homes! California serves as a cautionary example for other states as they grapple with increasing density and widening disparities in prosperity. No place is immune.

By relying on outdated paradigms and applying policies as mere band-aids, the core issue remains: unless we move beyond the 1950s infrastructural framework, we will never have enough affordable housing in this country. Whether politicians enact good or bad policies, they cannot stop the impending avalanche that suburban infrastructure will bring to their state as density increases.

The Middle Class

Our sprawling infrastructure and dependence on cars are not only harming the poor but eroding the middle class. Suburbia—once the most sought-after and peaceful place for middle-class families to raise their children—is becoming increasingly unattainable. Suburban neighborhoods that were once lively and filled with children are now aging, as young families can no longer afford to live near their parents. With older demographics dominating these areas, the local economy dwindles. Even with affordable housing options, these towns risk dying out without the influx of younger residents needed to sustain economic growth. The few suburban neighborhoods that are attainable to young residents will likely face the same challenge in due time.

As urbanist Richard Florida states in his book *The New Urban Crisis*, modern city building erases the middle class.[63] Without understanding the effects of suburban infrastructure, older middle-class suburbanites may wonder why they could afford their homes for 'pennies' while their children struggle just to find affordable rent. They may blame their children, even when they've followed the traditional path of success: graduating high school, obtaining a college degree, finding stable employment, etc.

Older generations might argue... 'Well—if you had only saved more.' 'I worked hard to get my house.' 'I didn't eat out as much as you guys do.' 'I could barely afford my house when I purchased it back in the day, so it's not different.' However, these arguments often overlook how dramatically today's economic conditions and housing market have changed.

In the last ten years, some areas have seen single-family house prices rise 200-350% compared to the previous decade.[64] Housing prices are up a whopping 33% from 2021 to 2023 alone.[65] It's burdensome to buy a house now in productive and economically thriving counties; money has reduced power, and people are losing access to the beautiful areas their parents lived in. Recognizing this shifting dynamic and its root cause is crucial for our nation's prosperity.

To tackle the affordable housing shortage, we need pedestrian-oriented cities. These cities naturally adapt to the community's needs without excessive regulation, allowing for an indefinite housing supply. By avoiding overreliance on congested highway systems, cities can expand outward or upward more effectively. Additionally, promoting mixed-use housing, which includes a variety of housing types like single-family houses, condos, apartments, and townhomes in one area, can help address housing challenges.

In other words, Americans must shift towards more community-centered, less regulated urban planning to make housing more affordable and accessible. By fostering the development of pedestrian-friendly villages and relaxing zoning laws, we can move away from viewing houses solely as ever-appreciating investments. We should revive the practices that once enabled families of different generations to live close together in American cities. Without these changes, we risk deepening America's economic divides and succumbing to corporate and housing elites. We must reform our infrastructure and urban planning to protect the middle class or else welcome a new era of feudalistic corporatism.

7

Dear Suburbia, I don't feel so good.

American adults are grappling with a range of chronic illnesses, both mental and physical. Here are a couple of sobering American health statistics. The Centers for Disease Control and Prevention (CDC) reports that heart disease remains the leading cause of death in the United States across most demographic groups, claiming 702,880 lives in 2022 alone. To put that into perspective, heart disease causes roughly 1 out of every 5 deaths.[66] This staggering number reflects the tragic reality that countless families are losing loved ones to a preventable condition.

In addition to our physical health crisis, we are also facing a similarly widespread mental health crisis. According to Mental Health America, nearly 20% of adults experienced some form of mental illness in 2022, which equates to nearly 50 million Americans.[67] This emotional and psychological toll on American citizens is staggering and only getting worse.

If you're an American reader, these numbers probably hit close to home. Whether it's you, a family member, or a dear friend, chances are someone in your life has suffered deeply from mental or physical health challenges. I know firsthand how painful that can be. The truth is that we rely too heavily on pharmaceuticals and medical institutions to treat symptoms rather than addressing the environmental factors that are making us unwell in the first place.

Suburban infrastructure has radically altered the natural environment and social structures that have been integral to human life for over a millennium. For a typical American, the day begins by leaving their half-million dollar box in a box—only to arrive at yet another, larger box. They work for eight hours, get back in their box, and return to a box that looks like every other box on the block. They may even watch a box for entertainment.

A new phrase has been coined to describe the sedentary lifestyle of American citizens: 'Sitting is the new smoking.'[68] In the U.S., the mere concept of traveling anywhere meaningful requires sitting. Moreover, the separation of physical activity from functional life begins to erode the social fabric necessary for people to feel whole. The fundamental pillars of health should be seamlessly woven into our lifestyles, becoming natural parts of our daily routines. In our current framework, Americans must exert excessive discipline and exhaustive planning to combat numerous chronic illnesses. How did preventing death by heart disease become such a struggle for Americans? Although this is an extreme consequence, many Americans can relate to frequently feeling unwell, constantly searching for the next gym or quick fix in a desperate attempt to reclaim their health. Basic health should be manageable and not be a battle requiring extraordinary effort and sacrifice.

American society can offer a practical alternative to our sedentary and social crisis by providing functional spaces for people to walk. Many common illnesses in the United States stem from our sedentary lifestyles and can be mitigated through daily physical activity and healthy eating. The suburban environment, dominated by concrete landscapes and limited public spaces, doesn't offer much to encourage staying active. For many Americans, there need to be more productive reasons to venture outside, especially during winter, when endless online entertainment is at our fingertips, and there's nowhere inviting to go.

Some might argue, 'But there's a pickleball court just down the road!' While I enjoy pickleball, menial recreational activities aren't enough to encourage physical activity in areas primarily designed to keep people off others' lawns and in their cars. Pickleball, originally a low-impact sport for seniors, has indeed become a national sensation, injecting some activity into our otherwise sedentary lifestyles. Yet I predict that once the novelty of this sport wears off, many Americans will slink back into the comfort of their homes. How else do we fill our days? Perhaps with short walks around the block or watching our kids play organized baseball from a park bench. If our most compelling reasons to go outside are the occasional gym visit or a solitary pickleball court, suburbia needs a make-over. These amenities won't break the monotony. Suburbanites will still be confined to cookie-cutter homes with limited opportunities for outdoor exploration—a life boxed in.

Some may blame Americans for our plight, suggesting that 30 minutes of daily exercise could solve everything. After long desk jobs and exhausting commutes, many Americans find it difficult to muster the motivation for 30 minutes of rigorous exercise. The Heart Foundation reports that only 1 in 5 Americans get enough physical activity to maintain well-being, highlighting the struggle to prioritize fitness in our current way of life.[69]

Even if most Americans miraculously improved their physical habits, "30 minutes a day" is an adaptive medical suggestion to a lifestyle that rejects normal movement outside of play. It creates the illusion that '30 minutes is all an individual needs.' It becomes a staggeringly overwhelming task when everything related to health must be a purposeful decision.

Such discipline should be reserved for exceptional endeavors, not just meeting the bare minimum. In fact, an active lifestyle builds the strength and motivation needed to pursue exceptional fitness. The Danes, who incorporate cycling into their daily routines, are among the most active populations in Europe.[70] As the old physics adage goes: 'Objects in motion stay in motion.' We need spaces and designs that encourage people to move naturally; relying on cars to shuttle us from one sedentary spot to another will never provide enough movement to maintain health.

Processed Foods

Our dietary habits contribute to these health challenges, as we rely on highly processed foods from corporate entities rather than locally sourced alternatives. According to a survey conducted by the CDC, one-third of Americans consume fast food on any given day.[71] I suspect this is because our infrastructure has made fast food our most convenient option. Most fast foods are ultra-processed, meaning they undergo extensive modification, making replication at home nearly impossible. These foods are designed to delay fullness and promote overeating through a meticulous combination of refined sugars, unhealthy fats, and excessive salt, all of which trigger addictive eating habits. Additionally, they are full of preservatives, flavor enhancers, artificial colors, synthetic sweeteners, and potentially carcinogenic compounds. For example, food activist Vani Hari claims that the Chick-fil-A sandwich boasts 45 ingredients, including dyes like Yellow 5, which is banned in Norway due to its studied link to genetic mutation.[72][73] It seems like many fast food companies believe their pickles require artificial dyeing to look palatable. Beyond that unsettling idea, I don't want to eat a pickle that potentially mutates my genes.

It's clear to me why there's a widespread fascination with social media influencers who prepare fresh meals from scratch. These influencers showcase their access to quality ingredients, such as eggs from their own chickens, fresh milk from local dairy farms poured into mason jars, and freshly ground flour. It all looks beautiful without a plastic container in sight. For the middle class, dependent on corporate grocery stores, it can be envy-inducing to see influencers create such wholesome meals. It's bizarre that cooking with fresh ingredients has become a spectacle reserved for the most privileged among us. This disparity highlights a significant divide between those who can easily access nutritious ingredients not wrapped in plastic and those who cannot. The dominance of 1950s-style box stores, driven by a car-centric culture, has promoted nearly poisonous processed foods under the guise of convenience and, more disturbingly, health.

The American Journal of Clinical Nutrition reports that 76% of U.S. grocery store shelves are stocked with processed or ultra-processed foods, contributing to health issues such as obesity, heart disease, type 2 diabetes, hypertension, digestive disorders, and certain types of cancer.[74] Michael Moss, in his book *Hooked: Food, Free Will, and How the Food Giants Exploit Our Addictions*, tells the story of Kellogg's and the salt additives in their cereal. The cereal was so processed that when he tried the unsalted version, it tasted like metal. Companies use salt and sugar to disguise the artificial and low-quality ingredients used in modern food engineering.[75] Though many of these foods are advertised as "health" items. This manipulation of ingredients isn't just about taste; it has profound implications for how we interact with food. In a study on rats and junk food, the food acted like a drug similar to cocaine. The more they consumed, the more they craved it, leading to a loss of interest in regular food. When reintroduced to their normal diet, they chose to nearly starve rather than eat it.[76] If human behavior mirrors that of these rats, it stands to reason that some Americans may need to detox from ultra-processed food entirely to heal from their disordered eating. Real food is not addictive. With such a deprivation of quality food, it's no wonder Americans feel so unwell.

The impact of ultra-processed foods also extends beyond physical health, significantly affecting mental well-being. Studies have shown a strong connection between diets high in ultra-processed foods and increased risks of mental health issues such as depression and anxiety. The excessive intake of refined sugars, unhealthy fats, and artificial additives in these foods is linked to inflammation and oxidative stress in the brain, impairing cognitive function and emotional stability. These foods often cause blood sugar spikes and crashes, leading to mood swings and irritability.[77] The detrimental effects of ultra-processed foods on mental health underscore the urgent need for access to healthier, more natural food choices.

Every day, I can't help but feel that the average food I consume in America is potentially contaminating me, and I suspect many others feel the same way. For Americans to achieve a healthier state of being, we must regain power from large conglomerate food companies. This is only possible by re-localizing our food production through walkability. Can a person access their nearby farmers' markets, butcher, baker, and dairy shop more conveniently than a bloated box store? This shift is crucial in combating the food industry's manipulative tactics and taking our health back.

It Starts Young

Our current way of life is failing our children, leaving them with a poor foundation for health and forcing them to fight a lifelong battle against its consequences. According to the CDC, nearly 20% of American children are struggling with obesity, starting from the age of two.[78] We are setting our children up for chronic health conditions that are extremely difficult to overcome. I've never struggled with excessive weight gain, but I can imagine the immense pain that comes with it, especially for a child who lacks the knowledge or power to combat it. In my youth, I despaired about my inability to be more active, believing it was entirely up to my sense of discipline. Desperate to get into shape and curb my sedentary lifestyle, I joined the track team. Yet, like many adults, I discovered that participating in organized sports doesn't necessarily translate into long-term fitness in American life, nor should it have to.

In addition to our quality food shortage and barren suburban landscape, cultural pressures keep children from engaging in meaningful outdoor activities. Much of children's exercise comes from simply being outside, yet we've made it increasingly difficult for them to 'touch grass' even when it's safe. Many Americans believe children are incapable of enduring the outside world unless they are fenced in a well-groomed yard under constant supervision. A woman perfectly illustrated these attitudes at a city planning meeting I attended. After I expressed how important walkability is, she stood up and scornfully responded, "I'm not going to let my children walk to school in the snow." I was astonished. I wanted to provide a safe pathway for children to walk, but she rejected the idea because of uncomfortable weather. In Nordic countries like Finland, it's common to see young children trekking or biking to school in the dead of winter despite the dark and below-freezing temperatures.[79] Children are more resilient than American parents often give them credit. And, of course, all of these ramifications have an impact on mental health, as children are supplied less and less of what they need to become emotionally resilient adults.

Crafting environments where children can independently move through their surroundings sets them up for a lifetime of mental and physical health. In my neighborhood, developers built an elementary school surrounded by a sea of single-family houses less than two blocks from my home. Absurdly, it's common for mothers on my street to drive their children to school. Our misplaced reliance on driving not only creates unnecessary and dangerous traffic but also deprives children of autonomy and valuable outdoor time with peers, hindering their social and physical development. Even though engaging with their environment offers clear health benefits, our unsatisfactory car-centric neighborhoods, coupled with strange American attitudes, prevent children from building a foundation of lifelong health and happiness.

Blue Zones

Some exceptional individuals might not relate to this chapter due to their high discipline or love for fitness; however, it's evident that the general public is suffering immensely, trying to endure in a system that constantly sells them a new exercise disk, a miracle diet pill, or a depression prescription.

So, what does an individual need to live a healthy and satisfactory life? The Blue Zone Study gives us insight. Dan Buettner, a National Geographic Explorer, Fellow, and journalist, coined the term *blue zones* following an observational project to identify areas with the healthiest, happiest, and longest-living people. The study focused on five locations: Okinawa Prefecture, Japan; Nuoro Province, Sardinia, Italy; the Nicoya Peninsula, Costa Rica; Icaria, Greece; and Loma Linda, California, United States. The researchers found that these communities shared four core principles, divided into nine sub-sections: movement, connection, the right outlook, and eating wisely. To save time, I will skip the diet section and focus on what I consider the most applicable principles. The six sub-sections are as follows:

1. To Move Naturally: to live in an environment where individuals don't need to schedule vigorous exercise but have numerous opportunities for consistent movement throughout the day. Examples include planting and harvesting in a garden, cooking dinner, walking to a shop, or biking to school.
2. Purpose: having a reason to get up in the morning. This could involve anything from family obligations and maintaining a small business to charity work or religious activities.
3. Downshift: to avoid chronic inflammation from stress, Blue Zone individuals create environments and rituals that promote peace. These can range from prayer to enjoying a beautiful view.
4. Belong: these communities are a part of some faith-based group. It didn't matter the denomination.
5. Loved Ones First: they put family first. They live with their aging parents, they commit to a lifelong partner, and they take care of their children.
6. Right Tribe: Blue Zone people are connected and surrounded by

individuals with healthy habits and behaviors.

As Buettner puts it, "The world's longevity all-stars not only live longer, they also tend to live better. They have strong connections with their family and friends. They're active. They wake up in the morning knowing that they have a purpose, and the world, in turn, reacts to them in a way that propels them along. An overwhelming majority of them still enjoy life."[80]

I once stumbled upon a divisive TikTok video detailing a young man's postgraduate daily routine. Reactions were polarized: some saw it as a nightmare dystopia, while others hailed it as a success. His day went as follows: Wake up, drive to his 9-5 job, work at a computer, drive home for lunch, eat lunch, play with his dog in his backyard, drive back to work, finish his 9-5, drive to the gym, work out, drive to get a haircut, drive home, spend time training his dog, tidy himself and his house, eat a quick frozen pizza for dinner with a bubbly drink, and end his day with some streaming services, all set to repeat the next day.[81]

I am in the camp that this man is indeed living in some dystopia. Sure, he has it all—for those who overly value American materialism: a house with a yard, a friendly dog, gym money, well-kept clothes, a 9-5 job, a nice car, TV dinners, a couch, and a television with a Hulu subscription. Even with all his modern comforts, he struck me as an incredibly sedentary and lonely man. Although he traveled extensively, he spent most of his day sitting. As I've iterated, Americans must possess the towering discipline to live somewhat healthy lives. While he may have the discipline to work out, he lacks the discipline to create a social community. Almost all Americans understand this social dilemma, but it is most acutely familiar to men. Our current society strips out many masculine activities besides work and recreation. Our culture makes it difficult for men to create social tribes, which leads to an epidemic of loneliness, especially if a man fails to marry a woman and has children who could innately provide that sociality. Loneliness has serious health ramifications, including the likelihood of premature death.

In essence, the TikTok postgraduate falls short of embodying the core principles of the Blue Zone theory, reflecting the reality for many Americans. He isn't connected to a tribe or surrounded by loved ones. What exactly is his sense of belonging and purpose? From what we can see in his daily life, he lives an isolated and monotonous existence filled with asphalt, driving, work screens, parking lots, and little to do but watch TV when he finishes his day. He has very little time or opportunity to be outside. His routine epitomizes the emptiness prevalent in modern American society and underscores the profound need for deeper social integration and purposeful living.

Pedestrian-first cities enable the healthy core lifestyles that the Blue Zone study promotes. These spaces have both productivity and sociality interwoven into the system, allowing individuals to develop a sense of community through organic and serendipitous interaction while staying physically active. Mixed-use zoning and housing provide many more opportunities for families to live and work near each other. Natural beautification, which is more easily prioritized in human-centered spaces, helps people feel more satisfied and less stressed. The inherently productive environment offers a variety of activities, reducing boredom and tediousness. Village societies may not be utopic, but they enable the principles needed for a healthy, fulfilling life, unlike car-centric societies.

8

Dear Suburbia, Mother Earth needs you.

Most of us are worried about the environment and the impact we have on it. We deeply disfavor it when developers pollute or tear down nature. We want clean water, air, and food. Dirty and plastic-riddled oceans fill us with dread, and trash-littered freeways upset us. Nevertheless, we feel so overwhelmed by our lifestyles that we question how to solve or stop environmental decay. Eco-friendly solutions promoted by large corporations often have negligible impact and may even be harmful. For example, the paper straw movement had almost no effect on plastic consumption and, as reported by NBC News, may inadvertently introduce chemical risks to consumers.[82] Fortunately, prioritizing pedestrian-first design effectively reduces plastic waste, minimizes air pollution, and highlights how localization can address these issues on a grand scale.

Infrastructures that value corporations over local economies perpetuate unsustainable waste practices with no signs of stopping. Instead, they shift blame and responsibility to the consumer. They guilt individuals and nations for not buying 'sustainably' while burdening them with the cost of ineffective recycling. Their message? 'It's not us! You refuse to take responsibility for recycling! You don't put your money where your mouth is!'

Even if these methods were effective on a grand scale—which they are not—any efforts to curb plastic waste are undercut by corporations that won't stop producing it and by governments that remain unwilling to regulate it.

Corporate America floods the market with unnecessary plastic materials, ranging from soap bottles to grocery bags, fueling relentless plastic packaging and resulting in astronomical waste. According to the University of California, nearly 8.3 billion metric tons of plastic have been dumped into landfills since the 1950s.[83] Annually, America contributes over 35 million tons, much of which is intended for single use.[84] It's almost certain that when you step outside, you'll find plastic littering natural landscapes or roads. Over the past two decades, plastic production has more than doubled, resulting in over 14 million tons of plastic entering our oceans yearly.[85] This trashes natural habitats and foreign communities. In this way, America tragically grinds the faces of the poor in foreign countries who lack the roads, money, or infrastructure to cope with our continual plastic production.

Plastic is ubiquitous in American life, and its unfortunate presence is nearly impossible to avoid. It is becoming increasingly difficult to find food that is not packaged in plastic, even something as basic as bread. Single-use plastic is so pervasive that individuals are often unaware they're even using it. For example, many Americans don't consider that the explosively popular Scrub Daddy sponge, made of a plastic polymer, slowly breaks into plastic pieces that settle into our water systems as they do dishes.[86]

Dear Dad,

I've tried to stop buying plastic, and I've discovered it's impossible. I can't even buy bananas without a plastic ring around them. All of my shampoo bottles have to be specially ordered, as do my detergent and cleaning spray bottles. Almost every container in my kitchen is made from plastic. I can't buy meat, cheese, or yogurt without a plastic encasing. Almost every toy we own, my makeup, and my pens are made of plastic. I keep forgetting to put the fabric bags in the car since the last trip for groceries, which is literally the least I could do. It's hopeless.

Americans are constantly trying to escape plastic. Suburbanites often attempt to mimic sustainable practices emulated by influencers by transferring food from plastic packaging into glass or other eco-friendly containers. This additional step only removes the plastic from view and adds more work. The fact that influencers capitalize on the idea of using sustainable materials for food only reiterates how deeply Americans wish to live a similar lifestyle.

Unfortunately, wrapping food in plastic and the invasion of plastic in our water systems impact physical health. On average, Americans consume 70,000 microplastics a year.[87] In a study conducted in the Netherlands, all the male subjects had microplastics in their sperm.[88] Scientists have yet to fully understand plastic's impact on the human body. According to a study in *Environmental Science & Technology*, microplastics have been found in human tissue. It's feared that this level of plastic invasion could result in a range of health issues, including infertility, hormone imbalances, and potentially more severe conditions such as cancer.[89]

Alternatives

Reusing containers used to be standard practice in America. For example, neighborhoods used glass bottles with local milkmen, setting out their empty bottles to be replaced and refilled.[90] Pharmacies would take back glass or tin bottles for reuse. Without the beck and call of plastic, they developed convenient methods for storing and transporting goods that worked just fine. Perhaps unsurprisingly, this common practice disappeared in the 1950s during the plastic revolution. This trend was part of a larger shift in American waste practices, as described by Susan Strasser in her book *Waste and Want: A Social History of Trash.*[91] By embracing such local practices and reclaiming sustainable traditions, communities can forge a path toward an environmentally responsible and clean future for their children.

In a pedestrian-first society, opportunities to avoid plastic are abundant. Local candy shops provide an alternative to pre-packaged candy. People can visit their local confectionery, enjoy beautifully displayed chocolates, and use their own containers or paper bags. Another example is bringing a refillable bottle to the local butcher instead of browsing aisles for processed barbecue sauces in plastic bottles. Likewise, a local makeup company could offer refillable containers that customers can return to be sanitized and reused.

In a village setting, we could also see the revival of sustainable practices like cloth diaper services, a personal favorite of mine that was once common in America. Twenty billion disposable diapers enter our landfills each year, and experts estimate that they take up to 500 years to decompose. Additionally, 200,000 trees are cut down annually to produce them. There's also the concern about the chemicals released into the air during decomposition and their potential effects on a baby's skin. Disposable diapers are not only expensive, costing around $900 a year, but they are also an incredibly wasteful form of childcare—completely unnecessary when there's a better alternative.[92] Cloth diapers are the obvious choice if we wish to reduce our waste to almost nothing. Today, options range from all-natural materials to hybrid cloth and polyurethane covers with extensive lifespans. While yesterday's cloth diapers were plain and required safety pins, today's versions are soft, stylish, and easily secured with buttons or Velcro.

Given the clear benefits of cloth diapers, why aren't more people using them? The most common complaint about cloth diapers is that they need to be cleaned rather than just thrown away. Suppose communities embrace sustainable living because local communities begin providing better services. Cloth diaper services can make a comeback, where families leave dirty diapers in a wet bag or bucket on their doorstep every few days and receive freshly laundered diapers in return. This service combines the convenience of disposable diapers with the sustainability of cloth. It's not only cheaper than disposable diapers, if not comparable, but it's also guilt-free!

The label "crunchy mom" is just a manipulative marketing tactic by big companies to make you feel othered or weird when choosing sustainable options. It's normal to want to avoid waste—what's truly strange is the expectation to engage in the environmentally destructive practices of the 21st century. (Cloth inserts also double as great menstrual products—which can also be extremely wasteful and toxic—just a thought!)

On a similar note, suppose a daily walk or bike ride to a local farmers market was a convenient option. In that case, a family can bring their own mason jars, cloth bags, or containers to fill up on flour, sugar, rice, beans, fresh vegetables, and even dairy products such as milk and cream— then return to refill. This is less plausible in large grocery stores that inevitably ship everything in plastic containers for safety and accessibility. Residents often travel to these stores every two to three weeks, returning with bulk quantities of groceries heavily encased in plastic packaging.

In contrast, opting for a more sustainable approach allows you to find fresher produce wrapped in eco-friendly materials such as biodegradable wax paper. Unlike supermarkets, where plastic packaging dominates, local businesses can encourage customers to use their own containers.

Promoting local economies provides a sustainable way to reduce plastic waste. Villages turn away from box stores that harm our planet and elevate local talents and goods. By giving precedence to local businesses, communities can make significant strides in reducing plastic usage and waste.

Plastic Things?

America can significantly reduce its plastic footprint by embracing community-centric production methods that prioritize durable, reusable goods over disposable, single-use items. By aligning more closely with the principles of local production, American communities can cultivate a more sustainable environment that values long-lasting goods and rejects the disposable culture promoted by large corporations. Such a transformation would lead to a marked decrease in plastic waste, helping to restore both local economies and the global ecosystem.

Children's toys serve as a prime example of our outrageous plastic materialism. While toys can be beneficial for a child's development, research indicates that an excess of toys can be detrimental. A surplus of toys can overwhelm children, stifling creativity and reducing overall play quality. In *Clutterfree with Kids*, Joshua Becker describes too many toys as a distraction from development.[93] Children quickly grow tired of their toys and must find another way to entertain their boredom... or buy more toys. As reported by Yale University, the overproduction of frivolous toys ends up in landfills at an alarming rate of around 80%.[94]

This pattern repeats with numerous other disposable items pushed by corporations, which hold little relevance to daily life and are swiftly discarded. One of the most striking examples I recall from my teenage years was the abundance of knick-knacks handed out during youth group gatherings. These trinkets, from plastic whistles to polyester hats, were intended as mood-boosting 'party favors.' Yet they ended up being more of a nuisance than anything else. I questioned why I was given these seemingly pointless and worthless items, only for them to be lost or thrown away shortly after. We have become so accustomed to the excesses promoted by

Corporate America that many of us don't even question the environmental impact of our frivolous consumption.

As American cities embrace localization, we can better afford higher-quality goods made within our communities rather than accumulating debt and waste. This could include anything from food, clothing, decorations, furniture to woodworking, quality non-plastic children's toys, beautiful housing, and more. Imagine living in a culture where you could buy a local washing machine that could potentially be passed down to your grandchildren, instead of buying from a corporation that deliberately designs it to break down after 15 years. For anyone who visits their local farmers market, it's incredible to see the diverse small business artistry from those constantly producing quality products in such small venues. Imagine the prosperity and sustainability if we put people above corporate America. Essentially, less is actually more.

I have wondered how I am supposed to be wiser about my plastic consumption, but America's current system has made it nearly impossible. Our international corporate world forces us to live in excess in almost all aspects of our lives. Even 'minimal' American consumption is over-consumption. Pedestrian-first cities create easier routes for cleaner and less wasteful behavior because they are driven by local people, not corporate America.

Air Pollution

Much of America's pollution comes from vehicle usage. Although personal car emissions have become cleaner over time since the 1960s, it's still a matter of how much Americans drive. For example, according to IQAir, 55% of Utah's air pollution comes from car traffic alone.[95] Surprisingly, only 25% of cars cause 90% of air pollution, with diesel trucks at the top of the list.[96] As particulate matter and carbon monoxide emissions float in the air, communities suffer health complications affecting their lungs and organs. Studies indicate that children who live near or attend school in high-traffic areas may experience slower cognitive development, suggesting that air pollution is a developmental neurotoxicant.[97] This finding underscores the need to reconsider the location of schools, avoiding proximity to busy roads where air pollution levels are high. Additionally, it underscores the importance of fostering communities that offer alternative transportation options for children's education, as reliance on car travel increases their exposure to harmful pollutants. By creating environments that support healthy air, we can better safeguard Americans' well-being, particularly that of our children.

The proposed solution to the air crisis, ubiquitous across the U.S., is to drive less. However, I've often wondered how this is even possible and have felt guilty for my lack of participation. Driving down the freeway, I frequently see blaring signs urging drivers to 'Limit driving,' 'Please carpool more,' or 'Don't drive on a bad inversion day.' While taking the train or bus is suggested, it remains problematic. These propositions often seem illogical, attempting to guilt drivers into driving less without providing feasible alternatives.

Fathers can't stop going to work because it's a lousy inversion day. Mothers won't stop taking their kids to school or soccer practice just because of the bad air. Carpooling is possible in some circumstances, but it is highly inconvenient. If I had to gather my friends to go grocery shopping, it would never get done. Individual lives move at a rapid and chaotic pace, requiring them to travel on their own time and dime.

Ironically, while natural elements like trees are essential for mitigating the effects of vehicle emissions, they are being torn down in tandem with increased car usage. This ongoing destruction of natural resources undermines the very efforts of political programs aimed at reducing car usage and promoting environmental sustainability. Unfortunately, these initiatives often rely on ambiguous or temporary measures, such as imposing higher taxes, subsidizing electric vehicles, and aggravating public anxiety.

Electric vehicles, for example, are heavily advertised as a solution to the world's air problem. (If only more people could afford them.) This top-down approach, driven by government and corporate interests, leaves citizens with less control and fewer resources as the air crisis worsens. None of these expensive government policies or electric vehicle propaganda adequately addresses the root problem. Although electric cars can reduce air pollutants if adopted widely, they cannot curb the infestation of cars, lessen the ever-growing traffic, reduce corporate aristocratic control, prevent the loss of farmland, or solve the housing crisis. While I am happy to see that technology is becoming cleaner—and this should be exciting news in moving toward a much healthier world—this cannot be the end-all, be-all solution to the air and car dilemma.

When addressing passionate electric vehicle lovers, it's important to note that we should encourage this type of technology as much as possible. Yet, we must remain moderate in viewing electric vehicles as an environmental solution. No— not every American needs to own an electric vehicle, nor should we push society in that direction through compulsion or policy. It would be the opposite of progress. Just as car and suburban infrastructure is currently leading us toward environmental destruction, the mass usage of electric vehicles will not be our deus ex machina.

Still, this type of electric technology is valuable and exciting. It will stretch far beyond personal car usage, and it should. For example, if diesel service trucks are causing so much air pollution, promoting electric vehicles for professional travel while we restore our cities would be a great win for environmentalists and Americans alike who wish to enjoy better air quality over time. Electric technology can also be harnessed for cleaner and more efficient public transportation as most urban and suburban areas in the United States are redeveloped to incorporate new, more convenient routes. Even more profoundly, electric technology will quiet transportation, so communities no longer have to deal with excessive sound pollution.

We must cultivate local and functional environments in which, over time, individuals no longer necessitate cars. Government policy should not aggressively remove cars based on a 'righteous counter-movement.' Propaganda against cars is evident when cities forcefully make driving much more difficult without infrastructural restoration that supports alternative modes of transportation. Bad policies only antagonize the public, leading them to question the value of having a public transportation system at all; in trying to address pollution, these policies convince people that the government is disregarding their freedoms. The reduction of unbridled and unnecessary car usage must be achieved organically through more thoughtful planning and under the will and demand of the free market.

Under a functioning society, cities put control back into the people's hands. Cities can reclaim precious farmland and replace endless concrete and asphalt with beautiful landscapes, new businesses, or housing developments. They can support wildlife and plant more trees that provide healthy air, shade, and enjoyment. In effect, the tons of gas emissions entering our air—from the manufacturing of new roads, torn-down cities, and car traffic—will be reduced immensely without coercion.

The true solution to better sustainability, beautiful natural environments, healthier air, protection from harmful chemicals, and less wasteful plastic consumption is restoring pedestrian-first societies. The heaping production of useless plastic has followed the trajectory of suburban infrastructure almost perfectly since the 1950s. As suburban infrastructure grew, so did the public's dependence on major corporations, which promoted wasteful behavior and are continuing to do so. All Americans would feel much more at ease if they *finally* had the power to reduce their petroleum product and carbon footprint, buy more biodegradable or quality products, and breathe fresher air. The health of our bodies will thank us, and so will the earth.

9

Dear Suburbia, why are you so expensive?

When discussing mixed-use zoning, a common sentiment is, 'I'd rather drive to Smith's for groceries because their prices are cheaper than local stores.' This mindset often fixates on the immediate cost of goods, such as the price of bread, without considering the broader, unseen expenses. While box stores indeed provide affordability through economies of scale, the actual cost becomes apparent when considering our economic, social, and personal well-being. Beyond the price of cars and infrastructure, Americans overspend to meet their emotional, physical, and daily needs, compensating for their dysfunctional environment.

The Cost of Car Ownership

Imagine a system where you must buy a car, then pay for insurance, gas, parking, infrastructure taxes, and, finally, a freeway toll to get to work and survive. You probably didn't have to stretch your imagination—it's just another day in the life of an American.

Owning a personal vehicle is a major expense for Americans. According to the American Automobile Association, the average American shells out approximately $12,000 annually for one vehicle, encompassing various costs like car payments, insurance, maintenance, and gas.[98] Add a second or third vehicle to the original cost, and we're looking at around $24,000 to $36,000 a year. These figures highlight just how expensive car ownership is.

The majority of Americans rely on a car to earn a living and meet their basic needs. Nearly 50 percent of U.S. households own more than one car, making two cars essential for many families.[99] As a teenager in my economics class, owning a car was a non-negotiable requirement in the financial drafting section of the course. We've accepted this financial burden because our infrastructure doesn't offer alternatives. It's as though we're forcing every adult in America to own and maintain a boat just to get by.

To achieve autonomy, Americans find themselves obligated to cover car expenses. For instance, fatigued parents, usually serving as designated chauffeurs, rejoice when teenagers can finally handle errands. They make the financial sacrifice to invest in getting their kids a car to reclaim a bit of their own time and sanity. Moreover, in households without a second car, stay-at-home parents frequently find themselves confined to their homes until the vehicle returns, compelling them to delay errands until its availability. This reliance on cars comes at a steep cost financially and in terms of personal freedom.

In a functional society, the loss of a car is not the loss of freedom. A family wanting to visit a remote seaside spot inaccessible by public transport will have access to a car. If they do not own a vehicle, they can rent one for the day and return it afterward. Their freedom remains intact, but their wallets are $10,000 fuller. The lowered demand for cars reduces the price of gas and the vehicle itself. In this world, shedding the need for car ownership saves money and fosters a sustainable and accessible transportation landscape for all.

Without car expenses, well-utilized alternative transportation saves consumers money and contributes to cities' economic abundance. For example, the average monthly bus or train subscription costs $58, representing a 200% decrease in transportation expenses compared to car ownership.[100] Cities can use surplus funds generated by public transportation to enhance infrastructure and improve the transportation system, turning public transit into a valued and luxurious amenity rather than an afterthought. When planned correctly and utilized efficiently, public transit decreases the cost of living and meets the community's needs.

Is a Car a Necessary Expense?

Of course, most Americans can't get away without a car in today's infrastructure, but it doesn't have to be this way. In a pedestrian-first environment, a car becomes unnecessary; walking, cycling, and public transportation offer practical alternatives for daily errands and activities. Though I live in a car-dependent world, my husband and I once cornered a mid-density area in Provo, Utah. We found that if we placed ourselves perfectly within a one-mile radius of essential amenities, we could function comfortably without a car.

We began walking, cycling, and using public transportation for our frequent errands and recreational activities. One day, I walked to my car to nab a piece of gum, but I was puzzled when I discovered it was missing. My husband and I had been using it so infrequently that we had forgotten where we last left it. As it turned out, my husband had driven it to work and walked home without realizing the car was still there. This disinterest in using our car for everyday tasks seems universal in walkable areas.

The need for a car barely crosses your mind in walkable spaces, like in Philadelphia, Pennsylvania. The historic Elfreth's Alley offers a glimpse into 1700s life, with narrow streets designed solely for pedestrians. People still live there today, embracing a lifestyle that prioritizes walking and community engagement. Parking is minimal, with small lots integrated nearby. One resident notes, "If you live in the city, you become more pedestrian-friendly, and you use public transportation; we do have a car, but it's parked a few blocks away."[101] Such sporadic car use underscores the success of pedestrian-friendly areas, though they remain rare in the U.S. Imagine if all communities prioritized creating beautiful, functional spaces, allowing people to forgo the need for car ownership.

It is becoming increasingly clear that while depending on personal cars is unsustainable for everyone, this doesn't mean that cars are unnecessary or obsolete. If America embraces urban innovation, only rural communities and specific professions, such as delivery services, plumbing, and electrical work, will require car reliance. Ultimately, adopting infrastructure that prioritizes alternative transportation will alleviate the significant financial burden of car ownership.

Cities and Bankruptcy

Car infrastructure relies on an economic system that continuously demands higher taxes. This is a huge part of our ever-growing price for car-dependent living. Reliance on cars leads to higher taxes because roads fail to generate economic returns and deteriorate, requiring costly maintenance every 5-20 years. As a result, cities impose tolls or hike taxes, shifting the cost to suburban residents to fund expensive road projects like the $2.8 billion Katy Highway in Texas.[102] This extravagant expense raises the question: who can afford to pay for these projects? According to engineer Charles Marohn, no one can. Cities fall into a debt cycle as they struggle to meet increasing demands for roads. Freeway expansions require billions in upfront costs, leading cities to take on loans. To handle this rising debt, they attract new investors by promising more improvements, typically through further road projects or expanding franchises. This reliance on cars strains city finances and deepens the cycle of debt.[103]

Neglected roads, abandoned buildings, and decaying urban areas highlight the crushing weight of the debt burden. Citizens are puzzled by the lack of infrastructure maintenance, unaware that cities deceptively subsidize their taxes. Funds meant for local improvements, businesses, homes, and beautification projects are diverted to maintain sprawling suburban infrastructure and roads that offer no economic return. Even with perfect government spending, there will never be enough tax revenue to sustain such a system. Despite the harmful consequences for residents, city developers persist in the chaotic expansion of roads until they inevitably face bankruptcy. This unsustainable cycle of debt began in the 1950s with the rapid road expansion across the U.S. The accumulated bill is now due, and the current system cannot pay it.

Charles Marohn also found that suburban infrastructure acts as an all-consuming black hole for city resources like roads, water, gas, and electricity. Cities subsidize suburban living through property taxes, diverting resources from those who cannot afford or choose not to live in suburban areas. For example, it's common for hundreds of apartment dwellers to contribute property taxes for services like water, yet these funds only benefit a few suburban households. This is because suburban communities, due to their sprawled nature, pay relatively little in property taxes back to the city. Consequently, suburban areas with single-family households create scarcity by consuming disproportionate resources. If suburban residents were to pay taxes proportionate to the amenities they currently enjoy their taxes would likely quintuple.

During a case study of Lafayette, Louisiana, as they attempted to balance their $32 billion infrastructure costs, Strong Towns found that the average family tax bill would jump from $1,500 to $9,200 a year.[104] If cities were direct and transparent about how their money was being used, suburbia would not exist—because nobody could afford it.

Not all subsidies are bad. For example, it makes sense for urban cities to subsidize low-density, productive rural communities because farming districts provide essential food and economic benefits that support both rural and urban residents. By channeling subsidies into these areas, local rural communities could achieve greater sustainability and significantly bolster the broader economy. On the other hand, suburbia has nothing to offer financially; therefore, in all fairness, it should not receive cheaper utilities than more economically productive areas.

Sprawling franchises also contribute very little to property taxes. Instead of a plethora of mom-and-pop shops intermingled with residential housing, franchises monopolize vast lot spaces that could house other businesses that contribute significantly more in taxes. For example, according to Bloomberg, a 2013 study across 17 U.S. municipalities found that Walmart paid only $2,000 in taxes annually, while single-family houses paid around $2,800. In stark contrast, a 6-story mixed-use, mixed-housing development paid $100,000 to the city.[105] It's shocking and absurd that a giant corporation like Walmart pays less in taxes than an average family home. Walmart's negligible tax contribution is especially unnerving given that cities often subsidize its entry. As discussed, this corporate dependence devastates local economies. Being compact, local businesses pay significantly more tax revenue, allowing them to multiply within an area and provide ample funds to reinvest in the city's prosperity and infrastructure.

There's a prevailing myth that implementing walkability in cities will increase taxes. Statements like 'I don't want to pay taxes for public transportation!' or 'The new infrastructure is too expensive' perpetuate this misconception. However, the reality is quite the opposite. Walking trails, public transportation, and bike-friendly infrastructure notably enhance livability while lowering residents' tax burdens compared to car-centric infrastructure. These alternatives are cheaper to build and easier to maintain, lasting generations with minimal upkeep when implemented correctly. For example, investments in durable materials like brick for walkable spaces result in minimal maintenance costs over time, potentially lasting centuries. Similarly, simple measures like installing semi-temporary traffic bumpers, such as flower boxes, can create new spaces for bikers and pedestrians without requiring extensive construction. By prioritizing walkability, cities can reduce tax burdens while promoting sustainable urban development.

Unlike car-centric infrastructure, well-designed urban spaces can attract smart investments from third-party investors, resulting in a surplus rather than unmanageable debt. For example, cities can partner with investors to enhance the beautification of an area and establish walkability as a lasting feature. As the area becomes more attractive, it will draw further investment, enabling cities to repay investors over time using surpluses generated from housing, business property taxes, or public transportation revenues. While car infrastructure drives taxes up over time, pedestrian-first cities typically see taxes decrease gradually. Remarkably, pedestrian-first societies are healthier, more attractive, prosperous, and cheaper to build than our current infrastructure.

Car Injury

In addition to the direct costs of car ownership and infrastructure, numerous secondary expenses arise from our reliance on automobiles, including substantial healthcare costs. Motor injuries, in particular, have devastating and costly consequences. In my home state of Utah, for instance, there were 319 fatalities and 25,325 injuries within a population of 3 million in 2022.[106] To put this into perspective, Switzerland, which has one of Europe's most expansive train systems, reported an average of only 20 train deaths among its 8 million residents, compared to 200 vehicle deaths in 2021.[107] Due to their diversified infrastructure, Switzerland's death and injury rates are significantly lower than ours.

Consider the case of a father who, after flipping his car in the snow, becomes paralyzed from the neck down. This tragic event not only results in overwhelming medical bills but also limits his ability to work and requires costly modifications to accommodate his disability. Depending on the severity of a vehicle injury, individuals may face expensive medical interventions, a lifetime of chronic pain, or, worst of all, funeral expenses. A mother of two could tragically run over her toddler in the driveway or be killed by a drunk driver. While no one expects to encounter such tragedies, Americans must confront the relatively high frequency of these situations. Every day, I worry whether my husband will come home safely from work. Offering Americans more transportation choices could save many of us from unimaginable heartache and financial burdens.

Gym Membership and Healthcare

Our dependence on car infrastructure promotes a sedentary lifestyle, leading to unnecessary health-related expenses. Many Americans drive to expensive gyms to prioritize their well-being, while those who are less ambitious or cannot afford such luxuries often see their health fall through the cracks. When we aren't deliberate about our choices, we pay a premium to fix diseases that our environment could have helped prevent.

The health trends aimed at addressing these issues are both persistent and costly. From diet pills and supplements to gym memberships and home exercise equipment, Americans spend significant time and money trying to counteract the effects of our restrictive lifestyles. Despite my efforts to stay active, I've spent thousands of dollars on my health due to issues caused by a lack of movement. Think about the extremes you have personally gone to in pursuit of better health and satisfaction. How much time and money must we spend to find peace with our modern existence?

Considering the vast amount of money Americans spend on healthcare, our outcomes are abysmally poor. According to the General Wellness Institute, Americans spend over $828 billion annually on fitness-related expenses, yet we only rank 20th worldwide in exercise participation.[108] Despite the booming fitness market, GWI senior researcher Ophelia Yeung reports that American chronic illness and sedentary lifestyles are increasing rather than decreasing. We need to address the core issue. Mixed zoning can alleviate and even eliminate many of these problems as physical exercise becomes a natural part of daily life. Americans are far less likely to pay millions in healthcare costs if we aren't sitting in rush hour traffic day after day.

Mental Health

It's alarming to learn that one in five Americans struggles with mental health issues, leading to an annual expenditure of $225 billion on mental health services, according to Cision PR Newswire.[109] Paradoxically, despite our wealth and privilege, average Americans—who should be equipped to handle life's everyday stresses—find themselves grappling with mild to severe mental afflictions.

It's crucial to view mental health as the bare minimum for a fulfilling life. Witnessing so many who struggle to rise in the morning is disheartening, especially knowing that many suffer in silence due to an inability to afford help. With supportive environments, Americans can reduce the costly burden of poor mental health and move beyond mere survival.

To safeguard against mental afflictions in a harsh world, our ancestors valued community by building cities, villages, and towns that prioritized walkability. Walkable environments naturally encourage community interaction, physical exercise, access to natural beauty, and a sense of purpose—crucial building blocks for mental health. Without these elements, Americans must work hard to overcome sedentary lifestyles and foster social connections, a discipline that many find overwhelming. Instead, many of us spend our lives languid, glued to screens filled with a deluge of information and entertainment. By cultivating healthier environments, we can reduce mental illness and redirect our hard-earned money toward more fulfilling pursuits.

Entertainment

As our reliance on cars limits access to local amenities and outdoor activities, we end up shelling out money to escape—whether it's on pricier hobbies, streaming services, fancy entertainment systems, or trips to see distant family and friends. Bottom line: Americans are bored.

Entertainment once was more accessible and didn't demand hefty spending. I appreciate the movie *The Sandlot* because it captures a time when this was common. The film is set during the early days of suburbia before its spiraling effects had fully degenerated the culture. When parents felt safe letting their children wander. In the film, the two main characters bond with other boys over their shared love of baseball without any formal organization or expense. With one leader responsible for the baseball's safekeeping, their shared ownership leads to various adventures and mishaps.[110]

In the movie, the depiction of communal enjoyment and resourcefulness starkly contrasts with today's reality. There's a charming quality to children independently finding resources and creating entertainment spaces nearby. However, with the dispersal of communities and the rise of technology, such experiences have become increasingly rare. Nowadays, children often rely on structured activities with a price tag, like joining organized sports leagues or participating in paid recreational outings such as ice skating, museum visits, or arcade trips. As a result, the spontaneous and cost-free leisure of *The Sandlot* era has largely disappeared, replaced by activities that require both financial investment and transportation. No wonder people believe having children is too expensive in our day and age.

With the loneliness epidemic in the United States, adults face similar challenges. The lack of spontaneous encounters during daily routines erodes the chances to connect with others. Regular face-to-face interactions are crucial for fostering friendships and encouraging social gatherings. Yet, when these opportunities are scarce, people often resort to renewing their monthly Netflix subscription, choosing solitude over the struggle to socialize.

The Real Cost

The popular belief, "I'd rather drive to Smith's for groceries because their prices are cheaper than local stores," displays tunnel vision. It overlooks the extensive costs tied to our car-dependent lifestyle, including the high expenses and dangers of car ownership, insurmountable infrastructure taxes, and escalating mental and physical healthcare costs. This reliance impacts our daily lives, even limiting what we can do for fun. Many of us find ourselves unfulfilled, struggling to build close friendships, and exhausted from constantly seeking ways to meet our social and physical needs. Our environment has left us broken, clearly demonstrating that the true costs of car dependency far outweigh the benefits of interconnected villages. Sustainable infrastructure makes living more affordable and transforms our investments into fruitful assets, allowing cities to flourish rather than becoming depreciating entities.

10

Dear Suburbia, it's time.

As we reach the end of part one, it's important to reiterate that the costs of our current infrastructure extend far beyond the issues highlighted in the previous chapter; they permeate every aspect of our lives, as discussed throughout the beginning of this book. We live in a society where the car-centric design of our cities has led to unsafe roads, the destruction of local businesses, and an ever-widening gap between the promise of the "Land of the Free" and the reality of life for many Americans. This design perpetuates a cycle of dependency on corporations, degrades our environment, and strips away the beauty that once made our communities vibrant. The suburban sprawl is a framework that fosters isolation, sedentary lifestyles, and a sense of emptiness. It exacerbates societal issues like housing crises, gentrification, and even crime. The convenience of driving to a big-box store may seem like a small choice, but it carries with it the hidden costs of infrastructure taxes, healthcare expenses, and a loss of meaningful human connections. We are trapped in an environment that demands more from us while giving less in return.

The time has come to reprioritize our investments to create spaces where people can walk and connect again. By shifting our focus toward sustainable infrastructure and supporting local economies, we not only restore the safety, peace, and choice that have been stripped away, but we also free up resources that can be redirected toward exquisite craftsmanship and artistry. This will allow us to live in enchanting places once more, turning our investments into lasting, valuable assets for future generations.

As we continue, we'll explore how these consequences have shaped our cultural attitudes. We'll then outline step-by-step principles for restoring suburban environments into an American village. Finally, we'll examine how the American family must shed the negative cultural adaptations imposed by suburban ideals to thrive in new environments, ultimately improving mental and emotional health, especially for children.

II

Disconnected Lives: The Cultural Ripple Effects of Suburban Living

11

Dear Suburbia, you've turned us against each other.

As we transition into part two of this book, we will explore the generational divide that has emerged from the suburban experiment. Each generation has encountered suburbia differently, with older generations often nostalgic about the suburban dream while younger generations find such fantasies inaccessible or unappealing. This contrast in experiences has led people to have conflicting views on suburban life, turning an ideal cherished by some into a hollow disappointment for others. In the chapters ahead, we will investigate how this divergence has diluted our culture, eroded our shared sense of identity, and contributed to the widespread feeling that we have lost our way as Americans. By understanding these shifts, we can work towards a society with a renewed sense of purpose and belonging.

Here is a simple analogy to illustrate the different perspectives on suburbia: The King's Feast. A young king emerges and promises an opulent feast, inviting all his subjects to partake in his generosity. When the first group arrives, they find a surplus of food to enjoy and leave with full stomachs. However, as the subsequent groups arrive, the scene shifts dramatically. The plates become less bountiful, and essential staples begin to dwindle. Confusion and disappointment cloud the once jubilant atmosphere as villagers wonder why the king has failed to uphold his promise. Only meager scraps remain on the table by the time the last group arrives, igniting tensions and conflict among the hungry and disillusioned villagers.

In this analogy, the king represents the suburban landscape, controlling the allocation of resources and shaping the lived experiences of its inhabitants. The varied perceptions of the feast mirror how each generation views suburbia through their unique realities and experiences. Here, we will discuss each generation and explore why they have struggled to relate to one another since the inception of the suburban experiment.

Greatest Generation

The Greatest Generation is one of the most highly respected generations in American history, partly due to the infrastructure they experienced. They were born between 1901 and 1927.[111] They were the last generation to live in a pedestrian-first society, whether in rural America or major urban cities. Many fought valiantly in World War I, while others contributed to the rapid industrialization and economic growth that defined the early 20th century. Raised in close-knit communities where personal responsibility, hard work, and sacrifice were esteemed virtues, they laid the groundwork for the prosperity and stability that would characterize post-war America.[112] Their environment fostered resilience, patriotism, and communal solidarity, forming the bedrock of American society and leaving a lasting mark on the nation's future.

The Silent Generation

Between 1928 and 1945, many of our current zoning laws began to take shape. The Silent Generation mostly grew up in pedestrian-first cities, largely untouched by suburban sprawl. They ushered in much of the civil rights movements in the 60s.[113] They maintained high religiosity and were generally loyal to institutions. Many sacrificed their lives in the Korean

War. They grew up during wartime rationing, the Dust Bowl, and the Great Depression.

For this reason, they are known for being loyal, thrifty, and respectful. As adults, they embraced the allure of suburbia, with ample rural land available. Coerced into car dependency during the 1950s, they fervently believed in the freedom symbolized by the American automobile. They saw affordable suburban homes as a birthright. Properties and cars were inexpensive, fueling their enthusiasm for the new status quo. Since this generation represents suburbia and we've already addressed its broader historical context, we'll now discuss suburbia's impact on the family.

Children

Children from this era were active and competent members of society who contributed to the workforce. Years of advocacy eventually led to the Fair Labor Standards Act of 1938, which prioritized education over work for those under 16. As a result, children were increasingly funneled into the public school system, fundamentally altering societal expectations of their roles. However, in rural areas, many children continued to work for their families during or after school, as child labor laws were not effectively enforced.[114] This allowed them to retain valuable industrial and social skills, even as cultural norms began to shift before the rise of suburbia.

Mothers

Due to suburbia, motherhood experienced a profound shift, relegating mothers from active participants in society to glorified housewives. Suburban motherhood became an exclusively domestic role, with mothers focused solely on childcare and household duties. Appliances became ubiquitous, streamlining domestic tasks. This lifestyle separated mothers and children from regular society and established a dynamic where women were left to care for the children until the father returned in the evening.[115]

The Silent Generation significantly shaped modern attitudes about motherhood through how they coped with suburban life. The once glamorous title of 'the suburban housewife' has radically impacted cultural and economic practices, particularly in shaping religious views on gender norms.

The influence of suburbia on mothers' roles has been significant, with religious communities now equating being a stay-at-home mom with being a good mom. Most faiths expect mothers to be close to their children during their formative years. To meet this expectation and live in suburbia, women were confined to their homes and discouraged from pursuing interests outside of it. This perpetuated the misconception that the roles of 'housewife' and 'mom' are interchangeable, cementing the idea that being homebound is central to a mother's place in American society.

The stagnant and isolated lives of mothers in suburbia sparked a new wave of feminism, which likened the roles of wife and mother to slavery. The perfect 1950s housewife effortlessly maintains a spotless home, nurtures the children with boundless grace, and presents dinner punctually, all while radiating beauty and ease. Feminists rejected the notion that women's roles should be confined only to domestic labor, often attributing this limitation to religious rhetoric. The crux of the matter lies not in the belief that nurturing children is valuable but rather in the oppressive environment of suburbia. To compensate, women actively sought social enrichment by participating in "mom" groups, clubs, church activities, block parties, public school functions, and more. The feminists were correct in their assertion that this was not enough. Women deserve an environment that blends the demands of motherhood with opportunities for broader societal engagement. Instead, the moment women become mothers, America sentences them to a life behind a white picket fence.

Fathers

While often seen as purely patriarchal, the 1950s homemaker role had strong matriarchal undertones. In his book *Life Without Father*, David Popenoe argues that this is because men were conspicuously absent in suburbia, leaving a void in familial presence and influence. Consequently, children had fewer interactions with men, as they no longer worked nearby, resulting in a decrease in masculine role models.[116]

This dynamic greatly diminished a father's influence on his children since he had fewer opportunities to interact with them. For example, rather than a child spending time with his father doing farm work or helping with the family business, his father was away all day, only present for a few hours after a long shift and on weekends. When fathers from this era returned from work, they were likely burnt out, making it difficult to give their children the same level of attention they could have provided throughout the day.

This limited their influence and took an emotional toll as they struggled to balance work and family life. Men generally form connections through shared activities and tasks, yet suburban infrastructure does not adequately support this form of bonding.[117] In pedestrian-first societies, as previously seen in American history, men could actively and passively interact with children in their community while engaging in productive and everyday tasks. With suburbia demanding mothers to take on the majority of child-rearing and domestic labor, fathers had fewer opportunities for meaningful engagement with their children.

Fathers in suburban settings have a couple of responsibilities: providing financial support and engaging in recreational activities with their children. Although essential, these responsibilities often lack depth, not quite tapping into the deeper involvement that brings true fulfillment to family life. More roles include serving as a leader, mentor, and emotional support within the family dynamic.

Suburbia reduced a father's participation in domestic life, leading to negative stereotypes like "dumb dad" or "incompetent husband." Suburbia has saddled fathers with a narrow identity, where they're mainly seen as the family's wallet and weekend sports coach. This limited scope of involvement not only undermines the diversity of fatherhood but also perpetuates stereotypes that equate masculinity with only breadwinning and leisure. Men better equipped to create connections alongside their children, rather than solely through recreational 'play,' were often perceived as neglectful. They may struggle to establish meaningful bonds with their children beyond surface-level interactions. Imbalanced responsibility in child-rearing was placed on mothers, often without the support of a strong community to assist them. This situation embedded itself deeply into the American psyche of what proper gender order looked like.

This 1950s spousal dichotomy is often considered the epitome of the "traditional wife and husband." It is either falsely romanticized by some highly religious communities or scornfully despised by critical representatives of the feminist movement. Both groups react fiercely to the vast imbalance that car dependency creates in family life. Considering the challenges posed by these shifting societal norms, the Silent Generation managed them remarkably well. However, they did not fully understand the cultural and generational influence their new lifestyle would have over time—a perspective more easily seen in hindsight.

Boomers

Suburban infrastructure bestowed upon this generation perhaps the most abundant resources and prosperity.[118] The Baby Boomer generation, born between 1946 and 1964, stands out as one of the most influential and populous generations in the U.S. They have played a pivotal role in shaping political policies. However, despite their substantial political power, they show little interest in ending car dependency. This is because suburbia influenced the equation for the "American Dream" in this generation:

110

- Go to school.
- Get a degree.
- Get a job with a pension.
- Buy a family car.
- Buy a suburban home.
- Start a family.
- Attend church (and maybe get a family dog).

While Baby Boomers embraced suburban living, they did so at a time when many of the challenges now associated with suburban life had yet to emerge. For instance, the rapid population growth that often leads to resource shortages and traffic congestion was not yet a significant concern. As a result, undeveloped areas made housing relatively affordable. This allowed many Boomers to enjoy spacious homes surrounded by picturesque rural landscapes. Access to farmland for exploration was more readily available, allowing Boomers to engage with nature and exercise autonomy.[119] Furthermore, during their childhoods, technological advancements that are now ubiquitous, such as online video platforms and unlimited television networks, had not yet permeated homes, preserving a sense of local community and identity.

Boomers' nostalgia for "better times" is widespread.[120] Underneath an old picture of Orem, Utah, that I found before it became urbanized, several comments from individuals of Boomer age expressed longingly: "I miss the old Orem where my brother and I would roam the apple orchards. Now it's a chaotic mess."

Today, Boomers often struggle to understand the importance of mental health because their childhoods were more holistic, encompassing the enjoyment of nature, community, and autonomy. Trade skills were still prevalent in households, providing children with hands-on learning experiences and ample mentorship. With around 10-12 years to navigate

111

the transition to adulthood, Boomers were well-prepared to embrace responsibilities, often taking on major life commitments like marriage and family earlier than later generations.

The rise in formal education played a major role in fueling the feminist counterculture of the 1970s. This counter-movement challenged suburban gender roles, notably highlighted in Betty Friedan's book *The Feminine Mystique*.[121] Despite the societal push to reject traditionalism, Boomers held on to Judeo-Christian beliefs, which is evident in the strong religiosity prevalent among their generation.[122] This contrast illustrates the complex blend of social change and enduring traditional values that shaped the Baby Boomer identity, as shared religious involvement was a major source of community and sociality for them.

The Baby Boomer generation has witnessed the peak of technological advancement and enjoyed nearly every modern amenity of the 21st century. They also have relished the accumulated wealth that the housing crisis has bestowed on them through climbing real estate prices.[123] As Boomers grapple with the challenges of the 21st century, including technological advancements and economic upheavals, they often find it difficult to reconcile their prosperity with their grandchildren's financial challenges. They typically attribute these challenges to the rise of social media or corruption in government and school systems. However, like the Silent Generation, many have yet to grasp the negative impacts of the suburban experiment.

Having enjoyed a period of perceived cultural prosperity and stability, this group often resists acknowledging that the system that gave them so much might be flawed. They represent a blend of suburban ideals, traditional values, and societal shifts that have influenced American culture and politics. Despite their understandable reluctance to confront these underlying issues, Boomers have the potential to shape America's landscape for the better.

Gen X

Generation X, a unique cohort born from 1965 to 1980, has accepted suburbia as the status quo. They have never known anything different. This generation is fiercely independent and highly distrustful of government institutions. Born after the civil rights movement, they readily embraced and defended the narrative of racial equality. This generation places a high value on consumerism and the free market, often exhibiting more materialistic tendencies than previous generations.[124] They watched more television than their parents and were introduced to personal computers and cell phones earlier in their lives. This generation was far edgier in clothing and behavior, engaging in a rebellious counter-movement to the pristine and suffocating norms of suburbia. An explosion of franchises, corporatism, advertisements, music videos, MTV, magazines, self-help books, and Hollywood movies was shaping the cultural landscape. They approached higher institutions of power with cynicism and skepticism. While social institutions like churches and public schools were generally chugging along, this generation trusted and valued them less.[125]

The culture surrounding Gen X children underwent a significant change during this period. Unlike previous generations, they were less likely to be involved in family businesses or farming in their youth. As a result, they were perceived as unskilled and given less respect. Still, Gen X-ers maintained a degree of autonomy during their childhood. With the influx of working parents, much of this generation was left unsupervised, sometimes verging on neglect. They were gifted a house key, usually between the ages of 8 and 12, to access their empty homes, earning them the nickname "latchkey kids."[126] While this absence of parental influence came with challenges, it also allowed them to develop independence and resilience. Unlimited outdoor autonomy gave this generation 6 to 10 years to practice becoming adults. In turn, they were more prepared for adulthood than their millennial children. They eagerly embraced the opportunity to leave the house and drive a car.

Gen X participated less in local community gatherings and clubs than their parents. Malls emerged as popular social hubs for this generation, emphasizing the importance of car ownership for socially active teenagers. As the suburban landscape widened physical and social interactions between neighbors, they began to experience the first effects of community isolation.[127] Social attitudes toward neighbors evolved, with Generation X showing less interest in nurturing relationships compared to the Boomer and Silent generations. This detachment was considered "cool."

As the job market evolved and demand for trade skills decreased, Gen X-ers prioritized higher education and became considerably more college-educated. Their media exposure to culture and politics led to reduced political activity compared to their parents. Instead, they chose to pursue prosperous and consumer-driven lifestyles with their college degrees. Gen X-ers mark the last generation for whom home ownership was within reach for those with a college degree or a decent job.

Despite Gen X-ers spending a good amount of time outdoors as young adults, their diets and physical health suffered due to the prevalence of highly processed foods from corporate box stores, an expanding fast-food network, and increased reliance on cars for travel. According to Dr. Keith Kantor, creator of *Nutritional Addiction Mitigation Eating and Drinking*, Gen X was labeled as the unhealthiest generation.[128] Consequently, a rising fitness culture exploded across the nation. Alongside these physical health challenges, Gen X-ers also faced mental health issues. Their mental health was worse than that of their parents, though not as severe as their millennial children's. They attribute cultural degeneration and declining mental health to the influence of social media and technology.

For a Gen X-er, car dependency is central to American life. They have never experienced a world outside of suburbanization or seen effective examples of alternative infrastructure in the U.S. Due to their independent streak, this generation is more open to changing infrastructure. They are frustrated by rising traffic and concerns about government overreach. Additionally, seeing their children struggle financially and emotionally has fueled their willingness to consider alternative solutions.

Millennials

Millennials were born between 1981 and 1996 and are the first group to suffer the most severe consequences of suburban infrastructure. They remember a time before the digital age. However, online and smartphone devices inculcated much of their adolescent or young adult life. Despite being one of the most college-educated groups in America, they can't seem to catch a break economically and are less emotionally stable. This generation is often characterized as lazy, financially illiterate, and silly.

According to PBS, Millennials have lived with their parents in droves since 2020.[129] As previously discussed, the growing population density in suburban areas is beginning to cap housing markets. Millennials, in particular, are feeling the impact of these issues as they struggle with limited and unaffordable housing options despite having decent jobs.

Although half of this group grew up without significant digital influence, their childhoods differed radically from their parents. Millennial children were culturally and environmentally infantilized until the age of sixteen when they were abruptly expected to "grow up" after receiving a driver's license. Strict child labor laws and regulated environments confined them to "child-only spaces" like schools and parks.

Adding to this conundrum, Gen X-ers and Boomers were led to believe that American children were being abducted at alarming rates, often depicted as being snatched by white vans. In reality, child abductions were statistically unchanged and remain quite rare.[130] Perhaps this fear was a reaction to the more unregulated childhoods of late Boomers and Gen X. Regardless, Millennials were heavily supervised and restricted from roaming the streets.

Even if they had the opportunity, there were fewer places to explore. Suburbia's expansion had replaced much of the open rural land of previous generations with endless rows of uniform houses. Their environment grew increasingly unnatural, dull, and noisy, particularly in the expanding downtown areas.

These factors impeded Millennials' competency and contributed to self-esteem issues, which prompted the implementation of programs like 'No Child Left Behind'. However, the practice of awarding every child a trophy, regardless of performance, proved ineffective for teaching emotional regulation and life skills—skills that develop naturally in more constructive environments.[131] Overall, these stifling childhoods hindered Millennials' development of independence and resilience.

For this generation, receiving a college education was everything. They focused heavily on building an extensive extracurricular portfolio to enhance their college applications, becoming deeply involved in organized sports and academic activities. In contrast to the greater autonomy enjoyed by previous generations, Millennials were confined to highly regulated and institutionalized environments.[132] This shift was driven by the rise of ubiquitous franchises and the decline of local businesses. Parents prioritized formal education to prevent their children from being stuck in a low-wage job like a McDonald's cashier for the rest of their lives. The erosion of local opportunities meant parents could no longer encourage their children to join family businesses or develop trade skills.

Gen X and late Boomer parents, facing immense pressure to prioritize academic success, often excused their overscheduled children from basic household responsibilities. As a result, many Millennials lacked essential skills like cooking and cleaning when they reached adulthood. Instead of managing practical tasks, they were overwhelmed by heavy emotional and mental demands, struggling without sufficient opportunities for autonomous discovery or regular outdoor activity.

As the digital age took hold and suburbia remained as dull and regulated as ever, this generation spent dramatically more time indoors compared to their parents. They immersed themselves in an array of screen-based activities, including television, pornography, video games, and the insipid world of social media.

The deprivation of organic community in suburbia drastically diminished Millenial's social skills. Unlike previous generations who frequently rubbed shoulders with their neighborhood friends, it was abnormal for Millennial children to gather serendipitously in the suburban sprawl. As adults, they are less likely to participate in community events or find any satisfaction in them. Even a Millennial who is skilled at socializing may struggle to find the time and discipline needed to gather others in this splintered social climate.[133]

Millennial adolescents gobbled up social media because it promised to fulfill a much-needed desire for social connection with minimal risk or effort. It allowed them to observe others from the safety of their iPhones, offering a pseudo-form of relationship-building without the challenges of direct human interaction but with less reward.

The Millennial generation is rapidly abandoning religion, which was once a central source of social and emotional support.[134] Many Millennials feel it has not fulfilled its promises. This disappointment partly arises from the expectation that religious institutions should be the sole providers of community and hope. However, these institutions struggle to carry this burden alone, especially when broader societal systems fail.

Hyper-dependent on parental authority, Millennials were confined to their homes until the age of 16, relying on their parents to shuttle them to various activities, including college application extracurriculars. Treated like children until they received their driver's license, Millennials had a brief window of two years to explore the world before being expected to become fully-fledged adults. This transition proved challenging for many as they faced the complexities of life beyond the protective bubble of public school. Consequently, Millennials have come to embody the saying, '30s are the new 20s,' spending a decade after high school graduation catching up on emotional regulation and essential life skills that they were deprived of during their childhood.

This delayed development is often falsely attributed to the shortcomings of the public school system, leaving Millennials ill-prepared for the practicalities of adult life. Questions like, 'Why didn't they teach us how to manage taxes? How to finance a house? How to handle student debt?' reflect the frustration of a generation struggling with real-world skills.

Millennials faced the first widespread mental health crisis in America and went to great lengths to destigmatize mental health issues while seeking personal relief.[135] Their own experiences and fears with mental health have shaped their approach to life and parenting. As part of their ongoing infantilization, they were encouraged to delay marriage or avoid it altogether. Driven by a deep fear of divorce—often rooted in their own childhood experiences—combined with emotional immaturity, they extended their dating years before marriage. They also postponed having children until their thirties, feeling unprepared emotionally and mentally for parenthood. To address the psychological pitfalls of their upbringing, Millennials frequently embrace trends like 'gentle parenting' to safeguard the emotional health of their children.

This generation also struggled to stay physically active amidst a predominantly sedentary lifestyle. The increase in media use also exacerbated expectations for beauty standards and fitness. As a result, many Millennials grappled with eating disorders, body dysmorphia, exercise obsessions, and a mania for clean living and food.[136]

There is a large disconnect between Boomer/Gen X parents and their

Millennial/Gen Z children because the older generation lived completely different suburban lives, and they cannot fathom why their children are struggling to cope. The term "Okay Boomer" comes from a bitter group of Millennials who feel their parents' generation let them down.[137] They believe they were not emotionally or mentally equipped to handle life's challenges, especially the escalating economic crisis. They are tired of being mocked by older generations as they were inadvertently confined to an environment that left them emotionally and physically dependent.

They feel deeply misunderstood and don't know how to handle being continually shunned out of the "American Dream"—even when they did everything 'right.' Ironically, this generation still relies on dependency, hoping that mass government intervention will solve their problems. Millennials don't feel as proud to be Americans as their parents, and they longingly look to other countries they believe are doing better.[138] Many don't cherish their culture, which has become so industrialized, negative, sexualized, fragmented, and chaotic that they often don't know where to turn for information or peace. It's not difficult for this generation to be convinced that America needs drastic infrastructural changes as they profoundly feel their environment is over-stimulating, corporatized, and shallow. Many dread driving a car, especially in traffic, and they spend a lot of time online searching for more beautiful, peaceful, and exciting places to be. They are highly enthusiastic, if not hopeless, in reorganizing American life so that they and their children do not continue to suffer.

Gen Z

Generation Z, born between 1997 and 2010, represents an intensification of the cultural trajectory set by Millennials. Having grown up with technology permeating every aspect of daily life, Gen Z has never known a time without digital influence. This reliance on technology has resulted in a generation with limited social skills, especially when interacting with people outside their age group.

"Big Brother" is their lifestyle. They are passively shuttled from place to place by cars or parental chauffeurs. Gen Z navigates a landscape increasingly dominated by suburban sprawl. This lack of stimulating or accessible destinations further isolates them and exacerbates the mental health issues that are already on the rise within this demographic.

With their lives steeped in intense online stimulation, Gen Z may be experiencing burnout or apathy. For instance, many in Gen Z are eschewing traditional milestones like marriage, driving, and even sexual intimacy.[139][140] They are tuning into the digital world more than the physical one. This disconnect from real life makes them increasingly bored and unfulfilled, with even work or academic pursuits failing to spark their interest. What's to get excited about when everything feels so monotonous?

This dependence on online platforms and public institutions has also led to early ideological politicization, with Gen Z embracing intersectional coalitions at younger ages than previous generations.

Compared to previous generations, who typically enjoyed a decade or more to transition into adulthood, Gen Z often finds itself thrust into independence with almost no preparation, particularly for those who delay obtaining employment or driving until they are 18. This lack of preparation sometimes leaves them drowning, often yearning for meaning and purpose, and frequently feeling empty and alone.[141]

If America is not careful, this generation may be so desperate for change that they could give all their power to corrupt and powerful institutions that promise quick fixes but deliver tyranny.

They may be so impatient for infrastructural changes that they encourage a top-down approach where walkable cities are instantly planted and controlled by international entities rather than local governments and individuals. They must recognize that a bottom-up approach is the better alternative, one that promises meaningful change within their lifetime.

Gen Alpha

Generation Alpha, born after 2010, represents the future. As children, they are currently in their formative years. Societal and economic trends suggest they may face unprecedented difficulties if we don't address our infrastructural crisis.

Given the social climate of our modern environment, Gen Alpha is likely to struggle with developing the emotional stability needed for adulthood. They face limited opportunities to connect with their community or develop meaningful skills. Generation Alpha will encounter technologies like Artificial Intelligence without the necessary buffers to navigate its complexities. This dependence on digital technologies may leave them highly reliant on government institutions for support. Without a restoration of the American village and a rejection of car dependency, Generation Alpha faces a bleak future marked by housing affordability issues, diminished political power, compromised mental health, and restricted prosperity.

Everyone Suffers

There's no use in generations blaming each other. The suburban experiment is a complex phenomenon that defies easy categorization—a place of both promise and peril. Many American parents are desperate to provide healthy and happy lives for their children but must compensate for how our environment has failed us. How could any generation anticipate the breadth of technological advancement or what the suburban experiment would lead to? Most societies have multiple lifetimes to figure out what works in their culture. In the last 70 years, Americans have had what feels like a matter of seconds to figure out the best way to maneuver our advancing world.

Despite the varying levels of success from the suburban experiment, all six living generations have suffered to one degree or another. We have lost prosperity, beautification, creativity, interesting places, farmland, and political power. The infrastructure has separated us from our communities and even families. Each generation must deal with the destructive course of the current zoning and infrastructural failures. We must confront the cultural degeneration and difficulties the suburban experiment has placed on us.

No matter when we arrived at the feast, we are still ruled by a tyrannical king. It is our collective responsibility to take back control and shape a better future.

12

Dear Suburbia, you've stolen our culture and identity.

Sadly, the discord we've observed among generations is just one aspect of a broader cultural erosion. Our infrastructure acts like a vampire, draining the lifeblood from America and slowly shutting down its organs. The aftermath leaves us culturally destitute and searching for meaning. It wasn't always this way.

As we examine the cultural casualties of car-centricity, we'll also rekindle hope by exploring how pedestrian-first cities can restore richness to our culture and rebuild a unified American identity.

Institutions

Car infrastructure has weakened our institutions by creating millions of non-functional spaces that offer no meaningful interactions. While the modern workforce provides some opportunity for socialization, it no longer serves as a significant source of deep community ties. The 'Great Resignation' of 2021, marked by Millennials and Gen Z-ers frequently job hopping, underscores the diminished value Americans place on their 'corporate families.'[142] Working for large corporations simply can't provide the same level of intimacy that local businesses can, and it's clear that people are feeling the difference.

If our suburban neighborhoods are cultural dead zones and our corporate jobs are similarly underwhelming, Americans are left with churches and public schools to meet their need for connection. However, these institutions are also losing their impact. The pool of people participating in religious services is at an all-time low. Our corporate families might be stronger than our church families at this point—which is saying something. This decline is unfortunate, given research by *Religion, Families, and Health: Population-Based Research in the United States* indicates that religion can positively impact individual and community well-being. Benefits include reduced crime and drug use, longer life expectancy, economic prosperity, increased charitable donations, and better mental health outcomes.[143] Religion helps unify community values typically for the net good. Since religion can foster communal and personal well-being, it's clear that abandoning these kinds of institutions puts communities at risk of further deterioration.

At least we can count on formal education to keep us connected, right? Not exactly. Homeschooling is on the rise as more families turn away from the public school system due to various criticisms, including its perceived corporate structure. Interest in universities is also fading as people question the skyrocketing costs and diminishing returns. If this trend continues, all the traditional avenues for social engagement will wither away.

Essentially, without environments that elevate organic connections, workplaces, churches, and schools begin to suffocate. As American culture is increasingly replaced by car culture, the significance of these institutions wanes. Fortunately, pedestrian-first environments can revive these institutions, as local businesses and mixed-use housing naturally hold our communities together.

Holidays

The start of many cultural dilemmas can be tied back to the 1950s when suburban zoning exploded into American life. A striking example of how suburban infrastructure has diluted our culture is the corporatization of American holidays. Christmas, a beloved Christian holiday, has rejuvenated the human spirit for centuries. Unsurprisingly, as suburban infrastructure has uplifted corporate dependence, the Christmas spirit has continually diminished in favor of consumerism.[144]

In pedestrian-first communities, people celebrate holidays through service projects, religious rituals, music festivals, caroling, sharing with the less fortunate, giving gifts, making crafts, writing letters, and preparing festive food. Both religious and non-religious members of the community enjoy these traditions. These practices are still happening but with less vigor over time. Instead, Americans are essentially harassed every time they walk into an ugly box store and are forced to listen to the same Mariah Carey Christmas album for months at a time.

Our approach to Easter is similarly corporatized and demoralizing. Consider the millions of plastic eggs discarded yearly and the single-use plastic candy wrappers accompanying them. This disposable behavior is gross, gluttonous, and cheap—especially given the holiday's deep meaning and value. With more thoughtful and creative gift-giving, these traditions could be both beautiful and sustainable. Imagine hunting for a personal basket filled with cheese, chocolate, grapes, and handmade letters instead—nothing goes to waste; everything is meaningful.

Or think about the average American birthday party, where we buy single-use plastics, like balloons, table covers, and trinkets. These items end up in the trash mere moments after they're used, threatening our environment with unnecessary litter and pollution. We could opt for more sustainable alternatives like paper or fabric decorations. For instance, beautiful and

125

intricate foldable sphere lanterns can closely resemble balloon displays and be stored for future use or passed down. How much more enriching would our holidays and traditions be if they weren't driven by wasteful consumerism? I would be ecstatic—personally.

The prevalence of consumerism leaves individuals feeling isolated and fiscally stressed during the holidays. Instead of living in a society where everyone, regardless of wealth, can enjoy the generous traditions passed down through generations, many feel like America prioritizes their dollar over their heart.

Pedestrian-first communities foster meaningful holiday engagement in ways that car-centric societies simply cannot. Here are a few examples of how a village would celebrate a holiday like Christmas: the library invites Santa Claus to read Christmas stories to neighborhood children; a local bakery offers free hot chocolate every year on Christmas Eve; a soap boutique donates shampoo bars to a local or international charity; a theatre troupe puts on an annual puppet show, a butcher gives away five free turkeys to neighbors in need; a high school choir sings Christmas hymns in courtyards around town; and a local millionaire donates Christmas lights to beautify the city. The list can go on in much more creative ways than I could voice. Whatever the tradition, it should turn our hearts to each other rather than to corporations to act as our intermediaries with the less fortunate.

Will these practices happen in our current environment? Not likely. We no longer have strong local communities to uplift them. We have replaced most of our cultural practices with large yellow arches and parking lots. While big businesses can mimic these traditions in some ways, in the end, their contribution is shallow. Since they are primarily motivated by profit rather than people, their efforts are deeply impersonal and lack genuine care.

In our corporate culture, the true meaning of holidays gets lost in translation. Potential bitterness toward these celebrations may arise as they fail to live up to their promises year after year. At this point, some question why we celebrate them at all.

Social Gatherings

In addition to diminishing our holiday spirit, the influence of commercialism is causing our social gatherings to fade. Our culture has become so national and watered down in the last three generations that sometimes it takes an imaginative and historical approach to explain what we've been missing and what is possible for future American heritage. There is a fictional book series that I have seen catch fire in recent years called *The Unselected Journals of Emma M. Lion*, set in 1883 London, written by American authoress Beth Bowers. It has attracted robust public affection because the author frankly has a gift for being both witty and hilarious while plausibly expressing what a pedestrian-first town, with its rich culture and traditions, can feel like.[145]

For example, one of the many well-known traditions in St. Crispian features an annual undisclosed performance of *Hamlet*, in which only the most passionate and lucky few can discover the venue's location if they decipher the supplied clues throughout the town. Certain established and respected business owners in the community are privy to specific clues and assist those with accurate information. If a person fails to receive a ticket, they can look forward to trying again with renewed effort and enjoy a fresh performance next year. In another, more darkly hilarious example, the town spends one day each year searching for the church vicar. Once found, they put him in the stocks and later 'hang' him. This tradition began after a church vicar betrayed the town during a war effort a few decades ago. The vicar cannot leave town for the day if the game rules are obeyed. St. Crispian's contemporary vicar is quite skilled at evading foraging citizens, but it seems everyone enjoys the sport of potentially capturing him. This is particularly poignant for the men in the town who giddily look forward to the yearly sleuthing event and relish the passive camaraderie and competition that occurs when they are on the hunt.

In a real-world example, we can see how localization can be powerful in assembling meaningful communities. Thomas Sowell, an American economist, social philosopher, and political commentator, noted this during the Civil Rights Era in his book *White Guilt: How Blacks and Whites Together Destroyed the Promise of the Civil Rights Era.* Segregation had many harmful consequences, but it fostered tightly-knit local communities among Black individuals.[146] The solidarity and resilience within the era of this Black culture inspired the hit show *Hairspray,* which sought to capture its strength and unity. It was the locality that enabled Black communities to stand in the face of tyranny and discrimination; that generation has left an enduring legacy that continues to influence racial movements today.

This kind of cultural lore can happen in pedestrian-first towns because the townspeople are constantly engaged with each other through worship, work, and recreation. Thanks to proper zoning and walkability, they experience the ease and advantages of proximity. Annual events and activities are almost self-organized through community gossip and expectations, bringing striking interest and happiness to daily monotony. The most fervent and trusted community members hold up local heritage like a sacred mantle. Car dependency makes forming tight communal ties much more difficult and sometimes impossible.

Social Dancing

One historical piece of American culture that I believe suburban infrastructure disintegrated, or at least heavily contributed to the erosion of, is social dancing. Social dancing has been a highly effective courting strategy between men and women across various societies and eras.

In pedestrian-first societies, it's common to have spaces where men and women can gather to express appropriate sensuality and physical prowess. Both genders spend time peacocking or wooing potential suitors, and it's simply just plain fun for everyone involved when there's enough mutual competency.

Social dancing used to be an incredibly important part of American culture. A 1907 *New York Times* article published a study that found that of the 1,097,503 people in the five countries they reviewed (the United States, Germany, Switzerland, France, and Greece), 80% of the married or soon-to-be-married couples had met at a dance.[147] This strongly opposes the Stanford study published in 2019, which found that the most popular way modern people meet their significant other is through online interaction rather than through neighbors, friends, or church meetings since the 1940s.[148] Online communication is a much drearier and more distant form of courting than social dance, which can be quite amusing and physically stimulating.

In 1919, 2,500 urban amusement parks provided pavilions for American teenagers to dance in, sometimes amassing 150,000 dancers a day. By the 1960s, there were only about 245 left.[149] It's amazing how quickly social dancing was lost after suburbia was created. The 1950s Lindy Hop and Jive are the last remnants of a strong casual dance culture. It's so sad this ordinary practice has faded—especially now, when modern men are stigmatized as less masculine for enjoying such a normal, human activity.

Dance band historian Leo Walker once noted, "The ten-year period comprising the 1950s was one of steady decline for the dance band business, from its once top position as a form of live entertainment to a situation where only a few of its former great names could prosper."[150] Instead of men and women engaging in romantic dancing traditions to a live band, today we see wasted college students with little dancing skill grinding against each other to stereo beats. Alas, we see another great loss in our culture.

Nostalgia

This cultural void is why there is a great yearning and profit for nostalgia. Americans constantly try to escape our modern world and return to a perceived 'better time.' This desire drives major corporations to leverage products, media, and services that take consumers "back" to whatever era holds the most interest to them. While nostalgia can be a sweet getaway, its pleasure is fleeting; it cannot quench the deep hunger for meaning many Americans experience.

Disney is an excellent example of a corporation that capitalizes on Americans' desire for nostalgia. The Walt Disney Company is an international success, and in its golden years, it represented incredible innovation, storytelling, and values for people of all ages. Today, Disney attempts to attract audiences with nostalgia-driven remakes that echo the past rather than crafting new films that reflect the present, possibly because we resent this era. Ultimately, both Americans and the intended products suffer while our money is siphoned off to billionaires who will simply create something trite once again.

Identity

Car-centricity is an overbearing lifestyle deteriorating our neighborhoods, workplaces, churches, schools, and beyond. Yet, somehow, most Americans seem to have an underlying sense of what true American culture is, even as corporate entities like Hollywood refract it in a thousand different directions. We're constantly searching for it, watching it slip away like sand in our fingers. Neighbors remain strangers unless they are deeply involved in their religious communities or make a concerted effort, such as hosting block parties or joining clubs. Our widespread loss of local engagement contributes to a growing identity crisis among Americans. As we stop participating in shared practices, we lose our ability to relate to one another and our country. This affects our view of American history, political beliefs, and core values and explains much of the generational and political divide; we don't even want to live near each other. Suburbia, the very space meant to bring us together, has torn us apart.

To put it lightly, the suburban experiment isn't good for us or our culture. Our culture is decaying; generations are at odds with each other, and traditional institutions are falling by the wayside. It's anguishing to see our holidays and customs, like social dancing, being reduced to the shadows of their former selves, especially since online communication is usurping face-to-face interaction. Our insatiable appetite for nostalgia shows we'd rather be anywhere but here. Americans yearn for a solution to this loss of self.

Moving forward, we must recognize the devastating impact that suburbanization has had on us. We must build infrastructure that uplifts connection over convenience, creativity over consumption, and community over individualism. Only then will a wholesome culture be returned to us. Ironically, the best way to unite the country is not done on a grand national scale but through local communities that each contribute something unique and beautiful to our society. By constructing places worth living in, we can become unified and feel what it truly means to be an American again.

III

Restoring the American Village: A bottom-up revolution

13

Dear Suburbia, it's all up to you.

For years after graduating college and maintaining a steady job, my husband and I clung to the hope of finding a home that wasn't just another condo by the freeway—one close to family, friends, and work. As a mother of young children, I insisted on having a yard; the thought of raising my children without one was unthinkable, and I was already struggling with the constraints of apartment living. In the wisdom of our current infrastructure, my uncle told me, "It doesn't matter if you're house-poor—just buy a house, *any* house. It's only going to get worse." But I couldn't accept the idea of potentially being trapped in a place I didn't love for the next twenty years under a crippling mortgage.

Desperation set in as I searched—frantic. I wondered if I could provide a healthy home for my little children. I even considered leaving the country. I found remote homes that were much closer to my price point outside of the state, but none of them seemed worth investing in. I now understand why it was so difficult for me to find a suitable home beyond affordability— which was tight. I was searching for something far more significant than four walls. I didn't want a single-family home that was isolated from meaningful interaction, even if it was spacious or picturesque. I truly craved a community—a thriving ecosystem of productivity, beauty, and human connection. To my disappointment, I was searching for something that doesn't quite exist.

While every American deserves access to shelter, we shouldn't settle for a mere roof over our heads. We should demand homes embedded in beautiful, operative environments that allow us to raise our children, connect with our elders, and enjoy a high-quality life. Anything less is a disservice to ourselves and the future we're trying to build. In other words, it's never been just about the *house*.

How Do We Get There?

While entertaining the concept of restoring the American village, you may have wondered, "How are we supposed to fit villages into a world entrenched by Walmart super centers and 26-lane freeways?" It's no wonder people respond to me with forlorn faces when I bring up the possibility. They often exhale and say, "Yeah, living in a village sounds nice, but it's too late for us." As I've said before, it's most certainly not too late!

Rather than trying to uproot major corporations or freeways, the middle class can reclaim village life by enacting zoning laws that allow them to work where they live. In a truly free market, major corporations could lose their stronghold over the American people as more community-focused alternatives emerge, which would also reduce reliance on expansive freeways.

If our entire infrastructure needed to be torn down, it would be too difficult, expensive, and time-consuming. However, we don't need to buy land from large governments or commercial businesses; we just need to allow people to contribute to the economy from their own neighborhoods. Villages are a product of the working middle class. Essentially, village rehabilitation starts from the bottom up, beginning in residential areas—A.K.A., the suburbs.

I don't love suburbia for what it is but for what it could be. This is my

Love Letter to Suburbia because suburbanites are at the heart of restoring the American village. I'm not putting my faith in big government or corporations to solve the American infrastructure problem but in my fellow Americans. We don't need to depend on grand institutions but on each other. The "loophole," so to speak, to resolving our issues is giving the middle class the freedom to do what they do best—build strong communities, drive economic growth, and uphold the values that make our nation great. They are the "American Dream." With all of its faults, suburbia holds the keys to saving our nation.

This movement must start in the suburbs because, unlike commercial downtowns and surrounding freeways, they don't require drastic infrastructural overhauls. They can be incrementally improved through individual and city efforts. As they currently exist, suburbs are nonfunctional, low-density, isolating, and dull, displacing farmland in favor of tract housing. However, with a strong vision for prosperity and changes to current zoning laws, they can become lively, functional, self-sufficient, and affordable villages. Because of how villages handle density, they can protect farmland and preserve the natural beauty of the area. In this system, locals are prioritized over billionaires, and people have dynamic transportation options instead of enduring traffic day after day. As economic prosperity shifts away from commercial downtown areas, infrastructure is bound to follow. Therefore, to organically meet the needs of the American people, we must transform American suburbs into magnificent American villages.

There are three key strategies to turn American suburbs into vibrant and functional villages. They should be tackled in a specific order and applied wisely.

1. Provide mixed-use zoning (mixed-use, mixed-house, mixed-wealth)
2. Create walkability and redesign infrastructural road failures.
3. Lastly, communities should supplement newly created walkability with efficient, speedy, and reliable public transportation within the

village limits and eventually connect cities.

If any of these steps are done out of order—such as prioritizing public transportation or allowing governments to densify residential areas without including businesses—the efforts will fail. Cities often start and end with the last step, which frequently infuriates drivers who are already greatly inconvenienced by nonstop driving and traffic. I will preface that I am not an urbanist nor an engineer, and I cannot provide solutions for every city or suburb. Even if I could, this book would be much too long and tedious. Every municipality has its own laws and red tape to reconfigure or dismantle. However, this three-step process is based on strong urban theories that will help restore villages across the United States.[151]

Mixed-use, Mixed-house, Mixed-wealth

Evolving R1 zoning areas into villages requires a commitment to mixed-use zoning, flexible density, and local businesses. A main facet of village life is people should work near their homes.

I once visited a beautiful Victorian house in a small downtown area that had traces of mixed-use zoning. The bottom of the store was dedicated to selling dance gear, while the owners lived on the top floor. Despite the store being in a house and the owners living there, it did not detract from the experience. The store was beautiful inside and out, improving the community rather than infringing upon it.

This design helps keep villages attractive and successful because people care for and maintain the places where they live. Since individuals have no invested interest in their commuting destinations, they are indifferent about whether these places become decrepit. They will happily encourage more ugly roads to make their commutes faster, even at the expense of other areas. Because these roads are outside their own community, they're less concerned about their impact. However, no community should endure higher taxes and road expansions near their homes just so outside drivers can use their streets for daily commutes.

For example, a friend of mine, who recently bought a house and has invested significant time and money into it, is now fighting the expansion of a road in front of her home because the city wants to build *another* road for easier freeway access. The value of her home will inevitably depreciate, and suburban degeneration will continue to spiral.

Suburbs must adopt mixed-housing and mixed-use zoning to reduce the ever-increasing congestion from car commuting. This approach would bring back the flexibility in land use that characterized America before the first zoning restrictions in 1907. As renowned urbanist Jane Jacobs remarked in her book *The Life and Death of Great American Cities*, mixed-use environments enable convenient walkability, which negates the need to drive to designated commercial areas.

For instance, a house could be converted into a shoe shop and later back into a residence, just as an apartment complex could become a general store, or a millionaire might buy three lots to build a chateau. People would be allowed to use land according to free market principles, with the public and local government making balanced decisions about which businesses best contribute to the community. With these new zoning freedoms, suburban areas would naturally evolve into villages where everything is within walking distance.

Take a Moment to Imagine

Here's a vision of how mixed-zoning could transform a suburb into a village:

A woman who loves to sew starts a formalwear business in her neighborhood. As her business expands, she moves her family to the second floor of her house and remodels the first floor to serve as her business. She is pleased that more people are moving into the neighborhood, which bolsters her business. She makes a decent living and hires three new employees to help her. As a side gig, she begins specializing in historical costumes. A growing professional theater company notices her talent and commissions her to make costumes for their shows. She decides to focus on this full-time. She is thrilled to be near her family while contributing to her community and pursuing her dreams.

A bored and retired accountant wants a closer grocery store so he doesn't have to drive. He decides he's the man for the job. He buys a home a couple of blocks from himself and guts it. He works with local farmers and vendors to get fresh produce. Various small vans arrive early in the morning to restock. He hires 6-7 community members to work for him as cashiers, stockers, and building care. The community uses his store for daily needs because it is convenient and well-stocked.

Another man realizes the local grocer has fewer dairy products than the community wants. He buys an old law firm in the community and transforms it into a dairy shop. He provides fresh cheeses daily. Customers bring their own glass bottles and fill them with fresh milk.

A knowledgeable butcher moves into the neighborhood and opens a business. Neighbors begin asking him questions about his various meats and how to cook them best. Multiple bakeries spring up across neighborhoods, providing fresh sourdough, pastries, and sweet rolls.

A flower shop arrives a few blocks away, followed by a yoga studio. The community needs a family doctor, so a man starts a small practice and hires 3 to 4 nurses; his son cleans the offices after school. A gynecologist follows suit, then a local dentist. A woman wants to provide better spaces for youth to congregate. She buys a cheap, beat-up home, fixes it up, and installs a ballroom floor. She uses it as a wedding venue and charges a small fee for social dance nights. The beautiful venue is an excellent reason for the community to gather frequently.

A local immigrant opens an Italian café nearby to complement the crowd. It is a great place to grab a bite to eat or people-watch. Confectioneries, home improvement centers, mini-law firms, thrift stores, sports gear outlets, music shops, and programming services begin to arrive. People buy homes or lots at affordable prices and renovate them according to their needs.

As more people move in, the city begins building spacious and architecturally impressive apartments. Discovering this, a sizable tech company realizes it is losing employees to small businesses. Additionally, more than half of its workers live in areas where they are reluctant to commute by car. The company responds by splitting its offices and placing them in villages throughout the area.

It buys three homes and transforms them to fit the village aesthetic. While the company occasionally gathers in the city, it primarily operates from these local villages and communicates with other departments via video conference as needed. A dad at the company is thrilled to bike to work rather than drive, and with so much to see, he enjoys his daily commute for the first time in his life.

The city hires architects to add character to bland buildings and encourages facade improvement programs for tract homes. It also hires local landscapers for public maintenance, like restoring a rarely used grass field. The landscapers start by planting trees and installing a fountain. They also add lamps along several brick pathways to enhance the area. Small vendors visit the site frequently, and there are plenty of places to sit.

Part of this park is used for recreation like soccer, frisbee, or dog walking, while the other is designated for musical or theatrical entertainment. People frequently walk by and stumble upon a community event. Over time, it becomes a beloved hub, well-maintained and bustling with activities throughout the year.

A small lake operates as an ice skating rink in the winter and a fishery in the summer. A man runs a shop to manage both, and people can buy fishing gear or ice skates depending on the season. Several community gardens pop up around the area, allowing people to grow their own food. During Christmas time, lights are strung up in the trees, and clothes are donated to those in need.

Children and teens suddenly have many spaces to go. They begin gathering all over the neighborhood, exploring different areas. They congregate and make their own spaces for socialization and fun. They start running errands for their parents, buying gifts and treats for friends, and acquiring jobs.

Rather than aimlessly walking through suburbia, parents and adults venture outside to discover interesting places to shop, curious about who they might encounter or what they might find.

This vision for village transformation can happen in current suburban neighborhoods through small businesses and flexible density. The village then accumulates wealth, which can be reinvested into the community.

Businesses and Chains

In villages, zoning for businesses can get pretty complicated as they try to strike a balance between community values and economic growth. As villages mirror family values, like suburbia hopes to do now, they can discourage smoking shops or seedy alcohol joints from entering the space— promoting them in metropolitan areas instead. The underlying principles for small businesses should always be as follows: "Does this business bring prosperity to our village?" "Is this business low traffic for cars?" "Do they maintain peace?" "Are they causing pollution or ire among the citizens?" "Are they overbearingly loud?" "Are they attractive?" "Will they add value?"

And finally, "Are too many similar businesses trying to compete in the same space?"

One of the points that Jacobs iterates is that economic diversity is key to village life. Villages are a bit like natural ecosystems; just as ecosystems require a balance of various species to function properly, a village needs a mix of businesses, services, and community activities to remain vibrant. If a village loses its diversity, it will likely stagnate and decline.

Consider the impact of a species that becomes too dominant; it turns invasive and disrupts the balance of the entire ecosystem. Likewise, when a business becomes overwhelmingly large without the proper density to accommodate it, it starts infringing upon smaller businesses and compromising the economic stability of the entire village. It would benefit such a business to move to a denser area or expand elsewhere. The same principle applies to companies that compete right next to each other. Jacobs observes that none of these businesses perform well if an area has multiple deli shops or barber shops on one street. Diversifying businesses is essential for maintaining broader community interest and economic prosperity.

What about businesses like franchises? Franchises and chains pose similar risks to suburban areas aspiring to become villages. They undermine local economic independence and are generally considered undesirable. Suburbanites don't want to live near enterprises like Arby's. Major franchises should be reserved for the densest areas in the state. To keep our local economy diverse and preserve the unique character of our towns, it makes sense to prevent corporations like Dollar Tree from moving in. These big companies will kill any efforts to transform a suburb into a vibrant village. With all this in mind, some villages may allow local chains to enter with the understanding that they can still maintain economic diversity and identity. Hopefully, the barrier to entry for these chains will be stiffer due to the explosion of middle-class businesses.

143

Individuals and communities must advocate for mixed-zoning policies in their neighborhoods. While positive change may begin incrementally, with collective effort, it can happen faster than we imagine.

Density

Density is not an inherent virtue, as many urbanists believe. Plopping down six skyscrapers in a suburban town to fill the state's density quota is problematic; it aggravates car infestation in a car-dependent place. This type of reactionary planning creates desolate projects that fail to resolve the cost of living crisis. Suburbanites are utterly terrified of growing populations, and for a good reason: density does not inherently bring the amenities, conveniences, and wealth they seek.

However, density and convenience become cyclical when a city is well-designed. As the prosperity and beauty of a village grow, density naturally follows suit and vice versa. Our current framework is split into three distinct parts: urban, suburban, and rural. As suburban areas get more crowded, they become chaotic, and people feel like they must flee to rural areas to find peace. And thus, the cycle of infrastructure sprawl continues. People are constantly running from what they consider 'high density,' but the reality is they are running from car traffic, disorder, industrialization, crime, and stiflingly regulated environments. Ironically, most things suburbanites hate about higher density are the direct consequences of the zoning laws they keep fighting for.

This underscores the significance of designing developments that thoughtfully implement strategies to sustain prosperity and beauty as populations inevitably increase. Unlike what is observed in suburban areas, villages maintain their integrity and aesthetic appeal even as density rises. It's the difference between living in Florence, Italy, a city rich in history and art, or a town that keeps you addicted to fast food and makes it difficult for you to get home promptly after four o'clock.

From this point onward, when I mention density, I am advocating for density that comes from planned, thoughtful, incremental urban growth rather than as a last-ditch effort to deal with overcrowding or housing shortages. Villages must anticipate and prepare for increased density. They can do this in various ways, such as constructing more housing or adopting flexible zoning laws. The approach may differ depending on the specific circumstances of each city. For instance, if a village is concerned about infringing upon rural farmland, it may opt to expand vertically rather than horizontally.

Though other urbanists may fiercely disagree, I believe most villages should have a density cap—specifically in terms of building height and population size—to prevent overcrowding. Overly dense cities, like New York City, face challenges, such as strained sewer systems due to the burden of high-rise buildings. Therefore, it's preferable to have millions of self-sustaining, mid-density villages rather than a handful of overcrowded mega-cities. By setting these limitations, we can incentivize the development of new villages rather than overburdening existing ones. Cities with extreme density, like Chicago, New York City, and San Fransisco, should always be in the minority. In all ways, villages must be wise and responsible in their resource management relative to their density.

Benefits

There are many ways village life contributes to the ease and pleasantness of a place while accommodating a lot of people. For those who insist on living in semi-rural areas because they believe these are the only places that remain 'pretty,' that's simply not true. Extensive tree placement can make a village look quite beautiful and enchanting. As a bonus, some trees use 40-50% less water than some types of lawn grass, which reserves precious water for mass community consumption and other beneficial amenities.[152] When water bills and road development are not draining city funds, they can be allocated to aesthetic appeal, so that people are surrounded by stunning architecture and landmarks.

One of the biggest myths about high density is that it causes crime. In reality, low-density rural areas like the Appalachian Hills can be just as crime-riddled and poverty-stricken as the densest cities. In "Hillbilly Elegy," author J.D. Vance describes low-density communities steeped in drug abuse and crime, including a confrontation where a man puts an ax through a friend's back over a slur.[153] Single motherhood, drug abuse, limited education, and an inability to invest in one's own community are some of the most pivotal causes of crime, regardless of population density.[154][155]

Since villages handle mid- to high-density gracefully, they provide suburbanites with what they desire—easy access to businesses, schools, and convenience—without ruining the landscape they treasure. The walkability of villages enhances and preserves all the alluring aspects of suburbia—peace, family life, low traffic, privacy, and beauty.

Mid-density village life offers suburbanites all of these magnificent things without the need for a car or the consequences that come with it. Higher density means more stores and amenities. As a community becomes denser, more people engage in a wider variety of activities; with an influx of participants, the quality of these activities and events improves. Are you passionate about quilting? You'll find specialty quilt shops, fan groups, and live conventions. Love baseball? There are clubs and intramural leagues that cater to every age group. Are you a Harry Potter enthusiast? Join the Quidditch practice sessions held on Wednesday evenings at the recreation center! Enjoy theater? Denser populations create more opportunities for the performing arts, leading to exceptional quality productions and increased theater wealth. For suburbanites who wish for their children to go to good schools, play soccer, or take music lessons, gentle density in villages is where they will find those opportunities.

Everyone understands what it's like to attend an orchestra concert in a low-density rural or suburban town. With such a small pool of participants and fewer opportunities for growth—attending almost feels like an act of charity. Despite the beautiful backdrop a rural town may offer, which isn't understated, they are deficient in other capacities. When I was searching for a nature-centric home outside of my own urban chaos, I realized my growing family would lack the opportunities that I wanted for them. There are trade-offs to rural living, where the simplicity and serenity frequently come at the cost of educational, social, and professional opportunities I wished for in my own life. Suburbanites may have forgotten that people, through sharing their talents, breathe life into our culture; we should welcome them rather than push them away. When designed wisely, villages are lively, beautiful places where every street offers something interesting to explore and enjoy.

Higher density also allows more families and friends to live next to one another—another huge perk. Building strong familial ties can help re-establish support and community in our very lonely and struggling America. Higher density also spares rural land because it doesn't sprawl over it. Rural land is more easily protected for mass enjoyment, and it can become productive again as villages begin relying on local farmers. Suburban developments needlessly destroy rural land because it is useless to them while they are dependent on big box stores.

Lastly, having more people around means more job opportunities and better pay. There is a significant increase in employment opportunities within densely populated communities, such as retail, hospitality, healthcare, and technology. Studies have shown that areas with higher population densities tend to attract a more diverse range of businesses and industries, leading to a broader job market[156] and higher average wages for residents.[157]

Nature has a way of creating laws that bring health, freedom, and prosperity. As we can see, suburban areas cannot be low-density and have all the amenities of urban living without a whole host of problems. Similar to a stroad, trying to have it both ways can result in both falling short. Suburbia, as Firenze in Harry Potter says, is 'a half-life, a cursed life.'[158] We must realize that if we want specific amenities and conveniences, they inevitably come from people.

Suburbanites have removed people from amenities as faceless corporations have taken their place. The suburban experiment artificially separates individuals from the economy while a village recognizes they are at the heart of the economy. Villagers celebrate when people come in because that could mean a butcher, yoga instructor, or choir director is a part of their community. When locality is returned to people, they no longer view the economy through the lens of estranged corporations; they understand people are bringing these perks.

While higher density can enhance communities, there is a sweet spot. Too high a density may feel chaotic and cramped, whereas too low may feel boring and inconvenient. Given what I know about suburbanites, they truly desire communities that resemble villages—a balanced density that supports small businesses, cultural vibrancy, and camaraderie among residents. Suburbanites need not fear density when towns are well-designed; they may find... they even prefer it.

Propinquity verses Togetherness

As someone raised in suburbia, I was indoctrinated into believing "togetherness" was crucial to being a good neighbor. I realized I held this belief after reading Jane Jacobs' book, *The Death and Life of Great American Cities.* Jacobs gave me the language to describe the cherished suburbanite concept of "togetherness," which emphasizes the need for neighbors to maintain high levels of intimacy. Suburbanites understand that dissimilar value systems strain 'intimacy', so homogeneity is a key pillar in how suburban communities form and function. This attitude is evident in their willingness to pay extra taxes for Homeowners Associations (HOAs) and adhere to strict neighborhood regulations. From my experience, I now understand how difficult and ineffective it is to apply "togetherness" on a grand scale, like in an entire neighborhood.[159]

An alternative to mass "togethernesses" is propinquity. Propinquity emphasizes physical proximity over forced intimacy, allowing for greater variety and flexibility in social interactions. By contrasting these two approaches, we can explore how propinquity fosters healthier and more sustainable communities. Moving forward, it's crucial to recognize that walkability and localization are essential ingredients to propinquity.

Suburbanites build intimacy by participating in activities like block parties, dinner dates, public schools, and religious meetings. Historically, religion served as the foundation of community connection for middle-class Americans, leading many to closely associate it with suburbia. While you can develop a sense of community by participating in religious communion, you gain stronger religious ties through social interactions.

Our infrastructure discourages effortless connection, so suburban areas are witnessing declining religious participation, even in regions with strong religious roots. As a result, the traditional methods of conserving "togetherness" in suburban environments are becoming increasingly less effective.

The problem with mass "togetherness" is that it requires a level of intimacy most adults aren't willing to participate in, especially now. People generally don't want their entire lives open for public consumption and judgment (with the apparent exception of family vloggers). Preserving intimacy also becomes more challenging as more people enter the sphere. Togetherness can cause cliques, discrimination, and exclusivity toward those who don't fit the mold, whether intended or not. This can be especially painful when the excluded member doesn't have other outlets for socialization.

Humans are not meant to be intimate with everyone, nor can they be. People tend to feel intimate with a few close friends, typically ranging from about 2 to 3 people and occasionally extending to 5 to 6. The more people you add, the harder it is to sustain intimacy. When the idea of togetherness is imposed upon everyone, important relationships fall through the cracks as individuals fail to juggle all sorts of ties, whether with their next-door neighbor or an old college friend.

As a result, individuals often find themselves on social media, longing to stay connected with friends yet overwhelmed by the extensive list of people they feel obligated to engage with. The lack of alternative socialization permits technology to dominate our interpersonal relationships. Online platforms enable individuals to connect indefinitely, often at the expense of depth and authenticity. As America paradoxically becomes more isolated through online activity, individuals feel compelled to bridge the gap in real life. However, in their efforts to stay connected with too many people, they often become inadvertently detached, leading to flakiness or complete absence in others' lives.

Social media is the new online village. I believe social media emerged as a response to the lack of propinquity in American life. It's effortless to people-watch when you need only 'swipe'. It used to be that all a person had to do to get social interaction was walk outside; now, planned dinner dates, playgroups, and extracurriculars are the only way adults can spend time with others. They have very little interest in knowing their neighbor, as that would add to their intimacy circle, but they are quite happy to examine them online.

Though an individual understands the shallowness and time-wasting endeavor of following distant acquaintances or online influencers, it may be the only non-invasive form of sociality they have, which, to them, is worth it. Online life can also be unnecessarily cynical, particularly when people begin forming para-social relationships with influencers they will never meet and who do not care for them. They often only see the most polarizing and extreme content, which distorts their perception of reality. Most exchanges in real life are not so cruel or numerous. If most of an individual's social interaction is online, they are experiencing an abnormal level of negativity that can greatly hurt them. The only way to counter this dire need for sociality is to re-establish healthy environments for the human soul.

Suburban influence has promoted the idea of "togetherness" too extensively, which leads many people to fall through our social fabric. It requires too much effort; we have overextended our intimacy capacity. Suppose a person meets someone new and believes they must have an intimate relationship with them to establish a connection. In that case, they may completely ignore that person, unwilling to add yet another individual to their already burdensome and ever-growing list of people to keep in touch with.

The Benefits of Propinquity

What communities really need is propinquity or 'physical closeness.' Unlike intimacy, propinquity allows people to be near others without the pressure to form close relationships with them. Think of people working side by side or passing each other on the street. This kind of casual, everyday interaction helps build social connections naturally, without any heavy expectations. Essentially, propinquity lets people interact throughout the day effortlessly, creating a sense of community where everyone gets a little social boost— enough to help others or connect across different backgrounds—without needing to maintain deep personal connections.

This already occurs frequently in public spaces, such as when a friendly stranger helps a new mother with her toddler onto a plane. It's easier to offer someone a hand when there are no deeper obligations to that person. You can simply bid them a warm farewell and be on your way. These small social interactions give a slight dopamine hit and help boost morale. I often think back to a sweet moment between my two-year-old son and a friendly Chinese man we'd just met on the train. We had only known each other for a brief five minutes when he offered to give my son his first 'kung fu' lesson. Much to my son's delight, the man plucked him off the floor and playfully swung his foot into a roundhouse kick to the amusement of everyone watching. We left with warm feelings, and I thought about how we would never have met him had we driven instead.

The freedom to withhold information about their private lives enables individuals to engage with people of diverse backgrounds, each with their own experiences and values. It's not their deep attachment that brings them together but the shared love of their environment. Right now, this only happens in a mega-city or state-wide scope. Two New Yorkers may have no idea who the other is. Still, if you ask them their thoughts on the other individual, they may respond, 'He may be Jewish while I'm Catholic, but we're *New Yorkers*, for Pete's sake! We got each other's backs.' Or consider the seemingly obsessive 'fandom' of anyone from Texas. Their community belonging, not private lives, binds them together and transcends differences. They become happy or tolerant of living next to one another so long as they uphold what attaches them: their home.

Propinquity creates communities where people may not be intimate, but they aren't suspicious of each other either. For example, if I routinely walk to the local hardware store, I will sense familiarity among those who also frequent the store. There are too many people to be intimate with, but trust and kinship will develop because we see each other often. We are not obligated to share intimate details or even say hello. From this example, we can see that a community becomes stronger through passive propinquity; they develop a higher trust in their neighbors simply because they are a part of their everyday lives[160]. This can be highly beneficial because communities having more awareness of local problems increases their political influence as well.

The concept of propinquity is not reserved for planned events or scheduled activities; it permeates everyday life. From college campuses to local gyms, propinquity builds trust and camaraderie among individuals, transcending differences and promoting a sense of belonging. College spirit is an excellent example of this. A college campus may have 20,000 to 50,000 students pursuing different careers and majors. Yet, they're all willing to gather in a giant stadium with strangers, paint their faces in school colors, and join together in a shared celebration of their alma mater. Since they care about the same institution, they mourn or celebrate the game's outcome together. When the game is over, they return to their diverse lives, content to live under the unity of the school they attend.

I believe part of the reason people spend thousands of dollars to pursue higher education, even after they've essentially finished their degrees, is because college is the only place in the United States that resembles a village. Everything is generally walkable and functional. The campuses are beautiful, and each student leads a very interesting life through various studies. They constantly meet people serendipitously and can talk to those they will never meet again with ease and intrigue.

The walkability of villages fosters propinquity through organic interactions, preserving energy for intimacy among those who genuinely need it, such as spouses, children, and close friends. In contrast, suburbia often struggles to cultivate balanced and healthy social environments. It's not like togetherness has no place in our society. Being intimate with friends and family is good, but people cannot sustain that level of care with everyone. Togetherness is crucial for immediate relationships, whereas propinquity benefits the wider community. Propinquity is a complementary approach to togetherness that embraces diversity and encourages casual interactions in community life. By striking a balance between the two, we can create social environments that are dynamic and resilient. In doing so, we can authentically affirm to our fellow neighbors, 'He's an American, for Pete's sake! We've got each other's backs!'

153

Mixed-Housing

Unlike the rigid restrictions central to suburbia, villages implement flexible housing policies that promote multi-generational living and address housing shortages. These policies encourage stronger family and community connections by allowing diverse and adaptable land uses.

Consider this scenario: An aging father wishes to downsize. Instead of moving into a rest home, he sells his house to his youngest son and builds a 400-square-foot home in the backyard. He maintains his own space with a separate entry while staying close to family, allowing him to keep some independence and the life he's built. The family spends ten more years with him before he passes away; his grandchildren know him intimately and learn a great deal from him. After his passing, his house becomes his granddaughter's and her husband's first home, where they start their family. She remains close to her parents, continuing a beautiful cycle of family life.

Why not allow families to be reunited? Cities and states shouldn't separate them just because they can't afford to live close to one another due to a lack of housing or job opportunities. Mixed-use housing enables multi-generational families to support each other and the economy. This way, grandparents can be near grandchildren, and people of all ages can be active participants in everyday society.

Dear City Councilman,

    My married, college-educated, and successful son can't afford a home. He started living with us, and we've enjoyed it so much that we want to remodel a larger mother-in-law apartment with a separate door for privacy and autonomy. I just found out that our HOA will not allow it. He's already here, so I cannot see why I can't add another door to my property.

Here are some other ways people could benefit from flexible zoning laws. An artist constructs a small studio in her yard, where she works on her craft and hosts community art classes. A retired couple converts their garage into a small rental unit, providing affordable housing for a college student while earning extra income. A millionaire buys an apartment complex for extended family to live near him; each family owns a separate unit and enjoys extravagant shared spaces. Six families build what's commonly known in Mexico as a vecindad, a traditional housing structure featuring several units arranged around a picturesque central courtyard, often with a fountain to help cool the area. A teacher converts her spare room into a tutoring center, offering after-school help to neighborhood children. The possibilities are endless.

As we can see, villages do not stunt healthy social and economic development through intense housing restrictions. People are free to innovate and adapt their living spaces as needed. A friend of mine once argued that villages are only affordable to the extravagantly wealthy. This is not true. Flexible zoning lowers the barrier to entry, making housing much more affordable and accessible for everyone. As a young married student, I would have happily lived in a 'tiny home' like a renovated garage or studio, especially if that meant gaining equity or ownership. People desire all sorts of living arrangements. While some individuals want a 4,000-square-foot single-family house, I am not one of them. I am far more interested in pursuing my ambitions than taking care of a large house. Housekeeping would be a poor use of my time, especially since my small children don't require a lot of living space at the moment. On the other hand, my mother of twelve children loves keeping house and happily lives in a big space where she can accommodate her visiting children and grandchildren. If suburbanites wish to solve the housing crisis, they must allow greater flexibility in housing of all kinds.

Hey Bestie!

I know we were hoping to turn a cheaper house into a duplex, but it turns out the zoning won't allow it. Since neither of us can afford an actual duplex, it looks like we won't be able to live next to each other after all. Ben found a cheap apartment near the freeway, but it's not ideal. I'm really sorry we couldn't be closer. I wanted our kids to have easy access to each other for play dates, but I guess we'll just have to plan things and drive back and forth.

Due to the recent under supply caused by zoning laws, housing has generally become an ever-appreciating asset. However, housing is similar to a new car in that its physical structure loses value if it isn't maintained, much like a car begins to depreciate the moment it leaves the lot. Yet, unlike most depreciating assets, housing prices continue to rise because of the scarcity exacerbated by suburban development. Locations may also appreciate at an exponential and unjustifiable rate because we aren't building enough desirable and prosperous places to meet demand for the middle class. This creates a paradox where even homes built in the 1900s, with higher risks of plumbing or infrastructural failures, are often priced similarly to brand-new houses. Developers, aware of this paradox, often exploit it by deliberately slowing down construction to keep prices high. This should not be the case—everyone deserves access to shelter without facing an insurmountable price tag. If this trend continues, the middle class will eventually lose access to home ownership altogether. Flexible zoning can help address this issue by empowering individuals to build the housing they need, ensuring supply meets demand. This, in turn, would discourage large corporations from buying up housing units, as they would be less profitable to upkeep. Ultimately, the only way to keep prices affordable is to produce enough profitable and desirable places to live underpinned by flexible zoning laws.

Regulations? Maybe

156

Like with most things, we need a balanced approach to regulations. Overregulation can stifle economic growth and innovation. But when applied wisely, regulations can protect communities from unsustainable development and cultural decay. Villages should impose height restrictions on buildings, regulate short-term rentals, eliminate unnecessary lawn requirements, and promote walkability. Additionally, cities should be responsible for maintaining parks, public spaces, and other amenities rather than placing the entire burden on HOAs. These measures will help keep communities healthy and affordable, but most importantly, they will prioritize people over cars and concrete.

If a village wishes to maintain its character as density increases, it should avoid building anything taller than five stories, except in downtown areas, and prohibit skyscrapers. Jan Gehl, a renowned Danish urbanist, argues that structures taller than five stories begin to infringe upon natural light and are not designed for human scale.[161] As mentioned earlier, excessive building height can lead to several issues. These include increased energy consumption and strain on infrastructure, limited sunlight resulting in poor vegetation, and increased wind turbulence at street level, known as the "canyon effect." This phenomenon occurs when tall buildings channel air down to the ground, making walking or cycling difficult—ultimately discouraging people from being outside. Keeping building heights in check can prevent a host of issues and help maintain a community's quality of life.

Additionally, we must regulate renting laws and home-sharing services to protect a community's wealth and culture from being destroyed. Hood River, Oregon, a tourist hotspot and robust orchard town, intuitively understands the dangers of short-term rentals. To balance tourism with preserving its orchards and local life, Hood River makes short-term rentals illegal for half of the year.[162] This is a good example of how restrictions on renting can protect a community's long-term vision. Villages should promote ownership above all else because stable community members are more likely to give back to their communities than renters or vacationing visitors. Most Americans should own their homes, not be forced to rent from others indefinitely. In theory, if villages were widespread and affordable, a 70/30 owner-to-renter ratio would be ideal. 70% homeownership keeps the community stable, while 30% renting provides dynamic housing needs. This can be seen in some places like Spain, where over 70% of citizens own their homes.[163] While renting can be a valuable source of income for a community, there needs to be a balance of ownership and rental opportunities for a village to remain healthy and prosperous.

One of the most effective ways to enhance suburban areas is to eliminate pointless lawn regulations. When driving through a suburban neighborhood, many areas legally require 10 to 20 feet of front and side lawns. Owners are not allowed to build closer to the edge of their properties. What's the point of a front lawn beyond looks and needless labor? I rarely, if ever, see children playing in front lawns and even if children did, a backyard or lively street could serve the same purpose. Suburbanites scarcely sit out on their front lawns to socialize or people-watch because... there's nothing to do and no one to see. One of my favorite quotes is from a movie called *The Burbs* with Tom Hanks, which illustrates the pointlessness of a front yard. The movie is a humorous commentary on the monotonous life of suburbanites who are so bored that they begin suspecting that their neighbor is a murderer. 'Remember what you were saying about people in the 'burbs, Art... people like Skip? People who mow their lawn for the 800th time, and then snap? WELL, THAT'S US!'[164]

This unnecessary amount of front lawns is particularly challenging for me as a mother. I have to be extra vigilant to keep my toddler off these lawns and other private property, even though the street isn't safe either. I have a deceptively limited amount of public space to maneuver through, making it hard to safely manage multiple young children. With the amount of caretaking I have to do, it would be nice if, when I stepped outside, my children could *at least* roam within sight without feeling like they might be hit by a car or caught trespassing. It's no wonder parents are desperate for yards. However, when I try to keep my son in his grandma's yard, he cries at the gate, wanting to explore the wider world. Unfortunately, in suburbia, that means...*other* people's lawns or left-open garages. It's great fun for him and a lot of work for me.

The regulations requiring houses to be set so far back from the street waste perfectly good land that could be used for more homes. The front of our homes can be just as beautiful and functional without the need for excessive mowing. In the absence of these yard restrictions, a person could expand their home to accommodate their growing family, add a new property to their land, or move their home forward to create a larger backyard. For example, the walkable nature of English suburban areas makes it safe and functional for homes to be situated close to the street. Instead of maintaining expensive lawns that require mass watering, English homeowners use flowered planter boxes and tree-lined sidewalks to provide shade and visual appeal. In Canada, some homeowners allow businesses to turn their front lawns into micro-farms. In exchange for land use, they receive free weekly produce, such as fruits and vegetables. Laws shouldn't prevent people from transforming their front lawns into creative and functional spaces that better serve their needs and neighborhoods. Our current approach to front lawns tends to be more demanding and expensive than necessary; we can beautify our front homes in ways that make better use of space.

Another way we're wasting space is with our over-reliance on cars, which feeds into the American belief that we need large front yards. More driving means more parking, and for many families, a garage alone isn't enough anymore. This has led to increasingly expansive driveways. My mother, for instance, has a three-car garage, a driveway with three or four additional spots, and a parking island for guests. Vehicles take over all that space, leaving little room for anything else.

Front lawns also waste excessive amounts of water, and Homeowners

Associations (HOAs) can be pretty strict about keeping lawns 'up to standard.' If a lawn looks dry or unkempt, the owner is slapped with a hefty fine to shape it up. Water is so scarce in the West that city officials have started promoting the idea of xeriscaping. Homeowners are being encouraged to replace their green lawns with rocks, bark, and shrubbery to save water. While this conserves a precious resource, it renders the yard practically useless, turning a huge space into something that's not even comfortable to spend time in. Is it really necessary to force homeowners to slave over a big grassy front yard, with the only escape being to replace it with un-walkable landscaping? I suppose you could always opt for plastic turf, which is wasteful, hot, and challenging to keep clean. Pick your poison. Regulations can prevent front doors from being just centimeters from the road, but why force every suburbanite to labor over a front or side lawn if they don't want to?

Lastly, cities are diverting the burden of maintaining parks, public spaces, trails, and amenities onto HOAs, consequently imposing a double tax on residents. This approach allows cities to shirk their obligations, leaving homeowners to bear the cost of services that should be publicly funded and maintained. HOAs should be viewed as a neighborhood supplement, not the end-all-be-all of a community's local amenities. It makes me wonder if the growing popularity of HOAs is because people actually want one or feel they *need* one to have their community function.[165]

Suburban areas need to take a thoughtful approach to regulations that prioritize people over infrastructure. Villages place height restrictions on buildings, regulate short-term rentals, cut out unnecessary lawn require-ments, and make areas more walkable. Additionally, pedestrian-first cities maintain parks, public spaces, and other amenities instead of dumping that responsibility entirely on HOAs. These measures help us waste less water, use space more effectively, produce more engaging neighborhoods, and ultimately design timeless communities.

Mixed-Wealth

The dark history of suburbia is often overlooked by the middle class, with much of its heritage rooted in racial discrimination through classism.[166] This greatly impacted our culture and showed up in various laws until the Fair Housing Act came along. While all races can live in suburbia today, we have not eradicated the origin of the problem. Despite the middle class briefly enjoying the benefits of single-family home districts, suburban zoning is, and always will be, a form of legalized classism with unfortunate outcomes. Our zoning laws haven't suddenly started catering to the wealthy elite; they've always been for the wealthy elite.

As housing development slows down and developed land gets maxed out, zoning laws are reverting to their original, more sinister intent. With so many unaffordable homes, corporate billionaires buy real estate and then rent it back to the public.[167] America is reaching the point where, even if a person could afford a suburban home, their options to buy and own are limited. As briefly mentioned, some suburban divisions are mass-produced with only the intent to rent—creating a forever dollar bill for the developer. Through crony capitalism, fueled by classist zoning laws, Americans are bowing down to new kings who prevent them from owning property.

Americans are slowly turning into serfs—peasants who, in the past, were bound to the lord's land. Today, it's corporate billionaires who guzzle our hard-earned salaries and prevent us from becoming masters of our property. If this continues, the American middle class will disappear forever. They will become slaves to what I call 'suburban capitalism,' a framework where the very few who own anything will likely own everything.

The essence of the "American Dream" is like a well-designed irrigation system, with water flowing freely everywhere. Opportunities for prosperity are abundant; everyone can receive enough water. However, classist zoning laws, industrialism, corporatism, box stores, and franchises are corrupting the irrigation system by redirecting water to themselves, all while promising to return it to us. If we continue down this road, only a select few will have access to clean water. The American people, torn by drought, will need to beg for water from people with complete power over life-sustaining resources. We have seen this kind of imbalance throughout history. America could succumb to a civil war between the classes, much like the French Revolution. These divisions could even weaken our country, making us more vulnerable to external threats.

This is the dark path of Suburban zoning, and we are already seeing its economic effects. Unless we abolish the red tape surrounding fair housing and economic opportunity, no government entity will be able to stop the poverty-stricken enslavement of the American people. The wealthy cannot and should not be allowed to put laws in place that segregate themselves from everyone else. They must learn to coexist with their fellow Americans. R1 zoning not only legalizes special economic privileges but also encourages the dominance of mass corporate powers like box stores. This is especially poignant when one learns that suburban neighborhoods and billion-dollar corporations are given massive tax subsidies to maintain lifestyles that ultimately harm those around them. As surprising as it may seem, even 'middle-class' suburbanites have become part of the wealthy elite. They hold the unique power to restore and revitalize society. Likewise, if they remain apathetic, they will cause immense damage.

Village life abolishes legalized classism. There is no legal separation between the wealthy and the poor. All can coexist together, and all benefit from one another. Since zoning laws do not separate them, villages include those with extravagant homes and those living in tiny 400-square-foot spaces. Both groups shop at the same stores and sit in the same parks, enjoying their village's unique culture. The wealthy have many opportunities to ground themselves in ordinary life and serve their fellow residents as they see fit. Being near those who are less fortunate creates opportunities for the wealthy to offer service and practice humility. This proximity to one another builds empathy and encourages collaborative problem-solving to address issues before they escalate. The poor also benefit from village life because it's productive and often lavishly invested in by those with more resources. Instead of being confined to unattractive housing projects they don't care about, where their children have no place to roam, village life provides them with various economic opportunities and a better quality of life.

Most Americans once lived in what we would consider today as abject poverty, yet they were still part of the American fabric. Though poverty looks different now, we should not discriminate against the poor; we should always discriminate against crime. When the poor are provided with equal opportunities and intermingled with those who are already well off, they often pull themselves out of poverty and become the middle class.

This is possible because mixed-wealth communities create a plethora of job types and crafts. Everyone becomes wealthier and more prosperous when the free market is allowed to flourish. In a village with a large middle class as the buffer, all types of wealth can coexist healthily and serve each other. A poor man gets paid if he decides to shine a wealthy man's shoes. If he gets paid enough, he could open a booth. If his booth is popular enough, he might open a shop. One day, he may become the wealthy man getting his shoes shined, and the cycle continues.

Mixed wealth is imperative in village life because it allows all types of economic growth and creates lovely places to live. Under this framework, various jobs exist in towns, and small businesses, rather than large corporations, reign supreme. When the free market does what it does best, everyone benefits from it. Suburban zoning limits the free market in many ways; it is the antithesis of the "American Dream"—an ideal where everyone 'receives water' and cares for one another.

Beautification

There's no excuse why we shouldn't strive to make our communities beautiful. Given beautification's significant economic, emotional, and health benefits, it should be one of our top priorities. It's worth the investment. As mentioned before, merely beautifying an area can lift a community out of poverty and into the middle class. To my vexation, I frequently disagree with urbanists or economists who place practicality over beauty. There is usually a way to accomplish both. The human spirit longs to live in exquisite places; suburbia, however quaint, does not fulfill this desire. My personal social media vice is *Pinterest;* I spend a lot of time there because I long to live somewhere more beautiful. Villages offer many more opportunities for aesthetic enhancement, and there are steps that communities can take to achieve this. Here are just a few ideas.

1. Plant trees to enhance beauty. Not only do they provide shade, but there are hundreds of options for varying climates; they can offer both color and blossoms, as well as varying levels of height and interest. They often require less water than grass, and they are incredibly dynamic. We should prioritize trees far more than grass in productive areas.

2. Encourage biodiversity that invites wildlife into the village: shrubbery, hedges, varying types of grasses, flowers, and greenery in high-traffic foot areas to induce visual complexity.

3. Prioritize construction that features intricate architecture and values traditionalism. It never goes out of style. Our modern infrastructure is extremely drab and boring. As you can see—I'm not a big fan of modernism.

4. Construct buildings to their environmental strengths. Work with your climate and use natural materials such as brick, stone, and clay. I think many man-made materials like stucco look cheap and dirty. Don't even get me started on half-stucco, half-stone designs—tacky, that's all I'll say. Natural materials age like fine wine and last for centuries with proper upkeep.

5. Commission classy murals and art pieces on both buildings and

ground.

6. Allow color for external housing within reason. Not only does color create individuality, but it also makes neighborhoods incredibly interesting to look at.

7. Use brick or stone for pedestrian pathways instead of slab sidewalks. These materials are stunning and require minimal upkeep.

8. Ban or limit billboards—for obvious reasons.

9. Create extravagant public spaces. For example, a park should be far more than just a grass field. Most playgrounds and parks I visit are often empty, indicating they aren't compelling enough to visit. A park should be economically productive and interesting, having many moving parts, such as vendors, trees, fields, playgrounds, wooded trails, lakes, ponds, streams, bridges, courtyards, fountains, and art. The greater the diversity, the greater the enjoyment.

15 Minute Cities

The "15-minute city" concept is a manufactured metropolis that promises all amenities will be walkable within fifteen minutes. I'm personally not a fan of the idea of plopping down an 'immaculate' 15-minute city. I believe it is often an elitist power grab defined by a top-down approach. Since people are increasingly fed up with car dependency and long for more walkable options, powerful entities seek to capitalize on this desire by overtaking the real estate market and offering the walkable 'utopian city' that so many crave. The problem is the potential influence of third-party developers who may not act in the community's best interests. Many non-city folk are uncomfortable with the idea: they lack control in the planning process and fear the increased density and heavier car traffic. The combination of constantly feeling out of control and not fully grasping the benefits of reducing car dependency leads many to combat changes that could improve walkability.[168]

Regardless of who is funding the project, people are generally right about one thing: they aren't involved. This is why I promote village growth over 15-minute cities. Villages are created over time from the bottom up. The ownership of property and the ingenuity of local individuals make villages so functional and profound. The people create the culture and traditions within the area through shared experiences.

On the other hand, 15-minute cities certainly don't grow organically, and locals have limited control over what businesses are put in. Meticulously planning cities without community input can result in designs that don't work well in practice. Additionally, cities created by 'big money' for 'big money' cater to the wealthy rather than the average person living in the area. For example, if Utah were to plop down a 15-minute city, it's unlikely that most Utahns could afford to live in such a place. 15-minute cities invite a soft form of gentrification where precious land is overtaken by wealthy populations, likely from outside the state, who may not share the same values or political leanings.

Furthermore, those living in a 15-minute city are trapped if the rest of the state continues to rely on car infrastructure. Consequently, residents wishing to leave their 15-minute city and visit other places still need a car to function beyond their immediate area. Therefore, 15-minute cities do not absolve people of car dependency so long as car infrastructure dominates the rest of the state. We don't need 15-minute cities; we need millions of organically constructed villages that interconnect and offer dynamic experiences and amenities. These problems will never be solved in isolation. It will never be enough to create 15-minute cities here and there. We must have an entire infrastructural overhaul so that suburban areas are connected to one another and can diversify alternative transportation. Suburban areas that try to 'protect themselves' by remaining car-dependent halt the healing of infrastructure wounds.

I think 15-minute cities could work in some contexts, but I would not turn to them to solve the American infrastructure crisis. What these cities represent, and what many suburbanites may be blissfully unaware of, is the swelling demand for walkability; people will do anything to make it happen, even if that means giving away their freedom. Rather than be overtaken by the growing demand for walkability in promised 15-minute cities, suburbanites should fight for their future villages, where they will have much more economic and political power—before it's too late.

The first and most effective step in transforming your suburb is to work towards disentangling zoning laws that limit flexible housing and small businesses, as well as regulations that make growth difficult. In other words, the first step is implementing mixed-zoning. This will provide Americans with economic freedom, lively density, a balance of propinquity and togetherness, housing affordability, sustainable use of space, and incredible beauty.

14

Dear Suburbia, here's how to implement walkability and village infrastructure.

One of the most profound scientific experiments, Rat Park, was conducted in the 1970s to study addiction. Rats were given free access to either morphine or water. When the rats were isolated, they consumed the drug until they died. Amazingly, when the rats were provided with productive activities and strong communities, they left the morphine alone.[169] This doesn't just apply to addiction. The behavior of the rats serves as a lesson on the components of natural mammal health; village life embodies these essential elements for human thriving: productivity, interest, physical movement, and community. Walkability is key to this type of human flourishing.

In our modern infrastructure, increased density inevitably brings car traffic. To avoid this dilemma for suburbanites who treasure their low-traffic lives, walkable infrastructure must be at the forefront of urban planning. We should design infrastructure that discriminates against car traffic and encourages foot traffic to maintain peace and support local business prosperity. These design changes can happen incrementally as villages and cities progress.

Walkability, at its core, is a zoning framework. That means the zoning is designed for easy business access, not a three-hour trek to Walmart. That means sidewalks lead somewhere important rather than meandering around the neighborhood without purpose. That means a person walking is always prioritized over any other type of transportation. That means sidewalk areas are wide enough to accommodate multiple people. That means cars on the streets are slow enough for people to cross anywhere. That means there are ubiquitous biking and walking trails that cut corners and provide efficient passage. That means walking or biking is enjoyable, peaceful, and visually interesting. That means there are specified areas where cars are not even allowed to enter. That means people are safe from car traffic and have proper city lighting for adequate visibility, even at night. That means there are deliberate, separated spaces for high-speed roads, allowing drivers to travel long distances efficiently without interruption. That means only the most productive car traffic is encouraged (i.e., delivery trucks, government or service vehicles, emergency vehicles, etc.). That means places are more convenient for the walker than the driver in pedestrian spaces, and that means there are plentiful transportation options.

All of this is important to deter car infestation and provide a balance of transportation alternatives. If residents wish to keep traffic from infesting their towns, they must always put pedestrians first and work around them. It's similar to the concept of sand and rocks in a glass jar: if you put the sand in first, there is no room for the rocks, but if you put the rocks in first, the sand will fill every remaining crevice of the jar. If pedestrians are prioritized, everything else will fall into place.

When I talk to someone about walkability, they always insist their city is walkable, "There are sidewalks everywhere in my neighborhood!" Just because a person can walk somewhere doesn't make it a walkable space. Sidewalks do not automatically equal walkability either, and sometimes, a sidewalk can be so absurdly placed that I wonder why it was built at all.

If there is a thin sidewalk next to a highway that takes individuals to the downtown commercial area, that doesn't mean the city is walkable.

Many times, sidewalks are created with only half commitment. Sometimes, there aren't any sidewalks at all. Sometimes, they disappear entirely. I've seen neighborhoods where driveways, even with garages, are intentionally designed to encroach on the sidewalk. The sidewalk temporarily disappears for the sake of the driveway, forcing walking or biking individuals to divert into the street to avoid hitting the butt of a car.

Clearly, in situations like this, the convenience and importance of pedestrians are almost nonexistent. Villages should have sidewalks, but they should be purposeful and one of the most consequential elements in the infrastructure. Cities such as Seattle are instead implementing what they call "walkways," which are designated areas for pedestrians and are much wider than modern sidewalks.[170] Similarly, if a city wants to prioritize pedestrians over drivers, raised crosswalks and sidewalks are a fantastic way to keep pedestrians moving.[171] Meaning, the road is always lower than the pedestrian. Pedestrians don't have to come down to the street; instead, the car must slow down and come up to them. This helps those with accessibility issues, such as people in wheelchairs and average pedestrians with strollers and bikes.

Sidewalks should be generally wide and consistently flat, even when entering a street space. Once, while walking to grab an ice cream, I was disgruntled to find that if I wanted to walk next to my husband and the baby stroller rather than behind them, one of us had to step onto the grass because the sidewalk was too narrow. Wide and flat sidewalks speak volumes about whom a city values. Investing in well-designed sidewalks, pedestrian-friendly streets, and accessible crossings not only improves safety and accessibility but also demonstrates a city's commitment to creating vibrant, livable spaces that value and accommodate all its inhabitants.

Trails

Trails and wider streets are essential for biking and walking, which take longer than car travel. Cities should avoid designing stroad-sidewalk pairings and instead focus on the pedestrian infrastructure that efficiently cuts through areas to maximize access and speed. Streets and trails should always prioritize pedestrians over cars, with physical separation whenever possible. If vehicles have access to certain streets, those streets should be narrow enough to signal that bikers have precedence, or bikers should be separated entirely.

Walkability is a key factor in promoting bikeability, a faster and more convenient mode of transportation. Ensuring the safety of bikers is crucial. For instance, if a mother with small children feels unsafe biking on the street, the bike lane is likely not wide, safe, or peaceful enough. This is most likely due to heavy car congestion. Traffic moving too quickly or cars frequently crossing the bike lane creates a dangerous environment for bikers. Such conditions underscore the need for separate, safe bike lanes.

In my hometown, I'm often jokingly told that my city is one of the most walkable in the state (when, in reality, it's one of the worst). On one visit, I offered to bike down to the local gas station and grab a treat with my younger sister. I did not feel remotely safe on the road, so I took the trail instead.

I could not believe the effort it took to get there. Not only was the trail directly next to the loud, busy stroad, but it also curved side to side and up and down for no good reason. I felt like I was biking on a mountain trail while the cars next to me zipped by on a perfectly flat, straight road. Why does the car take precedence over the cyclist, who removes one less car from the road? Nobody was biking on the trail, and it's no wonder why. The city made it an utterly arduous endeavor. Why would anyone bike anywhere when the infrastructure makes the cycling trail feel like some long Olympic sport to nowhere? On top of everything, the winding trail added to my valuable time getting there. Who exactly is benefiting from this? If a city is going to design walkable trails so begrudgingly, knowing nobody is going to use them, why waste the money to put them there at all?

Currently, cities believe they are doing enough if they merely paint bike paths on busy roads. Firstly, when everything meaningful is at such a sprawling distance, it's far more convenient to drive. Secondly, painting bike paths on busy stroads is not infrastructure. These 'bike lines' are incredibly unsafe, so they only invite the most ambitious people to venture on them. Those up to the task are usually strapping young males with fancy electric bikes who, in their confidence, are willing to risk their lives next to speedy and distracted drivers. Painted infrastructure is generally very thin, meaning it's not created for the average family with young children. I once witnessed a father biking alongside his six-year-old daughter. For obvious reasons, he opted for the sidewalk instead of using the painted bike lane. Despite being off the busy road, it still seemed like he felt unsafe because he held onto his daughter's handlebars as they biked.

While talking to a city council member, I expressed concern that my city's newly implemented biking infrastructure amounted to nothing more than just paint on the road. I argued the deficiency of such a system. He responded with, "It's better than nothing." But is it really better than nothing? Most drivers ignore biking infrastructure on the road because it inconveniences them. Anyone biking is at high risk of being clipped or run down. Once, while biking to a local fair, I realized, to my horror, that the only way to get to the rural street was on a fifty-mile-per-hour stroad. Sidewalks had not been implemented on my side of the street, and there was no access on the other side. With my baby in tow, I feared for my life as I biked on a thin green line. A driver saw my plight and graciously drove behind me to protect us despite being angrily honked at by other vehicles. This type of unsafe infrastructure is completely unacceptable, and even drivers are wary of it.[172]

Cities also construct pedestrian infrastructure that treats the walking individual like a second-class citizen. This includes hawk crossings or flag stalls for pedestrians to wave before crossing the street so they won't get hit. Many pedestrian overpasses are a backhanded measure to walking individuals. They are massive, loud, and inconvenient. Few people want to trek up 30 stairs to cross a busy road. Those who use wheelchairs have difficulty navigating winding and steep ramps. These places can become graffitied and infested with crime or drug use because so few people use them. Again, a city should ask, "What is the absolute easiest way for a walking individual to get somewhere?" Most overpasses are not the solution.[173] Pedestrian infrastructure should not be treated like an afterthought; it's the main emphasis in a peopled space.

We cannot approach pedestrian infrastructure half-heartedly because it gets pedestrians killed. We also can't wholly inconvenience drivers within the existing system, as being an American driver is already extremely inconvenient. We must change the framework and pull as many cars off the roads as possible through the correct infrastructure. Then, we can begin discriminating against car traffic and prioritizing pedestrians. But if a city is going to implement biking infrastructure, they better do a decent job. They can do this by creating separate and adequate spaces for bikers. For the benefit of all residents, cities must invest in infrastructure that caters to the needs of pedestrians and cyclists, ensuring their safety above all else.

Traffic and Road Designs

Villages should establish a culture that discourages foreign traffic from entering their areas so that suburbanites don't have to deal with immense car traffic. They should also provide as many opportunities as possible for people to leave their cars outside the village.

One of the many problems for flourishing cities is the thousands of drivers who enter for work or to attend big events. The traffic is unbearable for everyone involved and disrupts those living there. If these areas restored themselves to villages, they would begin to insist through redesign that when people enter the city, they must make their way through without a car, whether by walking or using transit. That way, the city remains peaceful all year long, regardless of the crowds of people entering the space.

One of the best ways for a city to progress towards village culture and discourage immense car traffic is to narrow the roads. This can be done permanently through reconstruction or semi-permanently with cheaper alternatives, like concrete planter boxes, bollards, etc. If a driver knows it may be arduous and taxing to drive during high crowds, they will avoid taking their car if they have alternative means of transportation. Currently, people don't have much of a choice, so traffic becomes increasingly intolerable as populations rise.

Turning stroads into narrow streets or efficient roads will also greatly improve walkability and bikeability.[174] Stroads have shown that people and cars don't mix well. Therefore, most trails should be separate from cars unless they offer the fastest route for pedestrians.

Additionally, street lights and stop signs are unfriendly to walkers and bikers. Two minutes in a warm vehicle might be fine for a driver, but it really adds up for a person standing in the freezing cold, waiting for the dreaded light to allow them to move on. Once, while waiting to cross a road, a girl turned to me, aggravated, and asked, "Doesn't this light take forever!? I can't stand it!" The weather was quite lovely, but I understood her disgruntled attitude. It's frustrating to wait so long at a pedestrian light because, contrary to what most drivers believe, a pedestrian's time and comfort are valuable, too. By reducing the excessive number of traffic lights and stop signs, drivers can stop being unnecessarily angry when they are paused, especially when bikers ignore stop signs. I imagine most individuals would also find stop signs pointless and irritating if they biked places.

Canadian Jason Slaughter, the author of the YouTube channel *Not Just Bikes*, discovered that countries with better walking and cycling infrastructure, like the Netherlands, have street lights that sense an approaching pedestrian and immediately shift the light so that the person can continue uninterrupted. Dutch drivers are aware of this cultural phenomenon and are relatively patient with such systems because they are often pedestrians themselves. Additionally, if people use streets again, both drivers and pedestrians can better rely on roundabouts for streamlined travel.[175]

Protecting Residences from Car Infestation

When cities were first being built in America, one of the initial ideas for reducing car congestion was to create parking outside the city and provide extensive transportation options inside. This is an excellent idea for those in local areas who wish to maintain the peace of their homes. Why should outside drivers incessantly infringe upon their towns as they do now?

Metal traffic bollards, sturdy posts designed to restrict vehicle access or guide traffic flow, can also be installed in the ground to protect walkability. Only neighborhood cars or delivery trucks can enter through community authorization. This way, as density and businesses increase, cars do not begin to dominate the space as only local car owners would have room for their vehicles.

Cities should do away with minimum parking laws, as they encourage car drivers, waste precious land, and cause car infestation. If a village wishes to promote walkability, it should drastically limit parking so that small businesses have, for example, five stalls at most for those who are disabled, working, or delivering. If people know they will likely not get a parking spot, they won't immediately turn to their car for travel. This applies to on-street parking as well. Some American cities are removing substantial parking lots for better use of the space. To keep some locations clean, street parking should be prohibited entirely.

There are many creative ways to combat car infestation, and many have been successfully implemented in other countries. Cities should be both innovative and informed on how to taper off car congestion.

Pedestrian Infrastructure

I used to feel highly discouraged by our wide roads, believing we've taken far too much space. However, the beauty of our streets is that they can be reclaimed for public transportation and enhanced with pedestrian infrastructure like walkways and spacious bike lanes.

In a village, a driver must ask themselves, "Is driving to this location worth it?" "Would it be easier and more convenient to park my car on the outskirts and then use a bike, walk, or take the local streetcar to my destination?" Many infrastructural street changes can be accomplished with more creative and practical ideas than what I've listed here. Still, hopefully, this chapter will give you a sense of where to start or at least provide insights into the frustrations faced by pedestrians. As fabulous as it would be to place walking infrastructure everywhere, it is generally useless if people don't have places to walk. That's why zoning must come first while cities and individuals brainstorm how to make travel easier for people, not just cars. All infrastructure changes must be done with wisdom and timeliness as Americans work towards a common goal with understanding and vision.

15

Dear Suburbia, many transportation options are good.

After a district reestablishes zoning and communities esteem walkability, the final step is to supplement travel time with various public transportation options. This makes it possible to implement efficient alternative transportation systems that people actually use and love. As people travel consistently, villages can correctly establish public and private transportation options to the most visited destinations and then begin connecting other villages or cities. In this scenario, people can start visiting various places without using a car.

I find myself mourning the loss of alternative forms of transportation in America because I understand the innovative and technological spirit of American society. Consider that a hundred years ago, cities like Salt Lake City had 30 streetcar routes connecting just a few small districts.[176] I imagine that if the U.S. had declined the suburban experiment, we would have the most expansive and efficient transportation systems in the world.

I like to envision a United States map with seemingly endless train routes across every city in America. If we had exerted the same effort we've put into personal cars, I can only imagine what our train systems would look like today; they would be astoundingly faster, sleeker, quieter, and more efficient.

Our train systems would likely have become so advanced that they could compete in speed and convenience with airline systems. If we restored our train systems, air travel—currently becoming a monopoly—would finally have enough competition to keep prices low and quality high. In Japan, with the help of American ingenuity, bullet trains are being implemented that travel at incredible speeds of 300 mph using magnet technology. In theory, that type of train could get people from Washington, D.C., to New York City in under an hour. The drive takes over four hours.[177] Essentially, with all our ingenuity and under the right frameworks, our public transportation system doesn't have to be a source of contention where so many Americans are divided about its value. Public transportation can be a luxury if things are infrastructurally sound and stabilized by functional zoning and walkability. We simply have to care about it once more.

Time and time again, city advocates clamor for public transportation or pedestrian infrastructure before they address zoning systems. There are many problems with this. The first problem is that an infrastructure dependent on cars makes all other transportation options generally obsolete. Even if an urban city begins implementing alternative transportation, hundreds of thousands of suburban cars enter that space for work, which slows down bus systems, trams, and streetcars. Public transportation will always lose if it has to compete with car congestion.

For example, a bus has many stops to make and deals with street lights. Unless a bus route is designed to be separate from regular traffic—like having its own dedicated lanes—it will always be slower than driving a car. If a person must take a bus out of necessity, who knows when they'll arrive at their destination if the bus system encounters rush hour traffic? A girlfriend shared an ironic story about someone she knew who faced this exact problem. The man was applying for a job as a bus driver but was late for his interview because the buses were delayed. Although the bus company begrudgingly gave him a second interview, the interviewer told him they wouldn't hire him unless he owned a car. It looks like not even bus companies have enough faith in their own system's reliability to get drivers to work on time.

There are ways to provide faster bus travel, but usually not within our current infrastructure. A bus should not be inconvenienced by stoplights, stop signs, or traffic like cars are. Instead, buses can rely on roundabouts to make their routes much faster. Additionally, to provide the bus systems with uninterrupted passage, unique lights can be added to roundabouts that prioritize the bus's time over a car's. Those lights would only be used when the bus is in sight, and the city deems it necessary. I've also seen some bus systems wholly separated from regular traffic and given the right of way at lights.

The second problem is that American alternative transportation routes are almost always incomplete or nonexistent. When they do exist, they rarely, if ever, reach suburban spaces. Yearning to be near my parents, I try to visit them often. My family could generally only leave during rush hour, so I longed for alternative options. Before my parents' suburban neighborhood exploded with development, my drive to their home took less than thirty minutes. Those days are long gone. Although there is a train on the outskirts of their development, no buses serve the suburban area. That means taking a bus to the train station and then biking to my parents' house would take an hour and forty minutes, compared to fifty minutes of driving in heavy traffic.

If you knew my baby, you'd know biking for an hour in the snow wasn't a real option. And I'm not exactly training for the Tour de France either. I realized my plan for relying on alternative transportation instead of driving was unfeasible and a complete waste of time. Not to mention, I'd be biking in the dark to get home. Despite this, I was determined to use the train. In a compromise, I asked my mother to pick us up from the station. If my mom got lucky, this would be a 30-minute commute. However, most days, the traffic was so heavy that when she dropped us off at the station, it would take her an hour to get home. We eventually scrapped that idea as well.

Instead of placing several train stations throughout neighborhoods to make them easily accessible from both homes and businesses, cities and states usually build only one or two stations. Furthermore, 90% of these stations tend to be located primarily in commercial areas. That means if a person wants to use the train, they need a car to get to the station. If a driver is already in their car, why wouldn't they just continue on their journey? They know full well that parking and taking the train would double or triple their travel time. I can only imagine this is what's running through their head, "Well, it's a 15-minute drive to the train, and then the train will take 20 minutes, and then I have to walk 20 more minutes... that's over an hour. I'll just drive—it will get me there in 30 minutes." I'm joking—nobody ever considers taking the train. That's a commentary from my head.

The lack of thoughtful planning and integration is widespread. Cities often waste money on extraordinarily limited transportation systems. I've seen train systems so clueless about their audience that it's almost impossible to access them as pedestrians. Train stations end up being surrounded by huge empty parking lots. Again, what is the point of the train if I need a car to get to it? This is why public transportation is so controversial. In our current infrastructure, taking a car everywhere is much faster. No wonder public transit is rarely used or appreciated.

American alternative transportation is notoriously unreliable because it's solely publicly funded; we simply don't care enough to maintain it because it has no place in our current framework. As much as I yearn to rely on the train systems in Utah, I know that I may end up waiting for a late or missing train. This is particularly frustrating as I have been delayed for long periods in the cold and heat at odd hours of the day. Non-drivers' lives and timetables also matter; this behavior is unacceptable.

Most Americans need to own a car. It's usually the absolute poorest who rely on alternative forms of transportation. On the other hand, Switzerland is famous for providing such an extensive and comfortable train system that the wealthy prefer it over personal vehicles. Many European train systems have a vigorous policy of never being more than five minutes late. In Switzerland, that number is reduced to three minutes because they have such a dependable reputation.[178] There are also many alternative transportation methods, and various options occur every 5-10 minutes. It makes sense why the public uses the trains consistently.

Unlike Americans, the Swiss need not wait every half hour or hour to reach a destination. If a person misses the tram, they know a short and dependable five-minute wait will get them back on track. When alternative transportation is valued, both private and public options become abundant. They can not only compete with driving but are also a terrific alternative to it. For those who insist that alternative transportation can't extend to rural areas, this is also disproven in Switzerland. Even some of the lowest-density areas have a bus or train system to pick them up every hour. Imagine the possibilities for people in rural areas who wish to travel to or visit prosperous villages without relying on a personal vehicle.

Villages and Transportation

As villages grow in scope, some places will inevitably be inconvenient to walk or bike to. This is where speedy and efficient alternative transportation comes in. Streetcars are a great example of a reliable alternative transportation source because they are built right into the road, consistently showing up on time.

A lovely commuting culture will naturally take root in society as a city expands its transportation options. The ins and outs of transit will become second nature; people will become familiar with where routes lead, how long they take, which companies offer the most comfort, and whether walking or cycling would be more efficient. One of the wonderful things about public transportation is that it allows people to relax, read a book, listen to music, work, or chat with friends rather than being tied to the intense focus that driving demands, especially in heavy traffic.

My favorite perk (a privilege I don't quite enjoy yet) is the idea that I can hold my baby while traveling. Mothers with access to public transit can play with their babies, show them the scenery outside, and let them socialize with the people around them. Babies get much-needed stimulation rather than suffering through a mundane car ride. Both my babies scream bloody murder the moment they're strapped into a car seat—well, let's just say we don't get out much.

There are innumerable benefits to public transit. Parents don't have to worry about transferring their baby from one environment to another like they would with a car seat. Their babies can sleep in a stroller in and out of transit for hours at a time, especially if they are used to everyday noises. In alternative transportation, people experience propinquity. They have the freedom to tune out the world or serendipitously connect with others. The elderly, whether they can drive, have much more mobility without intense supervision or trouble.

Alternative transportation like trains, trams, and streetcars is also safer for everyone involved, resulting in far fewer deaths and injuries.[179] Parents don't have to wait until their child turns sixteen for their child to start navigating the world on their own. They simply need to go about their lives, demonstrating how to use the transportation system to their children. When parents feel their children are ready, they can allow them to use these systems autonomously, an experience their children should already be very familiar with. These parents don't need to worry about their reckless teenage son, who has little experience behind the wheel, sliding headfirst into a pole during a winter storm. Thankfully, they have more reliable and safer transportation options for their children.

As mentioned before, cities become wealthier from public and private forms of transportation; the overall competition results in well-regulated and efficient systems that provide a substantial economic kickback to the community. An incredible number of jobs are available to villages that value public transportation, including roles for engineers, designers, city planners, conductors, cleaners, maintenance staff, and more.[180] Alternative transportation also eliminates the need for excessive parking lots, allowing that space to be repurposed for prosperous developments. On top of this, public transit not only saves money for the community but also for individuals. As previously discussed, alternative transportation is much cheaper than owning a personal vehicle.

I once spoke to a woman who was very disturbed by the idea of public transportation. She exclaimed, "That's how the government will control us! What if they took away all of our cars and then stopped running the trains? What then?" Well, in that apocalyptic society, we'd be ruined, but in a village, it wouldn't matter if the government stripped away every form of transportation we have because we'd still have our... legs! Theoretically, we'd have an environment where we could reach everything we need on foot with ease.

Besides, it's not as if cars protect us from government control; they are not the great banner of freedom they're often depicted as. The government would simply need to stop maintaining roads or cut off our gasoline supply to render our cars completely useless. We'd be confined to our homes, miles away from amenities, at the mercy of those in power.

On the other hand, village life is autonomous and wealth-building, with alternative transportation as an extra support rather than the end-all-be-all.

Still, to avoid potential corporate or government corruption, future villages should diversify their transportation options, striking a balance between the public and private sectors. Local governments must be intimately involved in their transportation systems and not rely solely on federal government intervention.

So Many Choices

I also want to highlight the amount of modern amenities available for getting around. We not only have bikes but electric bikes that are sleek, efficient, and comfortable. Many of these bikes have built-in wagons that accommodate children or groceries. We have long boards, skateboards, roller blades, scooters, Segways, one-wheels, mopeds, tiny cars, electric carts, etc. Modern America doesn't need new technology to help us get around; we need environments that facilitate quick and easy transportation without relying on a car.

When suburbs become walkable again, alternative transportation is no longer a burden or form of communist "slavery." It's an essential and enjoyable element of a wonderfully established village.

The Cost of Time

Time works differently in village life than in our current car culture. A suburbanite might argue, "I don't want to waste my time walking or using public transportation!" Right now, most Americans only think in terms of A to B. They emerge from their 'caves,' set out to a barren destination, and return as soon as possible. They likely check digital maps just to see how long it will take. Sitting in a mind-numbing car, usually by themselves, passing one ugly building after the other, how could they *not* think, 'I must get to my destination quickly'? However, when infrastructure is interesting, community-oriented, and beautiful, the journey becomes just as enriching as any other part of life.

Take, for example, a father driving his children to the dentist. The trip takes an hour and a half—15 minutes to get there, 45 minutes at the dental office, and 30 minutes to get home because, of course, he ran into rush hour traffic. He returns burnt out and wants to watch TV; his kids, on the other hand, are still wired and bored.

Now, imagine this scenario in a village setting. The trip might take longer, but it could be far more gratifying. The father and his kids take the tram to the dentist. The tram ride takes about 20 minutes. After getting off the tram, he stops by a local bakery to buy fresh bread for Sunday dinner. Following the dental visit, he takes his children to the park, where they discover a splash pad. The father runs into an old friend and catches up on their favorite basketball team. The kids enjoy the splash pad while they chat.

As the day comes to an end, the kids are happily worn out, and they head home on the tram. His toddler falls asleep in his arms, and he enjoys a peaceful moment before easily transferring his sleeping child inside. The whole outing took three hours. Between the two scenarios, one was filled with meaningful experiences, opportunities to stay active, and community, while the other was stressful and dull. Which sounds more appealing to you?

Take another example of my husband: though—perhaps this story should be taken with a grain of salt, as he doesn't live in a village and still has to travel long distances to reach his job.

His commute is an hour and a half, involving a 20-minute bike ride to the train and another bike ride to work. Unlike when he drives, he generally gets home on time. He usually comes home beaming for three reasons: he's thrilled to have already worked out for the day, excited about a story from someone he met on the train, and satisfied that he could work during his commute as a software engineer.

On the other hand, when he drives, he almost always returns frustrated. He's upset about sometimes spending over an hour behind the wheel and getting home much later than planned. On top of that, he usually tunes out the world with a podcast to make the drive bearable, which makes it harder for him to reconnect with me when he arrives.

Admittedly, public transportation isn't always seamless. In our case, buses and trains sometimes miss each other by seconds, causing aggravating delays—often because buses are stuck in rush hour traffic and train pickups are scheduled too infrequently. But unlike ever-lengthening traffic, these are solvable problems. The real issue is that Utah—like most states—hasn't made public transit a genuine priority. If America actually invested in these systems within a truly walkable framework—instead of mismashing them half-heartedly over a car-centric one—they could function beautifully.

Despite this, although biking and taking the train can take longer, the journey is often the best part of his day. It makes a big difference to his mood and physical health. (*He's even proudly mentioned his chiseling calves and abs!*)

There's nothing wrong with streamlining transportation, but we need to view time with new eyes. Is it slower for me to walk home from a church service than to take a car? Yes, but I chatted with my sister the entire way home; I felt the sun's warmth on my face and the rush of wind in my hair. Rather than pouring time into my car, it was invested in my health instead. Similarly, I'd rather bike to work for thirty minutes than drive for thirty minutes and have to work out later. Driving may be "quicker," but the experience is often empty or stressful. Pedestrian-first travel allows time to slow down in all the right ways, adding joy, health, and connection to the journey.

America's potential for a rich ecosystem of transportation fills me with hope — the hope of real choice. Finally, ridding ourselves of car dependence will give us more freedom than we ever had with just one mode of transportation.

16

Dear Suburbia, the Village awaits!

Rejecting suburban infrastructure will bring more health, happiness, interest, prosperity, culture, and fulfillment to the American people. There is a certain order to re-establishing the American village. Zoning needs to be prioritized over walkability and walkability over transit. Nevertheless, communities should advocate for implementing all three—zoning, walkability, and transit—as they should work together.

What can you do?

1. **Start Biking or Walking:** The first thing you can do is start biking or walking to places. This is how my husband and I discovered many of the deficiencies in our neighborhoods. Once we understood the troubles, we had a legitimate voice to make change. This is also how to make the movement visible to others!

2. **Fight for family-centric and flexible zoning:** If you want your adult children or extended family to live nearby, start advocating for flexible zoning laws. Push to eliminate restrictive regulations that prevent families from building additional units or homes on shared land. Zoning reform is essential to rebuilding multigenerational neighborhoods.

3. **Support Local Businesses:** Encourage local entrepreneurs to open studios, bakeries, childcare centers, artisan shops, and more. When you buy local, you invest in your community's economy and culture. Vibrant neighborhoods need more than houses—they need life at the street level.

4. **Invite Back Local Food Production:** Begin advocating for and incentivizing local food systems—this includes local and small-scale farmers, neighborhood butchers, dairies, bakers, and even backyard gardeners. A resilient local food network doesn't just provide healthier, fresher food—it strengthens community bonds, reduces environmental impact, and supports the local economy. Encourage the creation of community gardens and farmers' markets by pushing to reduce unnecessary regulatory barriers. Reviving local food sources increases resilience, autonomy, and connection—one tomato, egg, or loaf of bread at a time.

5. **Oppose Expanding Car-Centric Infrastructure:** Resist new highway expansions or widened roads that deepen car dependence. These projects are expensive, environmentally harmful, and often destroy the very neighborhoods they cut through. Advocate instead for infrastructure that centers people: transit, sidewalks, bike lanes, and shared spaces.

6. **Advocate for biodiversity:** Support policies that protect trees, encourage native landscaping, hedgerows, and promote eco-friendly lawns. Advocate for green spaces that support bees, butterflies, and other pollinators. Embracing natural biodiversity—even animals we aren't accustomed to—reduces the need for chemicals and makes walking through your neighborhood a richer, more beautiful experience.

7. **Fight against plastic:** Encourage businesses to move away from plastic packaging and disposable products. These materials litter our neighborhoods and threaten public health. Begin conversations about reusable alternatives and support policies that reduce single-use plastics. Revolutionize towards a plastic-free culture.

8. **Value Beauty:** When new buildings are proposed—especially public

spaces like libraries, schools, or city offices—advocate for architecture that is timeless, human-scaled, and beautiful. Our built environment shapes how we feel and interact with one another. Favor materials, designs, and craftsmanship that uplift the community and create a sense of place for generations to come.

9. **Invest in the Long-Term:** Support projects that are built to last—not just convenient, short-term solutions. Choose quality over speed, even if it takes more time or resources upfront. Whether it's infrastructure, homes, or landscaping, long-term investments signal care, permanence, and commitment to future generations.

10. **Collaborate: S**hare problems and solutions with your neighbors, friends, and family. Connecting with local people strengthens political power and paves the way for change. It starts with you.

11. **Engage with local politics:** Talk to city councilors, attend meetings, and let your voice be heard. This is how local change is made, and then national change. You don't need to attend all city council meetings, but being aware of potential infrastructure changes helps keep common goals in line.

12. **Patience:** Remember to be patient and kind when explaining your ideas. Sometimes, it takes several conversations before people begin resonating with what you're saying. As you work towards improving your locality, you'll find that regional areas will follow suit. As we work toward a common goal, we will inspire others and see positive changes rapidly unfold in many directions.

You'll know you're successful when you see signs of improvement: billboards coming down, your health improving, your community coming alive, and children running in the streets again. Every great movement starts with small, simple actions; you could be the snowflake that starts the avalanche.

While we strive for the ideal, it's important to understand that an American village will never be a utopia. The complete overhaul of our infrastructure will undoubtedly present challenges. However, these challenges will unite us as we transition towards village life. Together, we will iron out the kinks, and through shared experience, we will develop a culture that understands what works and what doesn't.

The suburban experiment has failed; only through the American village will we reach our full potential. Unique and ubiquitous American villages will help us feel proud of our country again. They will restore our identity and unite us. They will eschew the domination of corporate and political powers so wealth may be shared again. As suburbanites take these steps to become villagers, they will restore the very essence of American life.

IV

Restoring the American Family Through
Culture and Infrastructural Restoration

17

Dear Suburbia, villages need children.

Children used to be everywhere—playing in streams, taking turns with hopscotch, or wandering around with some kind of ball. Now, the streets are empty. While restoring the environment Americans have lost is important, it alone cannot secure our future. A society that no longer centers mothers and children is a society on borrowed time. If we stop having children, there is no future—no culture to inherit, no village to restore.

Consider Italy: many of its picturesque villages stand deserted due to a dwindling birth rate. In response to this cultural and economic decay, the Italian government introduced a program offering abandoned homes for *one* euro, hoping to incentivize people to move into the area. When the government is practically begging people—Italian or not—to repopulate the country, it's clear that Italy is facing demographic collapse.[181] Italians' ongoing reluctance to have children has taken a serious toll on the remaining populace, leading government officials to take drastic measures to combat the consequences of population decline.

Italy's plight is not occurring in a vacuum. The declining birth rate is a worldwide phenomenon, highlighted by Stephen J. Shaw in his documentary *Birthgap*. Countries like Japan, Germany, and Spain (just to name a few) are also shrinking in population and facing significant challenges. Low birth rates are associated with urban decay, geopolitical instability, and declining innovation. A lack of children puts societies at risk of economic collapse and cultural extinction as the aging population is left in complete isolation. Beyond these national upheavals, Shaw's biggest concern was personal suffering—women who had become involuntarily childless after waiting too long, as well as aging individuals who felt suicidal from loneliness and bearing the weight of a failing economy.[182] Whatever the rhetoric surrounding population control, it appears the neglect of family life hurts those left behind.

For those with suburban mindsets, it may seem logical to assume that there isn't enough space. I'm reminded of a comical moment from the hit show, *The Office* where Dwight Schrute walks into a crowded plaza and declares, 'We need a new plague.' It's funny— but it echoes a darker undercurrent of resentment toward population growth. Paradoxically, countless anti-urbanists have expressed to me that the country is too vast for walkability or alternative transit. Yet, they face cognitive dissonance when they also tend to believe that the population must be severely capped for their areas to "stay nice". This contradiction is even more stark when they want space preserved for *their* families, while implying that others' children should be kept out or not exist at all.

Yet, it has never been about population; it has always been about inefficient urban design. Cars require an incredible amount of space for road use and parking, as do ever-growing single-family homes with fixed yard sizes. These regulated car-centric designs are astronomically inefficient and repellent to live by except in conclave areas; therefore, they incite a frantic call to limit density. Yet, instead of focusing on the real problem at hand, we have blamed our children for coming into a world that has not created space for them. The same is true for resources. We have more than enough water, food, land, and clean air—it's just being squandered by systems designed to serve only a few.

What we really need are urban spaces that are both efficient and human-scale again. Designs that center themselves around walkable values take up drastically less space and function far more seamlessly. As I've said earlier in this book, we must reject urbanism that resembles cut flowers in a vase, destined to shrivel. We need a permacultural approach to urban life— a beautiful living garden, capable of expansion when space is needed.

Population control has never been our fight—it's a cover for failed design. So yes, I do agree with the critics. The United States is huge! There is more than enough space on this American continent to build better communities that coexist with our natural landscapes. Up to this point, we simply haven't imagined—or pursued—that possibility.

In light of the issues outlined, it's clear that the success and survival of villages depend on the continuation of families. Villages simply can't exist without the renewal of life, which raises an important question: why is our world progressively turning away from this fundamental need? Many would point to economic or environmental concerns to justify why birth rates continue to drop. While I would never deny these factors may play an important role in someone's decision not to have children, I'm convinced that culture is at the heart of why countless individuals no longer start families.

Our environment has gravely weakened the cultural pillars of healthy family life, with children being the primary victims. Americans are turning away from children because our environment tells us to. It tells us that children belong in fabricated 'child-only' spaces like schools, daycares, and parks— but not much anywhere else. Since the birth of the suburban experiment, children have been hidden behind white picket fences, and this distance has hindered their development and fostered a culture of resentment toward them. Children are not seen as integral parts of American society because our 50s-inspired infrastructure bars them from the real world.

Recognizing how our environment has harmed children can help correct our distorted view of them. Just as this book aims to inspire a paradigm shift in how Americans perceive their environments, this section seeks to transform our perspective on children. They are needed; they are good. If we invite children back into our everyday lives, we will see their value once more.

Children are the heart of any culture's joy and sociality. I have fond memories of my adult family members connecting with one another by relaying funny stories about their children's shenanigans from the day. They stir humor and wonder in disenfranchised adults, as well as hope for a better world. Children are unpredictable in their exploration, adorable in their affection, and boundless in their creativity. Without them, our world becomes more bland, predictable, and nihilistic. Whatever difficulties they impose upon us—being obnoxious or demanding—they refine us and push us to be better than we are. Through them, we experience true nostalgia, reliving our lives through their eyes—not through cheap trinkets or media.

Children create the wholesome culture that America so desperately yearns for. Take Martin Luther King Jr.'s most famous line from his riveting civil rights speech: "I have a dream that my four little children will one day live in a nation where they will not be judged by the color of their skin but by the content of their character."[183] The question then becomes: would Martin Luther King Jr. have possessed the same strength, perseverance, and vision if he had not been driven by the future of the little ones at his feet?

As a college student, I serendipitously discovered the joy and power of children. For years, I had only been around my peers and the question of whether I wanted to have kids plagued me. Being isolated from children only fed my disinterest in them. However, that attitude began to shift when I took several vacations where distant family members brought children along. Although I had taken no interest in them initially, I quickly discovered that all my trips with children were far more hilarious, endearing, and memorable than those without. On one trip, an unfamiliar young toddler—whom I was determined to avoid—showered me with so much undeserved affection that I eventually softened and spent most of my time with him. Another vacation with a separate family rang so joyfully in my mind that I wrote a five-page journal entry about my inadvertent adventures with some of these kiddos; I even sent the entry to their mother in gratitude. These experiences made me realize that my current narrative about children was making my life less full.

When I became a mother, I temporarily moved into my parents' home to receive the 'village' support I needed. My family was there to share my joys and challenges, and their presence made my chapter as a new mother a beautiful experience, as both my needs and my baby's needs were all met. Despite the lingering pains of labor and sleepless nights, I think back on that first month of holding my first son with a form of unknown bliss. Knowing myself before having children, this book would not exist. The moment I was on my own, the harsh reality of motherhood in a dysfunctional space became painfully clear. I quickly discovered that my lows during motherhood came from a lack of village support, while my highs came from its influence. A period of reflection led me to this realization: the American village is the key to restoring our society, and its survival hinges on the presence of families.

For most people, having children is the most fulfilling and adventurous path they can take. Parenthood is an earnest and life-changing journey that brings a previously unknown depth of joy, sorrow, and excitement. It defies easy explanation and can only be fully understood through firsthand experience. If you're a parent who does not resonate with what I am saying, I would assume it is because our culture has failed to give you the necessary framework to fully enjoy the richness of parenthood. I firmly believe that, given the right environmental support, becoming a parent can benefit most Americans in ways few other experiences can.

Several times during the writing process, I was told that this final section was unnecessary—that the only thing Americans need to address is our urban failures. However, I felt compelled to include this section because I knew this book would never drive home its purpose without it.

Restoring family life is the key to restoring the American Village; it is the culmination of *why* all of this matters. What is the point of building something beautiful, only for it to shortly stand forsaken and cold — untouched by the footsteps of our children and grandchildren? Americans need to feel supported in having children, so this section specifically discusses what families need for health and well-being.

I go through the essentials of care from infants to grandparents and address the support systems required at each stage. Why? Our infrastructure has distorted the roles of the American family, and we need multigenerational families to sustain villages. Everyone benefits when we value the most vulnerable members of society—starting with children and ending with all of us.

18

Dear Suburbia, you're disempowering our children.

If children are essential to the soul of a village, then it's no small tragedy that our current environment undermines their freedom, growth, and sense of purpose at every turn. Car dependency and its zoning destroy complex human habitats where children have ample time to practice adulthood safely. The "American Dream" of suburbia is not a dream for children but a nightmare in which every generation is weaker than the one before. Children should be well-integrated into society for healthy development, and walkability is imperative for them to exercise appropriate autonomy as they age. Stagnant and highly regulated school systems are not enough of a communal buffer, as they limit exposure to diverse experiences and age groups. Children become proficient, independent, and resilient through community, mentorship, outdoor play, and appropriate work. Village life gives children the diverse experiences they need to succeed, while suburbia disempowers them at every turn.

It feels like Americans have transferred our attitude about infants to kids, treating them as if they are incapable. In the U.S., the preliminary years to practice adulthood begin at sixteen when teens can finally start driving. A driver's license grants them their first taste of freedom and responsibility...

that is if they even want to drive or work. According to an article from USA Today, there has been a growing apathy toward getting a license in the last three generations.[184] For Gen Z, a driver's license would be the key to their liberation, but unlike previous generations, a disconcerting percentage of them no longer want it. This is because suburban environments instill dependency far longer than necessary.

One of the most life-altering books I've ever picked up was called *A Tree Grows in Brooklyn*. It's a semi-autobiographical novel by Betty Smith about a little girl named Francie Nolan in 1912 Brooklyn.[185] As a 21st-century suburbanite myself, it opened my eyes to an entirely new perspective of how the world used to operate from the lens of a child. My first observation was the mental health and competency of the protagonist, Francie Nolan, and her brother, Neeley. Despite living in poverty, being away from her working parents for long hours, and enduring cruel circumstances, Francie maintains strength and optimism.

Francie Nolan's mother, Katie, works much of the day as a cleaner out of necessity and, with the birth of her third child, continues to do so with her newborn by her side. Francie, a seven-year-old, spends much of her day exploring the streets of America, walking to school, interacting with other children, engaging in errands, reading at the library, and meeting with mentors and adults, including her family members. She has so much autonomy she even gets vaccinated on her own.

Francie seems to enjoy her independence, appreciating quality, and happy moments with her parents when they reunite. This arrangement is typical in historical narratives of young children who have been provided a world to function independently without constant parental supervision. Francie's mother tasks her and Neeley at tender ages with out-of-house errands, such as picking up sweet rolls, spices, or bones for dinner. This way, when Francie's mother returns home, she has fresh ingredients ready to prepare a warm meal.

Due to financial and family challenges, Francie and Neeley take on work responsibilities in their early teens. Francie's ambition and determination drive her to skip high school and enter college at 17. Despite her young age, she is mature enough to consider marriage. The book ends with a strong implication that she will get married to a loving neighborhood man.

Francie's life sharply contrasts what kids experience today, with their rigid paths and limited freedom. With ten years to practice adulthood, Francie explores her roles and responsibilities safely. Present-day children have little ability to self-determine their education or work timeline. Not to mention, our current culture neither emphasizes nor encourages young marriage. Francie's life highlights the importance of environments that allow young people to develop independence, take on age-appropriate responsibilities, and reach their full potential in a timely manner.

As a child whose life was centered around a highly structured public school setting, I couldn't believe families like Francie's existed in such a manner. A childhood in suburbia led me to assume that the 50s view of motherhood was the only way to raise children effectively. I had been brainwashed into believing children couldn't function without constant maternal care. This worldview was reinforced by the feminist narrative that I would become a slave to my children once I started my own family. If my children demand all of me for the next 18 years, how could I continue pursuing some of my talents or interests without being a neglectful mother? Reading *A Tree Grows in Brooklyn* amazed me because it suggested that children can flourish under a different framework than suburban living— one that may even be better for the health of both parties.

In addition to this book challenging my view of motherhood, it made me contemplate my life as a young millennial who felt perpetually weak and incompetent, especially compared to the resilient and capable Francie. Many bright and eager suburban children who wish to start exercising their autonomy are cut short during what could be a profound period of development. As these children naturally begin separating their identity from their parents, they realize that to do any meaningful adult mimicry, they must wait until they can drive. With little to explore beyond their homes—and parents often acting as chauffeurs—many kids lose interest in the outside world. Screens and structured activities fill the void, but offer little real autonomy.

By the time they are sixteen, they have been under complete parental control in every aspect, from visiting the bank to grocery shopping to attending school activities. Unless their parents spend a lot of deliberate time or money teaching them life skills, they lack other outlets to learn them. They no longer wish to work or drive because they haven't been gradually prepared to take on the weight of those responsibilities. This is the tragic and dull life of many American children—a defining circumstance that deeply affects their mental health and future trajectory.

No wonder the world treats young adults as though they are still children when they leave the house—they essentially are. A typical adolescent is given only two years to transition into adulthood before being urged into a university to 'grow up.' With limited real-world experiences to buffer the demands of adulthood, many enter this stage with the emotional maturity of a tender child. Ubiquitous technology has further exacerbated adolescents' lack of street smarts and emotional resilience. Millennials adopted the term 'adulting' because they felt like they were role-playing, rather than being stable and functional adults after leaving the nest.

It's as if becoming an 'adult' has turned into a child's game—a harsh and overwhelming game with no reprieve or prior experience to handle it. Instead of spending their early years gaining independence in the safety of a forgiving home and community, they are left to fill in the gaps during their 20s and early 30s. This gap in preparation and support has led to significant challenges among younger generations. Many struggle with mental illness, loneliness, sexually transmitted diseases, drug abuse, pornography addictions, unplanned pregnancies, unintended childlessness, single motherhood, and college debt.

I once spoke to an exceptionally bright teenager about this issue. He scoffed at the idea that other adolescents were struggling and pointed to their laziness. After listening to him, I realized he lived in a mostly rural suburban development, spent much of his time exploring outdoors, had extraordinarily involved and talented parents, was a highly successful teenage entrepreneur, and had the opportunity—thanks to his family's wealth—to pursue expensive passions like welding.

Another young man in a similar situation expressed the same sentiment to me. His wealth, semi-rural town, unusual intellect, and family stability barred him from truly empathizing with the plight of other American children. When he came of age, he was ready to enter the 'real world' because his father diligently and gradually introduced him to it. He worked under the table at his father's dental office for years, handling janitorial duties and landscaping. His industrious father also kept him engaged with extravagant backyard activities, where he taught him and his siblings various trades. This young man had a childhood full of meaningful work, community, religion, and household responsibilities. It's no surprise that he felt well-prepared to leave home.

Both young men were raised in environments that offered the freedom, mentorship, and meaningful work most children now lack. If we want to raise capable, resilient young people, we must rebuild those village conditions intentionally. In the pages ahead, I'll outline six essential elements children need to thrive—and how a restored village model can provide them. As we know, American rural areas will eventually be affected by suburban infrastructure, and children who live in those areas will lose the benefits of rural life. These young men were fortunate enough to escape the many disasters of suburban living with their mental health and competency intact for a variety of reasons. In this chapter, I address the six things children need to thrive and how village life can provide them with those things.

1. Appropriate Parental Involvement

Firstly, children need active and caring parents; a village helps them maintain healthy involvement. Every child deserves two loving and available parents for guidance, support, and counsel, but Suburban infrastructure breaks down the appropriate boundaries of parental involvement. Our environment makes it so that children cannot do productive things without parental assistance. Furthermore, parents feel their children are unsafe outside of the home. As a result, children become overly sheltered and dependent rather than being given opportunities to develop self-reliance. This manifests in two forms: overly involved helicopter parents or overly stressed absent parents. Suburbia has erased the middle ground between these extremes, leaving children without the necessary balance for healthy development.

In Jonathan Haidt's book, *The Coddling of the American Mind*, he highlights that millennial adults, in particular, lack emotional resiliency and are experiencing mental fragility in daily life. He uses the term "flight to safety" to describe a phenomenon where children are protected from all difficulties and offensive experiences. He argues that the overprotective behavior of American parents permeates cultural institutions like public schools or universities.[186]

This attitude toward children contributes to the pervasive mental health challenges among youth today, approaching adulthood. Even the U.S. Surgeon General has acknowledged the alarming rise in sadness, hopelessness, and mental health struggles among today's youth—a 40% increase in just one decade. [187]

Suburban environments bar children from real-world challenges, so parents must overcompensate to help them develop emotional resilience. How can parents ensure their children lead enriching lives without constant supervision? Where can parents find real-life settings where kids can engage autonomously, free from car reliance? How can they create spaces that mimic the resilience and social skills developed through hands-on learning? Environments where parents can step back and allow their children to mature holistically have disappeared from our culture.

The Forever Chauffeur

Parents rely upon extracurricular activities that nearly always require a car to provide a healthy amount of education and stimulation. As I've alluded to earlier in this book, I find it incredibly annoying that parents must spend hundreds of hours each year chauffeuring their children around just so they can be successful and well-rounded—or, at the very least, have something to occupy their time.

And if parents have multiple children—well, they often don't because more children equals more driving. I had a friend with eight children; her solution was that every child had only one extracurricular activity. Even then, juggling their schedules was exhausting and all-encompassing. I applaud her sacrifice, but this is an unacceptable burden—an infrastructural barrier that quietly discourages larger families.

While some parents may view chauffeuring as a generous use of time— appreciating the forced moments of proximity—it can be stifling for children. Kids are confined to a stuffy car, deprived of fresh air as they're passively shuttled between activities, usually glued to their phones. Unfortunately, there are no other alternatives. This situation is especially disheartening given many capable children would attend activities independently but cannot due to environmental limitations. If parents are unwilling to drive, children often miss out on the benefits of extracurriculars—one of the few social outlets available to suburban kids. This can be legitimately devastating for them, both emotionally and developmentally.

> *Dear Director,*
> *I really wanted to be in the ensemble of The Little Mermaid, but my mom said she's too tired to drive me—especially since I didn't get a lead and she has four little kids to take care of. Maybe I can try again next year. Thank you for the opportunity.*

Walkability solves the crippling issue of dependence. If children could bike to their sports or activities, they would develop essential life skills such as planning, time management, navigation, and practical abilities like dressing appropriately for the weather and getting outdoor time. When children can get to places on their own, both the parent and child have more time to focus on genuine connections later. Parents can still go along if they choose—but it becomes a choice, not a requirement.

I despise the idea that, at some point, I will have to give away my precious time to driving, knowing that my children would be better off if they could get places on their own. Not because I don't want to be with them, but because they deserve to live in a world that doesn't chain their growth to my schedule, or mine to theirs.

Endless Scheduling

Today's parents must be hyper-diligent, carefully crafting every aspect of their children's lives. They navigate highly regulated environments, meticulously planning costly activities—whether it's endless craft projects for young kids or organized sports for teenagers. Parents are pressured to provide comprehensive stimulation, wisdom, and skills. This is especially challenging in a culture where technology is pervasive, forcing parents to carefully balance screen time with other activities. The ability to curate experiences that don't exist in their communities comes at the cost of substantial money, time, and discipline.

I cannot fully express how rampant this idea is. Turn to any social media platform and you'll find mothers offering how to make 20 different sensory bins for babies, tutorials on raising toddler chefs, or how to craft the perfect Montessori shelf rotation. There are calm-down corners with curated baskets of wooden toys, baby yoga routines, toddler-friendly kitchenettes, themed educational book units, homemade non-toxic finger paints, color-coded snack drawers, bilingual flashcard systems, mini climbing walls, and home jungle gyms.

And it doesn't stop with toddlers. Older kids are expected to be enrolled in coding classes, STEM kits, nature journaling, foreign language apps, youth entrepreneurship programs, or theater camps with hours of volunteer work. The expectation is that every moment should be carefully planned—otherwise, your child will be bored, behind, or on a screen. It's not that these things aren't great supplements; it's their relentless accumulation. Parents are left scrambling to replace every minute of downtime with something beautiful, enriching, and constructive. But without community support or a functional environment, they're not even trying to do everything anymore—just surviving the guilt of falling short. Most are barely holding it together under the weight of expectations no one can meet.

Despite a parent's benevolent intentions, they cannot and should not be expected to do everything. A parent is not a playmate as modern culture would suggest, though they can fill that role occasionally. The time and money American parents invest in their children are why many people are baffled by the idea of a woman having more than four children. "Neglect!" they cry. "There's not enough time or resources for the children they already have! I would never divide my attention from my children by taking on more." Those who express such concerns misunderstand that children need intense attention only during the first few years. Then, allowing children the space to explore and develop independence is healthy and essential for their growth, even as young as five years old.

Rather than shouldering the entire burden, parents can find relief in villages that are infrastructurally capable of caring for children. For example, an eight-year-old boy could explore the world if, from a young age, he had walked where his parents walked, taken the same buses, talked to the same baker, and become familiar with his surroundings and the people in them. He feels he belongs and knows that people in the community care for him. Watchful and familiar eyes are everywhere, so he is quite safe and acquires mentors to help him through his journey to adulthood.

In another example, if a mother wanted to homeschool her children, she could spend 2-4 hours a day on school. Then, she could allow her children to explore the world: pick up groceries for dinner, drop off a mail package, make friends on the street, or wash windows at the local shoe store. They could save and spend money without her intense management, take themselves to band practice, bike around town, discover hobbies at the local library, visit the town's dynamic park or waterway, and be home in time for dinner.

Through these experiences, children become active participants in their education and learn responsibility. They encounter all types of feminine and masculine role models as they move about and learn the skills needed to take on adult roles. They can interact with all ages and watch how maturing adolescents transition into adult activities like dating, marriage, and career. Parents and children happily reunite with stories to tell after they acquire needed time away from one another.

While parents are the primary caretakers and should be available when needed, a child's village would also nurture their development. Villages provide children with ample opportunities to involve themselves in the world around them. The home should be a haven of comfort, counsel, rest, and security, but if it becomes the be-all and end-all of a child's education or recreation, it will fail in many ways. The parent and child will feel burnt out, and the child will miss out on critical growth.

I find it telling that the song 'It's Beginning to Look Like Christmas' written by Meredith Willson in 1951 emerged just as the suburban experiment soared and child labor laws were cemented into American life. One of the most famous lines is, 'And mom and dad can hardly wait for school to start again!' Parents are overly involved, and our culture realized this long ago.

Absent parent

On the opposite end of the spectrum, if a parent is not actively engaged in parenthood or the family is not functioning healthily, the neglected child cannot compensate simply by stepping outside their door in our modern day. It used to be that a child could find escape into a dynamic and functional environment, searching for other caring mentors to build trade competency, self-esteem, and emotional stability (however risky the outcome might be to them). Now, they are permanently trapped at home until they are 16 and are vulnerable to every failure of suburbia: weak life skills, lack of work ethic, online obsessions, poor social skills, addictions to porn or substances, limited appreciation for the outdoors, and a range of mental health challenges.

In the worst cases, they are imprisoned in homes with neglectful, physically abusive, or drug-addicted parents. Due to infrastructural failures, the culture becomes hands-off and utterly unaware of its local children's needs; it is the strangers of government, not community members, who have to step in at the very last moment to help rescue a child from disaster. Local communities protect children by giving them productive things to do away from home.

Spending time apart from their children at certain ages is healthy for both the parent and the child. Parents and children should have appropriate separation in which a child can safely explore the world, do meaningful work, and meet other people without a parent's ever-seeing eye. In this way, children can always return to their parents for needed support while still experiencing the world in a grounded and worthwhile way.

2. Young Outdoor Exploration and Free Play

Children need space to roam, climb, and explore the outdoors, and villages are some of the best places for it. An unprecedented lack of outdoor play is contributing to the mental health crisis in America. According to a study from the National Recreation and Park Association, the average American child spends at least seven hours on a screen and only four to seven minutes outside each day. [188] This is an egregious problem we must address. The benefits of outdoor play are unparalleled for children. Outdoor activities are a gateway to happiness, focus, and reduced anxiety. They foster brain development, social skills, fine motor skills, self-reliance, and respect for the environment. They are a powerful deterrent to chronic illness and childhood obesity. [189] The joy and freedom of outdoor exploration are paramount, and it's time we bring it back into our children's lives.

In *Balanced and Barefoot: How Unrestricted Outdoor Play Makes for Strong, Confident, and Capable Children*, Angela J. Hanscom writes, 'Kids of all ages should get at least three hours of free play outdoors a day.[190] We need our children outside—running, jumping, skipping, biking, and moving their bodies.'

Many Americans believe a private yard is necessary for their children to get enough time outdoors. This rational desire stems from car-dependent urbanism, which erodes public gathering spaces and undermines social safety. But children shouldn't need a yard to access safe outdoor spaces— and private yards simply aren't enough. Suburban yards are sterile and dormant, often filled with trampolines, plastic playgrounds, and other toys meant to compensate for their limitations. They're grassy but ecologically barren, lacking the hedgerows and wild vegetation that invite birds, insects, and a sense of wonder. I often think classics like *The Secret Garden* endure because they reflect a deep longing to roam rich, beautiful landscapes that spark imagination and heal the spirit. Many Americans ache for such spaces in real life, but instead, we've traded natural vitality for manicured lawns and plastic fences. Furthermore, what are children to do when they don't have a yard at all? In a culture of vacant neighborhoods and lifeless parks, the effort to reliably get them outside becomes a nearly impossible challenge.

(Note: Americans once used hedgerows—unlike today's decorative bushes—as a form of intricate, living fencing that invited nature into their neighborhoods. These were both beautiful and sustainable, but as car dependency rose, the artisan craft declined, replaced by cheap, disposable fencing. I hope to see this tradition revived.)[191]

While suburbia may offer some opportunities for outdoor play—especially for younger children with siblings or nearby friends—interest tends to fade as kids grow older and crave more stimulating experiences. How often do parents hear, 'I'm bored,' only to respond, 'Go outside,' and get the familiar reply: 'I don't want to'? Despite the serene façade of HOA suburbia, it's rare to see older children playing outdoors—because it's boring. Around fifth or sixth grade, many begin to shift their relationship with the outside world. Parks and backyard play lose their allure, replaced by screens and the comforts of indoor life.

Since opportunities for exploration aren't built into our environment, getting kids outside becomes a complicated, expensive and time-consuming task for parents. Some try to fill the gap with organized sports —but these curated experiences are no substitute for a world that no longer supports spontaneous, free play. Even if a parent can afford to send their 10-year-old to baseball three times a week, it can't make up for the long hours spent indoors—especially during winter. Once practice ends, that child retreats indoors, with no compelling reason to step outside again.

Parents often go to great lengths—camping trips, long drives to hiking trails, nature-themed weekends—to make up for what everyday life no longer provides. But these are short-lived escapes from a world where most kids lack regular, organic exposure to the outdoors. Some children are lucky enough to have attentive parents or extra resources—but many are not. What, then, are less fortunate children supposed to do?

> *Dear Daughter,*
> *I drive you forty minutes both ways for horseback riding twice a week. It's a great sacrifice for me and not everyone is as lucky. Be grateful.*

There are also many obstacles for safe passage. Narrow sidewalks, or the complete absence of sidewalks, often force children onto longer routes, navigating curbs and dangerous roads. This issue is more pronounced in limited townhomes and condos placed near busy intersections. I am continually saddened that more children are being relegated to denser areas that are designed around cars, rather than human functioning: too grim, unsafe, or uninviting for outdoor play. The suburban environment deprives children of sunshine, the earth under their feet, and the experience of weather of all kinds.

To encourage outdoor engagement, particularly among children, it's important to recognize that ecologically profound places— urban design that integrates its native climate and the wildness into its urban spaces- are crucial. I'm starting to believe that the destruction of native land that takes years to develop—rich in diversity and balance—for static water-reliant lawns is a quiet crime against our children and humanity. Instead, we must design in harmony with the earth, protecting regional beauty wherever possible.

Beyond this, the biggest factor that draws individuals outside is *purpose*. Whether a child grows up on a farm with access to creeks, ponds, and valleys or in a city with its array of outdoor opportunities, the key is creating pedestrian-friendly spaces where people can easily walk or bike to complete their daily tasks. There must be peaceful, practical reasons to leave the house. These environments include local shops, public institutions, architecturally rich neighborhoods, parks, and playgrounds. When judging whether an environment is truly effective, consider questions like: Can parents entrust their children with tasks like picking up milk or biking to school safely? Can children enjoy simple pleasures like wandering the streets or buying treats with friends? If the answer is no, then our neighborhoods are not built for children at all—they're built for cars, convenience, and quiet control.

No more should we tolerate developers tearing down hundreds of acres of unique ecological landscapes for endless rows of identical, cheap-looking houses. How we build villages should benefit everybody. If we do not stop, where shall children enjoy their birthright to the earth? How much more regulated suburban sprawl or subpar high-density housing near freeways will steal young people's access to worthwhile places? We blame our children for staying indoors, but the truth is, we've built a world where there's nothing worth going outside for.

3. The Autonomy to Adventure and Explore the World

Children need environments where they can learn and grow independently; villages provide this freedom. American psychologist Dr. Peter Gray states, "Children are designed by nature to play and explore on their own, independently of adults. They need freedom in order to develop; without it, they suffer."[192] In the same way a baby wanders around the house, pulling things out of cupboards, covering themselves in peanut butter, and shoving dirt in their mouth when parents aren't looking, maturing children need opportunities for self-discovery and adventure. Suburbia doesn't offer many of these opportunities. It's too "safe," dull, regulated, and empty. It has no soul, nothing to make it unique, and, without religious affiliation, very little organic community.

Villages provide the work, mentorship, beautification, culture, socialization, and outdoor play children need—that we all need. Children are just underdeveloped adults figuring out the world one step at a time and need a safe place to do so. Children learn emotional and physical boundaries when they are playing with other children or seeing adults in action. Children learn the value of money when they can earn it and spend it themselves. They learn trade skills by observation and participation.

I once encountered three children sitting on a neighborhood corner trying to sell lemonade and various snacks they had haphazardly placed in plastic bags. After generously giving them a dollar for four gummy worms, I asked them what they planned to do with the money. They said 25% of it was going to their downtrodden neighbor. I was humorously touched. Supposedly, 25 cents of my dollar was going to this cause. These suburbanite children were quite limited in their contribution with a skimpy lemonade stand, but they were intuitive and resourceful. They were trying to emulate adult behavior in the only way they knew how, and in doing so, they showed genuine concern and kindness. If only children were given more time and better means to hone these skills. Pedestrian hybrid societies allow exceptional children to become exceptional adults, as we can see from early American history. Suburbia and housing projects stunt exceptional children and sometimes create barely functioning adults.

Dear Son,

When I turned ten, my mom stopped buying my clothes, making me responsible for my own spending. I learned the hard way when I foolishly blew my money on two shirts for the whole year. I had to wash them every two days, and people kept calling me "shirt guy."

From that experience, I learned the value of money and how to be smarter with it. Now, I'm here to share those lessons with you. From now on, your clothing budget is your responsibility. I'm always here to offer advice, but it's time for you to take charge of your finances.

Teenagers are left to entertain themselves because they lack engaging opportunities in their community. When faced with the monotony of passing hundreds of identical houses or a local jungle gym they have little use for other than to vandalize, they turn to ulterior forms of stimulation. The National Center for Drug Abuse Statistics cites that 21.3% of 8th graders have tried illicit drugs at least once.[193] We can see that drug use starts early, right between the period of leaving childhood and entering adolescence. In this seven-year intermission, during which they must wait to 'grow up,' they are vulnerable to harmful substances.

Their dull environment neglects their basic needs. They are continually told they are spoiled or immature, sit for hours in failing school systems, and are indoctrinated with hundreds of hours of TikTok content. Of course, this age group is ripe for misbehavior and substance abuse under such circumstances. Children are anxiously waiting to join the world around them. If given proper outlets, they can learn the emotional and mental resiliency they need instead of becoming self-destructive or burdensome to society.

4. Continuous Age-Appropriate Work Inside and Outside of the Home

Children must engage in meaningful work to reach their full potential; villages provide this through community support. A couple of cultural misconceptions surrounding children can be solved through localization, education reform, and a shift in the perception of childhood participation in society. In modern American society, there's a widespread notion that childhood should revolve exclusively around play, lest we strip away their precious childhood. Play undoubtedly forms the bedrock for learning, nurturing creativity, socialization, and exploration. Yet much of the dichotomy between play and work is artificial in children's eyes. From their perspective, play and work are the same, offering exciting opportunities for learning and growth. Therefore, if given a choice, inviting an enthusiastic toddler to assist with doing the dishes is more valuable than buying them an expensive playset to 'pretend.' Both activities are just as fun for the child, but one teaches a skill, while the other tends to torture the parent when asked to participate.

In America, work for children should start as early as possible with household chores. Though it will initially be painfully slow or chaotic, and the child might lose interest, the ongoing invitation from a caring parent to collaborate on tasks without criticism can be immensely satisfying for the child. This approach builds confidence in their abilities and helps them develop a positive attitude toward work. To the glee of their parents, they also learn how to do chores early, gradually lightening the household load.

For modern hunter-gatherer communities like the Mayans, depicted in Michaeleen Doucleff's book *Hunt, Gather, Parent,* the earlier a child is engaged in daily work, the greater the sense of belonging.[194] Children who are excused from daily chores due to their young age or perceived incompetence often struggle to transition successfully into the community as they grow older. Therefore, children are expected to be highly engaged in collaborative activities such as hunting, gathering, and farming as soon as an infant can walk. As they leisurely work alongside their parents, they gradually increase their capability in more complex skills. They learn to fish, clean, cook, and repair household items during their early adolescence. Modern Mayan culture teaches children a mastery of skills that ready them for adulthood, helping them feel like they've always been valuable members of their community.

Consequently, their culture rarely struggles with disobedient adolescents because they develop what they call "acomadito." Over time, children acquire the combined skills of paying attention and acting; they notice when people need help or when a chore needs doing and assist willingly without being asked. This cultural expectation of work and belonging is so strong that it's embarrassing for a Mayan teenager to be asked to help.

Just as Mayan children seamlessly transition into Mayan adulthood by engaging in tasks akin to those of adults, American children should follow a similar trajectory. When a child is denied the ability to progress, they feel immense frustration and then languid resignation. As tasks pile up without being learned, even the most minor errands become overwhelming. This deprivation of basic skills leaves them ill-prepared for the adjustment to adulthood, resulting in unmanageable responsibilities and potential feelings of inadequacy.

Self-sufficient and mature qualities emerge early in cultures where children and adolescents are given meaningful work. This contrasts with the American philosophy of "just being a kid," which creates a fabricated childhood experience. This leads many American young adults to deeply mourn the loss of their sheltered childhood, making the transition into adulthood even more painful. Instead, for most of human history, children were not exempt from life, and today, they are still biologically wired to be productive. For a child, being accepted into societal work gives them a feeling of inclusion, which says, "This is life—we will help nurture the skills to manage it and succeed along the way," first in their home and then in broader society as they age.

It is time to contest the notion that work detracts from childhood innocence. Instead, engaging in meaningful work, especially alongside loved ones or friends, enriches the childhood experience. Children naturally see the world through rose-colored glasses, so introducing work at a young age helps them learn to value it as a positive and enjoyable part of life. Childhood is a time of exploration, growth, and purposeful engagement. Work should be celebrated and endorsed as a vital component of the journey to adulthood.

Children Then and Now

For a more grounded perspective, consider the lives of two young children: Mary and Jessica. Growing up in an industrial city in the early 1900s, Mary starts working at a textile mill at nine to support her struggling family. She perseveres through long hours of manual labor despite risks and hardships. The mills are unsafe, loud, and filled with musty air. After her father's death, Mary sacrifices her education and works tirelessly to provide for her family. After marrying and having children, she hopes that her children will one day receive an education and live better lives.

In contrast, Jessica, a privileged 21st-century suburban teenager, focuses on college aspirations and devotes hours to extracurricular activities like tennis and student government. Despite her achievements, she battles screen obsession, loneliness, body image issues, and an eating disorder. Her homework from AP and Honors classes is monumental, and the workload is often overwhelming. Her mother notices that she is stressed and excuses her from most household chores so she can maintain her grades and pursue her higher education goals.

After Jessica fails to get into her dream university, she spirals into a crippling depression. She also realizes she will never be a professional tennis player and struggles to find her identity and purpose. Due to the immense focus on her college trajectory, Jessica lacks essential household habits and abilities like cooking healthy food for herself. Despite eventually graduating and finding employment as a teacher, she faces overwhelming college debt and uncertainty about her future. She feels unprepared and childish despite being legally considered an adult.

Both children suffer in these circumstances. Mary and Jessica are cogs in a relentless machine: Mary is a faceless worker struggling for survival, and Jessica is a high performer with accolades that offer no real value. Mary confronts the harsh realities of early labor without the opportunity for education or personal fulfillment, while Jessica grapples with the pressures of academic achievement, restrained from developing necessary emotional fortitude and real-world skills. Both narratives underscore the absence of balance necessary for healthy development.

At first glance, it might seem unfair to compare Mary's grueling labor with Jessica's first-world distress—but trauma isn't always obvious, and affliction isn't always physical. Like Jessica, most American children are overscheduled, overstimulated, and deprived of meaningful work. Infrastructural limitations, outdated laws, and cultural attitudes compromise personal growth and development preparatory to adulthood.

Child's 'Work'

According to the National Research Council, the transition to adulthood has become increasingly challenging for younger generations, marked by declining practical skills, rising rates of mental illness, and increasing reliance on destructive coping mechanisms.[195] This multifaceted dilemma stems from the misguided belief that a child's 'work' should *only* consist of pursuits like higher education, extracurricular activities, and chores.

This cultural shift towards children is understandable in many ways. The unbearable exploitation of children during the Industrial Revolution is revealed in photographs of young boys covered in soot and toiling in dark mines for long hours. To address this, America replaced child labor in 1938 with mandatory education, setting the legal working age at sixteen. However, throughout history, children have been integral contributors to practical work alongside adults and were fully expected to be active participants. Such work cultivates essential life skills necessary for navigating adulthood.

With immense pressure to attend higher education, many children's 'work' is participating in extracurricular activities such as organized sports or music lessons to enhance their college applications. While these activities are beneficial for promoting discipline, physical exercise, and socialization, they fall short of providing children with holistic preparation for adulthood. Society inadvertently sets children on broken paths by encouraging them to emulate the top 1% of affluent athletes or musicians. Upon reaching adulthood, they experience a harsh reality check. Despite the time and effort spent away from their families, their sports participation rarely extends beyond recreation or, at best, college-level play. They leave home with a disillusionment of identity and the devastating realization they need to grow up and choose a 'real occupation.' They have poured thousands of hours into a skill that doesn't translate into adult work or responsibilities.

Furthermore, what is set aside for children without the means to participate in extracurriculars? As after-school lessons become increasingly expensive, they are also becoming insanely *competitive.* Many low-income and even middle-class families opt out due to the high costs, which can amount to thousands of dollars a year.[196] For example, when my sister joined her high school dance team, it cost a steep $2,000 a year. By the time my youngest sister tried, the price had doubled. Even with far more dance experience, she didn't make the team—the competition had intensified. One sister saw dance as fun; the other saw it as a high-stakes test of her worth—an unfortunate shift in culture.

This is a personal example of a teenager being priced out of an opportunity for development that was supposed to propel her forward—though unless she becomes a professional dancer, I'm not sure where. If organized sports are the only fruitful outlet for children, many will be shunted to the side due to increased costs and competition. As the middle class dwindles, statistically and tragically, these families may have nothing left but mindless entertainment. This underscores the severe lack of accessible and meaningful activities for all children.

Another form of work for children is household chores, but knowing how to sweep hardly prepares them for the complex challenges they'll face as adults. Many domestic skills related to cleaning and cooking can be acquired by the age of eight or nine. It doesn't help that modern amenities have made chores so easy. For example, a child can spend three minutes tossing in a load of laundry and then play video games for an hour while the machine runs. Children need more challenging tasks than domestic chores to foster maturity as they age. At the same time, many young people fail to develop these basic skills because school and extracurriculars demand so much of their time and attention. Preparing children for the demands of adulthood requires a better approach, one that integrates practical pursuits with essential life skills. Before children begin working with abstract tools like calculators, A.I., or coding software, they need real-world, tangible experiences. Digging in the dirt, measuring wood, sewing fabric, or writing a journal entry by hand gives them the physical discipline they need to later grasp digital tasks with confidence and clarity. It's a form of analog education desperately missing from modern childhood —one that takes its time. Most adults remember its value instinctively, even if they now struggle to pass it on.

The cultural attitude toward children's work is too narrow. While endeavors like extracurricular activities and chores are valuable, they alone are insufficient for preparing American children for adulthood. Children need meaningful labor, such as trade mentorship or family business involvement. Environments that allow children to practice adult roles until they are ready to be independent are vital for their success.

Corporate and Consumer Landscape

Our corporate landscape has deprived children of meaningful labor opportunities. The decline of local businesses and trades has left children without safe spaces to practice valuable skills and responsibilities. This lack of locality is the main reason why college has become the default pathway to success for most Americans. With a correction toward village life, children can work alongside adults and not depend upon college degrees to find success.

At sixteen, parents often encourage their children to start working 'real' jobs before heading to college. Yet, our corporate landscape has limited adolescents' opportunities to menial roles, such as cashiering at fast-food chains like Taco Bell. While parents may feel elated when their children begin 'working,' they are devastated if they remain in such roles long-term. This is an understandable attitude from parents, but it sends their kids a troubling message: "Your job is just another distraction on the road to adulthood rather than vital work experience."

Unfortunately, corporate consumer America offers few jobs that help children develop skills that lead to desired career paths as adults. Consider, for instance, the art of sewing. Every child should develop basic sewing competency (at least, home economics courses think so). Yet, our reliance on fast fashion—producing cheap, non-durable clothing—has rendered this skill nearly worthless. Why would a child want to learn how to mend a poorly made suit or dress when it is unlikely to last? Donating it to the thrift store or adding it to the growing landfill of cheap clothing polluting our planet is far more practical, even if it is wasteful. Our environment is not conducive to developing valuable skills or work experience. The incentive to 'grow up' is undermined at every turn. What meaningful work is there for our children to pursue?

If we truly want to commit to softening the transition from childhood to adulthood, we must rethink child labor. Sixteen is far too late to start engaging in adult occupations, particularly when considering the luxuries of modern society. A child should be legally allowed to start working around the age of nine. At this stage, children start to develop ambition and self-governance. If enabled correctly, they can exponentially grow in competency. This is a critical period when they are highly malleable and eager to learn from adults. I see no reason to bar them from rewarding work opportunities, especially given the stagnant years between nine and thirteen are often filled with screens, boredom, and other life-altering vices.

Most suburbanites sneer at the idea of such a young working age because suburban infrastructure creates environments in which children cannot function. All businesses are left to be relegated to the commercial downtown, where families do not live, and the asphalt wastelands are ripe for crime. As franchises explode and kill off small businesses, these places become more estranged and detached. They are barely safe and enjoyable for adults, let alone for children. The main issue is not the age at which children work but the absence of safe, community-centered environments. Even if America were to reconsider its stringent child labor laws today, reverting them would prove difficult. Children are not meant to be chauffeured to distant corporate franchises and work near strangers. Such scenarios pose significant risks and challenges.

Villages solve these concerns by giving children ample outlets to work safely near trusted adults. There are innumerable many ways this can be done. For example, a local businessman owns an art exhibit with whom the neighbors trust and are well acquainted. A 10-year-old child bikes from school to the art exhibit and works two hours mopping floors, wiping windows, and dusting artworks. When he finishes, he stops by the corner store and happily buys himself a caramel apple while picking up something for dinner. He returns home to a contented mother where he can rest, do homework, spend time with family, or play with friends.

In another scenario, an exceptional twelve-year-old shadows a dental assistant in a local office. After two years of learning about the dental assistant profession, she gets hired and works for four years while finishing school. She earns an associate's degree at eighteen. At twenty, she gets married and has children. She works part-time while her children are little. When her children become more independent, she has the opportunity to deepen her dental education and even pursue other careers, such as community politics.

In a final example, a homeschooled 13-year-old completes most of his schoolwork by noon every day. He applies for a job at the bike shop. He gets hired and handles front-customer orders and retrievals. He slowly begins learning more about bike mechanics through passive mentorship. He enjoys the work so much that he eventually becomes proficient and starts his own bike business with specialized locks and designs.

Of course, there would need to be boundaries placed on child labor. To avoid exploitation, America would establish the hours a child should be allowed to work. For example, perhaps a nine-year-old is only allowed 2-4 hours a week and works in specific services like janitorial work. However, a 12-year-old can work 6-10 hours a week with more complex alternatives as long as they acquire their core education. Seven-year-olds should never spend ten hours a day in textile factories, and twelve-year-olds should not skip school to sell newspapers in winter for family finances. Regardless of the direction we take, it's crucial to prioritize liberal attitudes toward childhood opportunities while also exercising wisdom and caution.

From an economic perspective, integrating children into the workforce could have far-reaching benefits by stimulating economic activity and providing businesses with a larger pool of potential employees, ultimately benefiting the economy as a whole. Additionally, children should be entitled to fair compensation for their work. Allowing children to earn pocket money grants them wonderful autonomy to spend or save, and existing laws already protect children from substance abuse.

While working with children poses potential challenges and trade-offs, the conclusion should not be that it's impossible to merge them into the workforce but rather that we need to integrate them thoughtfully and carefully. We must create solutions that ensure their safety and well-being. Beyond policy reform, the primary solution is to ensure children engage in work experiences within their own communities, where they benefit from familiar surroundings and local support.

The opportunity for children to engage in local age-appropriate work with suitable hours significantly enhances their self-esteem and prepares them for future careers. When children discover their interests and take ownership of their lives, there's little necessity for adults to endorse superficial school programs or condescending self-esteem initiatives. They are well on their way to building genuine self-esteem before reassurance ever escapes a parent's lips.

Children progress independently when guided by parental support, mentorship, work experience, or casual observation. This is especially true if a child can't find a supportive parent in their home where they would otherwise be trapped and stunted. Working within their communities gives children a sense of belonging and healthy outlets for maturation.

Reprioritizing localization challenges the belief that children shouldn't work and should only focus on obtaining a college education. Local businesses provide on-the-job training and mentorship, fostering competency at younger ages. The absence of relevant work for children delays essential preparation for adulthood, precisely when individuals are biologically primed to take on more mature roles, such as parenthood. In a village, parents can push their children toward work that leads to a holistic life. They need not fear that if their child chooses not to get a higher education, they will be stuck at an impersonal box store like Walmart, which is often not fulfilling or financially viable. Locality ensures children can engage in community-centered careers that support the pillars of adulthood: personal development, economic stability, and family life.

Safety

One pressing concern that I'm sure you've considered when thinking about children working is safety, particularly fears about them encountering harmful or predatory adults. Any mistreatment of children is abominable. Fortunately, villages can transform the environment and culture in ways that significantly enhance child safety. As always, part of the solution must include a society full of strong families and children.

Mixed-use environments can protect children by giving them a community where they are known, observed, and protected. Villages reduce opportunities for harmful behavior toward children because they surround children with watchful eyes that can quickly notice and address any threats. Integrating children into everyday life normalizes their presence, making it less likely for people to view them with malicious intent. The unique infrastructure of villages also enhances children's safety.

Anthropologist Sharon Heller's research has revealed that involving children in daily life reduces predatory behavior in societies rather than exacerbating it. She observed that cultures with a high number of children, where they are constantly held, touched, and cared for, score low on the predatory scale.[197] In these robust communities, it's difficult for individuals to emotionally distance themselves enough from the little ones they work with and care for to commit sexual atrocities against them. Maternal and paternal protection arises, and children are not 'forbidden.' When children are out and about with other adults, many hands and eyes will come to their rescue if a threat arises. Jacobs observed similar behavior in mixed-use communities in New York. She recounted a story of a little girl being compelled into a car by a man. Promptly, almost everyone on the block, including the local shop owner, came to help her. Fortunately, the man turned out to be her father.[198] Nevertheless, this anecdote underscores that children are safer when many eyes are on the street.

Separating children from working society is ineffective for their safety. As Americans become fearful of predators, there's a tendency to isolate children further. However, when children are segregated from everyday life, they end up confined to vulnerable, child-centered circles where predators can infiltrate. Integrating adults and children into shared environments can create a safer world for everyone.

The inherent infrastructural differences in villages also provide safety for children. For example, in vibrant communal spaces, it's difficult for a van to speed through a neighborhood, pick up a child, and disappear into a sea of cars. Empty suburbia, where there are rarely eyes on the street, is primed for speedy vehicles on wide roads to engage in this type of behavior. In contrast, villages emphasize design tactics prioritizing the safety of traveling children, such as narrowing roads, making it difficult for cars to speed through. In places like Germany, it's so common to see children navigating the streets that they sometimes create kiddie biking lanes with personalized streetlights to help them get through traffic safely. What a wonderful way to prepare a child for commuting and instill confidence in their ability to effectively maneuver through the world. Additionally, areas where pedestrians frequent are often well-lit, helping to deter dangerous activities.

Parents must ultimately use their discretion to determine how their children interact with the world. In the end, it's impossible to eliminate all the risks of children being hurt by menacing adults. Yet, we cannot confine our children to boxes and leave them to grow in darkness, or the harsh realities of adulthood will blind them. We must do our best to provide appropriate environments where they can develop naturally. Separating children from adult working environments is not the solution; it will exacerbate the safety issue... to say nothing of how it hurts kid's mental health. Children need communities, and communities need children for the safety of all.

Redefining Education in Village Life

America's regulated school system is deeply flawed. Academic outcomes are down, and teachers are leaving in droves due to poor working conditions.[199] Without a strong, localized foundation in K-12 education, higher education has increasingly monopolized employment opportunities, effectively replacing the essential learning that should occur during the primary and secondary school years. This has caused an oversaturation of modern degrees disconnected from real-world job requirements, making them a waste of time and money. One could argue that the failure of public schools has catapulted the idea that an educated person must be a college graduate and, therefore, the only person worthy of a decent job. This is driven by the fact that there are very few sustainable or desirable jobs that don't require a degree in this suburban economy.

A basic high school diploma used to be sufficient for a fulfilling middle-class life. However, prolonged childhood and regressive programs like 'No Child Left Behind' have lowered writing and math skills, making universities the default replacement for a decent education. If American children can achieve competence in their teens through a solid education, we can reduce the demand for unnecessary college degrees and debt. A high school diploma could regain the value of a bachelor's degree in today's culture.

In our car-centric infrastructure, public schools congregate children from all over the area into one place. In a village setting, there are more viable options. Public schools would operate more like campuses, with a central administration and sports facilities, but spread across multiple smaller branches. Having satellite campuses can reduce the risk of crowded school buildings and support homeschooling co-ops. This approach would offer personalized care, smaller classroom sizes, and allow children to safely and independently reach school without relying on a car or bus. As mentioned in Chapter 12, flexible zoning can help reduce costs by transforming suburban homes into interesting classroom settings. Children will have greater access to diverse learning spaces as schools carve themselves into the community.

Public K-12 education should prioritize a rigorous curriculum emphasizing only core subjects and integrating local community talents. In a village setting, this approach aims to ensure that, upon graduation, students possess the necessary competence to engage deeply with the fundamentals without relying on further higher education; higher education can mainly be tailored towards rigorous professions like law, medicine, and engineering.

In this setting, school days should be shortened, allowing more time for community involvement, electives, mentorship, or work. A child's education should have a strong base; any additional electives would merely be supplementary options designed to expand a child's horizons or interests. Streamlining the curricula would free up time for children to engage in broader communal learning. If a child is disinterested in pursuing other interests, however unlikely, they would finish school with a firm grasp of core subjects such as English, History, Science, and Mathematics.

Schools should rely heavily on community involvement to educate or mentor their students, especially since hands-on experience can be more effective than academic theory, particularly for children who are more geared toward physical labor or vocational studies. Take Jared, for example, the young son of a landscaper who could learn the trade from his father through vocational study after school. He would not need to pursue a college degree to hone his craft. Instead, he would acquire valuable skills from on-the-job experience, eventually taking over his father's business in the neighborhood where he grew up. By providing quality craftsmanship and personalized service, he continues a successful business that allows him and his family to live comfortably within their means.

Counselors can play a more significant role by facilitating these kinds of practical experiences. They would act as educational mentors, guiding students through hands-on learning opportunities and tailoring academic paths to students' interests. In addition to educators and local mentors, public schools should rely on part-time or retired working professionals willing to teach electives. This approach mimics what I've observed at universities like Ensign College and New York University, where part-time and retired professionals contribute to the teaching staff. It allows students to benefit from real-world expertise relevant to their career goals.

For example, Molly, an ambitious teenage girl hoping to graduate early, chooses sewing as her sole elective while completing her core subjects. Partnering with the school and a local seamstress, she gains practical skills and on-the-job experience. Unburdened by unnecessary electives, she graduates at sixteen with financial stability and a job she loves—creating beautiful, durable, and sustainable clothing. Years later, she returns to teach sewing at the same high school, bringing fifteen years of hands-on experience rather than just a college degree.

Jared and Molly highlight the power of practical learning outside the traditional academic path. When balance is restored to the education system, students can gain valuable experience and essential life skills through practical apprenticeships or employment. They can tailor their electives to align with their interests and potentially graduate earlier if they wish to enter the workforce. It's time to shift our focus away from car-centric school environments and toward villages that help our youth smoothly transition into adulthood, fully equipped with the education they need.

Working children?! Yes.

It's interesting to note that many suburbanites don't oppose their children working, provided they start their own businesses. Not every child possesses the skills, resources, or determination to become little entrepreneurs, but they shouldn't have to in order to access meaningful work opportunities.

Today, only a few children have safe access to long-term mentorship and monetary compensation for work. I often think of the young man who told me his peers weren't ready for adulthood due to laziness rather than infrastructural failures. Unlike other parents, this young man's father could circumvent the law and involve his children in his practice, offering them invaluable insights into his profession. The father's son even assisted him in surgeries for dental humanitarian work across the globe as a teenager. Unlike children who primarily interact with stay-at-home suburban mothers, this son had ample opportunities to observe and engage with male role models in action. He undertook weekend tasks, earned money for personal expenses, and gained hands-on experience in various trades and creative endeavors. So inspired by his experiences, this young man is now pursuing oral surgery and excelling in his medical degree.

This is all wonderful—it would be incredible if other children had access to similar opportunities. It is not fair to shunt most American children from this type of life just because their fathers are not successful small businessmen. It is an unfortunate form of classism perpetuated by suburban infrastructure and misguided beliefs about children that harms almost everybody.

Our current tendency to disempower children limits their access to diverse paths for exploration and hands-on experiences. Healthy work is not a problem for children; they desperately want and need it. As one of the world's most prosperous nations, why do we not invest more in our children's development? Why delay cultivating their competence? It's time to reimagine childhood—lest we continue to pump out children who are socially awkward, mentally ill, disinterested in work, and unskilled by the time they become adults. We must cultivate environments that balance education, work, recreation, and rest to ensure every child can reach their full potential.

5. The Importance of Socialization and Belonging

Children need to feel like they belong to something bigger than themselves; villages offer children a holistic form of socialization. In Gordon Neufeld and Gabor Maté's book *Hold On to Your Kids: Why Parents Need to Matter More Than Peers*, the authors argue that, without proper socialization, children can develop mild to severe behavioral issues that may continue to affect them throughout their lives.[200] Socialization helps develop a sense of self, empathy, emotional intelligence, and cultural understanding. It can mitigate destructive behaviors and enhance children's ability to interact with the world.

As previously discussed, suburban communities degenerate socially over time. So, where can kids turn to make friends and develop a sense of belonging? Their options are few—essentially, church, school, and maybe extracurriculars if they have the means.

As we have discussed, religion can bring about a whole host of benefits, but again, suburban infrastructure fragments religious institutions. Religious communities have historically provided children with service opportunities, communal activities, recreational programs, and avenues for togetherness. Suburban parents have relied heavily on religious institutions for their children's sake, not fully recognizing the environmental failures of suburbia itself. Since religious participation has declined, children are now more vulnerable to isolation. Parents have mistakenly assumed that suburbia would offer the same community benefits as religion. Many children have lost a strong sense of belonging because suburbia diminishes religious networks and offers no alternative communities.

Public schools have become the primary source of community for suburban children and have proved to be insufficient, particularly against the pervasive influence of technology. Children are not united by their school environment; they align themselves with others based on the views and opinions they develop online. This shift comes at a serious cost: extreme polarization with online groups becoming echo chambers for harmful ideologies. Online interactions lack the physical cues and human connections necessary for compromise and understanding. This form of socialization fails to develop real-life social skills and exposes children to distressing situations and damaging ideas. Children who spend most of their time on social media are more likely to experience loneliness and self-esteem issues. Public schools do not provide enough social gratification or belonging to deter children from tuning into online communities and forming their tribes there. This is a much riskier form of belonging and much less beneficial than personal relationships. Therefore, while being a good form of belonging, public schools are not succeeding in car-centric environments.

In contrast, village societies provide a constant stream of socialization through diverse, everyday encounters. Village social interactions are well-rounded, involving people of all ages, experiences, occupations, and talents. Children in these environments are not limited to interacting with peers of the same mental and emotional maturity level; they can engage with the broader community, learning from everyone around them.

Dear George,

   I just wanted to say thank you for helping me with my garbage yesterday on your way to school. It may seem like a small thing, but to an old widower like me, it meant a lot. You're such a good kid.

In a village setting, children can joke with the candy shop owner and haggle for a cheaper treat. They can sweep the floors in a dental office and observe social interactions, such as a scheduling conflict between a frustrated mother and a receptionist. They can learn social tactics by watching teenagers go on dates or attend dances. They can see tweens at skateparks and younger children wandering beside their mothers. These varied interactions help children develop social skills naturally and healthily.

When children receive proper socialization, they truly feel they belong in their community. Feeling they are a part of something bigger than themselves gives them great satisfaction and purpose. When walkable communities are restored, religiosity and schooling can be strengthened through proximity, allowing children to reap the benefits of these institutions once more. Without village life, children will continue to grapple with insecurity, isolation, and despair. They need well-functioning communities to build social skills organically and holistically.

6. Minimal Online or Media Entertainment

Finally, reducing screen time is critical for a child's well-being; villages naturally promote the real world over social media. It's becoming abundantly clear that children should be offline as much as possible. The online world can be dangerous, full of darkness and insensitivity.

Part of the reason children are drowning in online consumption is that parents are struggling to manage technology themselves. Isolated parents are overwhelmed and placing their babies in front of screens as young as five months old. According to Jennifer F. Cross, M.D., an expert on pediatric behavior and development, this type of screen consumption can delay social skills, fine motor skills, communication, and problem-solving.[201]

As parents struggle to maintain consistent technology limits, some children spend four hours a day in front of screens. Technology has become a second parent for many American children, interfering with their learning ability and diminishing their interest in the real world. Adolescents are wasting valuable time that could be used for productive work, play, personal talents, and socialization. And perhaps the most pressing issue, their attention spans are being obliterated. They can barely concentrate in educational settings, and they seem to only be able to complete tasks if they are "gamified".

So why are parents having a hard time with this? There are likely many factors, including mental health issues, parental screen addiction, overwhelming caregiving demands, and work-related pressures. Fortunately, creating environments where children and adults can find purpose outside will substantially mitigate the dangers of being chronically online.

Excessive screen use can overwhelm even the most mature children because children lack the mental and emotional capacity to combat its effects. Take a tween boy, for example. He loves playing video games and spends all his allowance on new games. He's a good kid—he completes his homework on time, is kind to his friends, does his chores, and plays on the basketball team. To his parents' delight, he is college-bound. However, he finds himself glued to a screen for hours on end. When Mom and Dad notice the over-consumption of video games, they start interfering and huge disputes arise. The young tween argues that he is doing everything he's been asked and the mother takes away his console for talking back. After weeks of contention regarding his desire to play video games, the parents realize that their familial relationships are much more peaceful when he's allowed to play. Eventually, the exasperated mother gives in and returns the console to him. She is too overwhelmed by her own screen obsessions, health issues, work concerns, and responsibilities with her other children to continue micromanaging her son. He is left with almost unlimited time on his console. She comforts herself with the thought, "At least it's better than drugs or crime."

Children and adolescents often search for something to do in unstimulating environments. Boys in particular gravitate toward video games for a myriad of reasons. Video games provide them an outlet for problem-solving, socialization, and excitement. Each time a kid completes a challenging video game task, they are rewarded with a dopamine hit.

At their stage of maturity, they crave new and interesting experiences. If given the opportunity, they would engage in work or exploration that builds a meaningful life. However, in suburban settings, where they have completed everything asked of them, these boys often retreat to the gaming community. That teenage angst that so many parents dread is partly due to rising hormones but mostly due to a lack of purpose, opportunity, and present male role models.

One of the main problems with excessive online consumption is that children become vulnerable to predatory behavior, including pornographic and sexual exploitation. The American Psychological Association found in a study that "among the group, the average age of first exposure was 13.37 years of age, with the youngest exposure as early as 5."[202] Such exposure to pornography creates distorted sexual education that can desensitize young minds and bodies, blurring the lines of healthy sexuality before they can even understand what healthy sexuality truly means. Pornography has been linked to a slew of negative consequences, including erectile dysfunction, emotional despair, loneliness, chemical alterations in the prefrontal cortex, addiction, desensitization, distortion of normal sexuality, driving sex trafficking, lowered satisfaction in relationships, tolerance of abnormal sexual interactions, and a proclivity towards sexual violence.[203] Marital couples are twice as likely to divorce if a partner watches pornography.[204] Additionally, those who deal with the most perverse pornography addictions may harbor an interest in sexual crime and child trafficking.

At tender ages, girls who are exposed to pornographic images may begin to believe their value comes solely from their sexuality. They become prime targets for older predators, who seek to exploit girls online in any way possible. This exploitation can also occur among peers.

If a child today is active online, it is nearly impossible to protect them from all pornographic material. Once, while looking up something about Snow White, I encountered an explicit computer-generated image of a threesome between Snow White and two of the dwarfs. Disturbingly, it appeared as early as the 10th image on a standard search engine. My benign search took me to an obscene picture I had no intention of seeing. I was disturbed by how easily any curious child could have clicked on that image and started down a dark hole of sexual content. Such explicit material is ubiquitous, even with the best protections in place. If a child is on a smart device, they are at continual risk, despite the most diligent efforts to shield them. With so many options for online exposure, it's easy for children to get lost in perverse *dark* sexual outlets, especially when they are emotionally hurting.

The battle to protect children from sexual content is ongoing. According to Newsweek, PornHub has blocked access to its platform in twelve states who require age-verification access to pornography.[205] The pornography industry is a multi-billion-dollar business primarily focused on profit. It will not implement measures to prevent children from being exposed to explicit content. It's mainly concerned with lining its pockets, regardless of what users it attracts.

Social media has also taken a deeply unsettling toll on young people, affecting everything from parasocial relationships to body dysmorphia. Young children and teens are constantly being introduced to very complex and highly inappropriate ideologies before they are emotionally or mentally ready to engage with them critically. These issues range from political movements to international conflicts to topics that shape everyday life, like body care, food consumption, family life, and dating. The result? A generation that struggles to navigate a world full of confusing and harmful influences.

Social media isn't even the end of our concerns; emerging technologies like A.I. pose unprecedented risks to our children that can only be left to the

239

imagination. All I can say is that America does not seem equipped to defend the growing generation from this unpredictable technology.

In a world where American children feel purposeless and lonely, villages bring a grounded sense of reality, work, community, and play that combats overwhelming online consumption. Car infrastructure has almost no buffers against rising technology. Villages can help preserve family values and the innocence of children. Children must receive instruction and guidance from personal family members, religious leaders, educators, community mentors, and local officials before exploring spaces beyond their immediate circle. It is only after children grow up in a stable and grounded environment that they are prepared to navigate broader concepts in online spaces as adults, particularly those of a sensitive or sexual nature.

The challenges faced by modern children demand serious attention. If America continues to neglect their mental and physical well-being, they may lack the resilience needed to lead future generations. Even the most fantastic parents have difficulty keeping their children offline. We live in a different world than 15 years ago, and technology is here to stay. If parents wish to protect their children from mental illness, addiction, sexual exposure, and wasted time aggravated by endless online influence, they must rethink their natural surroundings.

Not having a solid environmental buffer against technology has contributed to the notion that '30s are the new 20s.' Jean M. Twenge, author of *Generations: The Real Differences Between Gen Z, Millennials, Gen X, Boomers, and Silents—and What They Mean for America's Future*, cites social experts who plaintively express the view that prolonging adulthood is the natural consequence of technological advances and that there is nothing inherently wrong with this phenomenon.[206] This is not true.

American adults are becoming increasingly distressed because they are unprepared for adult responsibilities like parenthood. The 20s and

30s should be a time for establishing stability and responsibility rather than a 'party period' of prolonged education, work, and relationships. Having significant commitments would safeguard many young adults from common pitfalls, such as drug and alcohol abuse. We can stop the cycle of young adults getting into trouble and wasting valuable time by reforming our environments. Village life just takes a shift in priorities, and I believe people are eager to value more purposeful living—if not for their own sake, then for the sake of their children.

Our children are our most precious assets, and a world without them is empty. As we reevaluate the negative cultural attitudes we've developed toward children and create better environments for them, we will see how they delight our society. We will love them, be grateful for their presence, and allow them to inspire change in us. As we give children environments that give them the things they need to flourish—appropriate parental involvement, outdoor exploration, autonomous adventure, age-appropriate work, a sense of belonging, and minimal exposure to online entertainment—we will be awed by their competency and success. For this to happen, children must integrate into daily life and not be relegated to child-only spaces. Parents won't need to raise their children by themselves anymore, micromanaging every aspect of their lives, which causes mental and financial strain. They can finally rely on their communities to act as a village. This eases the burdens on parents and gives children healthy communities needed for growth. The solution is designing walkable, localized environments that captivate children's imagination. Are their surroundings interesting enough? Do they inspire wonder? Are they beautiful, peaceful, and dynamic? Are they more compelling than the endless scrolling available at their fingertips? If we send our children outside to play, will they find things to do? Will they be safe from predators and traffic? These are the critical questions suburbanites must ask themselves to save the next generation. Children are the key to establishing the American Village. Without them—we will fail.

19

Dear Suburbia, infants are worth the investment.

A village isn't just defined by where people live—it's defined by how they live, especially how they care for those who cannot care for themselves. The layout of a place shapes the kind of life its residents can lead. At the heart of any thriving village is a historical framework that nurtures its most vulnerable members: infants and their mothers. Without conscious support for their needs, no place—no matter how charming—can survive. When mothers and infants are neglected, cultures begin to decay.

Today, American mothers are suffering—isolated, exhausted, and unsupported by environments that do not account for the rigorous realities of early motherhood. To remedy this, we must address the needs of their babies. If we do not comprehend the unique demands of infants, we inevitably neglect both mother and child—hurting one or the other.

Infants require specific conditions to thrive: consistent, responsive care; close proximity to their caregivers; appropriate sensory input; and safe, enriching spaces to explore. It cannot be overstated enough that these are not just emotional needs; they are *physiological*. Meeting them goes beyond parenting preferences or styles, it's essential for healthy brain development.

Poorly designed places make responsive care oppressive, while thoughtful design makes it seamless.

Mothers, too, have essential needs: practical help, emotional support, social connection, and accessible resources. We will discuss these needs in more depth in the next chapter. For now, it's crucial to understand that whether a mother can meet her infant's demands depends largely on the physical and social structures surrounding her. The more disconnected, car-dependent, and isolating a place is, the more strenuous mothering becomes.

In this chapter, we'll first explore cultural infant practices and beliefs that undermine the health of children and provide alternative developmental care. We will then examine how certain types of urban design can either support or sabotage a mother-infant rhythm. Understanding infant physiology isn't an afterthought—it is *the* model for proper design.

Based on the prior section, one might still question the competency of children, especially considering the rise of mental illness and behavioral problems among American youth. According to the National Library of Medicine, in 2016, almost 20% of children in the United States ages 3–17 had a diagnosed mental, behavioral, or developmental disorder.[207] In addition to this regrettable statistic, many parents feel their children are not ready to practice adult roles. This is because our car-dependent environment has bolstered cultural myths that underestimate the demands of infants, leading to developmental delays in children. Children have been disempowered since birth, with this fragility extending into young adulthood. I believe these challenges stem from our diverse and often conflicting ideologies around infant care

By changing the cultural landscape around how we care for infants, we can lay a stronger mental, emotional, and physical foundation for American children. Early childhood experiences are deeply linked to long-term health. With a shift in environment and culture towards the needs of infants, our children will be capable of the independence we are seeking. Fully investing in the infant stage will drastically ease modern parents' challenges. Ultimately, when parents lay the proper groundwork, they benefit from the presence of mature and admirable children.

Proposed Shifts in American Culture

To promote timely maturation in children, I propose several cultural shifts toward responsive parenting. Responsive parenting involves tending to your infant swiftly and wholly at any time. This approach to infant care is the bedrock for their mental, emotional, and physical well-being. The principle of responsiveness is the basis of all the tactics I will mention in this section:

Revamping Sleep Practices: Replace conventional sleep training methods with approaches like breastsleeping. Modeling healthy sleep behaviors strengthens parent-child bonds, promotes healthier sleep patterns, and safeguards mental health.

Emphasizing Physical Touch and the Carrying of Children: Frequent carrying nurtures attachment and provides crucial physical and emotional support during formative years.

Reprioritizing Childcare Through Environment: In today's dysfunctional environment, we must create supportive communities emphasizing infants and mothers equally.

I often liken infant care to making investments or taking out loans. Just as you can deposit money into the bank, parents can consistently invest in their infants, sometimes depleting their own reserves for a greater long-term reward. If a parent gets to the point where they must prioritize their immediate needs over their infant's, this situation would be comparable to taking out a loan from a bank. Some loans may be easily repaid with a loving and present parent, while others might prove more difficult.

Managing the debt may become challenging depending on the child's disposition, temperament, or age at which these 'loans' are taken. The greater the loan and the longer it collects interest, the higher the risk for developmental delays, mental health struggles, and behavioral issues. Ultimately, it's up to parents to decide which loans they feel are necessary to survive, particularly in suburban isolation. Yet, we must understand that the more loans we take, the harder it may be for our children to recover and the more challenging our parenting experiences will become.

Investing in infants is not always easy or even feasible. Infants are incredibly demanding, and everyone's situation and support system varies. How a parent cares for their infant is up to their discretion, and I would assume most parents are doing their best. I have taken 'loans' myself. My newborn had a tongue tie that was so severe he couldn't eat without swallowing air, making feeding a painful ordeal for both of us. While the tongue tie surgery alleviated his eating discomfort, the three-week recovery period, during which I had to stretch his tongue four times a day to prevent the fibers from retightening, was an excruciating experience. I think back on it with horror, particularly because a newborn's mouth is their most sensory area, densely packed with nerve endings for learning.[208] My baby boy could never understand why his mother would put him through such torture, which was hard for me to reconcile. I may never know exactly how this affected him, though I believe it did because he had uncontrollable night terrors his first year of life. However, I took out the 'loan' because, in the long run, the surgery made it possible for him to eat and maintain a healthy weight.

I also did not breastfeed my babies for an entire year. I stopped at six months for both children because the pain was too great for me. I don't know what discrepancies this left in their nutritional or emotional health, but it was the best decision I could make for myself as a mother.

Lastly, I give my children binkies, which they do not necessarily need and which may cause oral and facial concavity later on. Yet, using a binkie to calm my anxious babies is a risk I am willing to take because it helps us all function a little easier. There are always braces... right? While we all wish to be flawless parents, what's most important is having a strong understanding of infants' needs to parent wisely and minimize long-term challenges. In the end, it's not perfection we seek—it's attunement. The more we understand, the better we can choose wisely within our own imperfect circumstances.

Myths Surrounding the 'Naughty Infant'

I'm biased because I'm in the thick of motherhood, but childcare sometimes feels like the most divisive topic on the internet. New mothers are constantly caught in the crossfires of the dreaded 'mommy wars.' The fact that American moms feel they must turn to the internet or parenting books for advice underscores a severe lack of confidence in their mothers' wisdom and, more importantly, reveals that America is missing a generationally sound approach to raising children. This contrasts with cultures where childcare is so unified that effective practices are common knowledge, passed down from mother to daughter for generations—seen mainly today in hunter-gatherer communities.[209] Lacking a cohesive historical tradition to draw upon, many parents have turned to popular American behaviorism, which is characterized by regressive infant practices that inflict grief on both mothers and children.

When exploring historical child-rearing practices, it's essential to debunk prevalent myths in American culture regarding infants' behavior and needs. Influential child psychologists like Dr. Luther Emmett Holt, John Watson, and Dr. Benjamin Spock perpetuated many misconceptions, such as the belief that infants are capable of manipulation, that crying is 'good for the lungs,' and that infants have the mental maturity for independence. Such ideas stigmatized infants as naughty and greedy beings requiring parental dominion.[210][211][212]

Many early 20th-century psychological theories about infants have been debunked by later experts like John Bowlby, Margaret Mahler, and James McKenna.[213][214][215] Over time, pediatricians have understood that infants' emotional and neurological development is extraordinarily delicate. This fragility primarily stems from their underdeveloped brains, which function vastly differently from adult brains. For this discussion, I will refer to infants as those under a year old, though the principles for responsive and present parenting apply up to the age of three.

Have you ever heard a seasoned mom give a new mom this kind of advice? "Be careful! They'll cry to be picked up. Don't let them abuse you." My own pediatrician gave me this advice. The idea that infants possess the cognitive capacity to manipulate has been disproven. Manipulation requires three cognitive milestones:

- **Future Planning:** Understanding abstract future events.
- **Theory of Mind:** Identifying emotions in people that differ from one's own.
- **Strategic Thinking:** Making calculated moves to influence the behavior of others.

Manipulation is an extremely complex skill that many adults never master. Forget about babies; the only thing manipulative about them is their cuteness, which is an evolutionary design that ensures we'll tend to them. This misconception of an infant's basic cognitive abilities and their complete dependence on adults underscores Western care's cultural shortcomings— knowledge considered common sense in many other societies.

Due to the underdeveloped prefrontal cortex and amygdala, an infant's ability to rationalize and regulate stress remains almost nonexistent, making crying extremely taxing on both their mind and body. A study by Ludington-Hoe, Cong, and Hashemi explores the nature of infant crying and its physiological consequences, including increased heart rate, elevated blood pressure, reduced oxygen levels, increased cerebral blood pressure, initiation of the stress response, depletion of energy reserves, and interruption of mother-infant interaction. These immediate physiological consequences were also linked to long-term effects, such as brain injury and cardiac dysfunction.[216]

Infants cannot calm themselves when experiencing fear or hysteria. A Harvard study suggests that prolonged crying can cause inflammation and damage to the amygdala.[217][218] Therefore, the popular but inaccurate notion that a baby can 'self-soothe,' even with gentle intervention, poses significant risks. Continuously leaving a crying baby to 'calm themselves' can lead to physical harm and developmental delays in children under a year.[219] Contrary to early 20th-century belief, the response to a crying infant should never be purposefully delayed. In other words, a mother's instinct to pick up her crying baby is hardwired into her to prevent emotional or even physical damage. Any childcare book that claims, "Trust us, hearing your baby cry is harder for you than for them," particularly regarding sleep, is intellectually dishonest.

The Infant Brain: A Foreign World

In all this cultural confusion, many American adults do not realize the vast physiological differences in how babies interact with the world. Here are a few key points to establish a foundational understanding of infant care:

Infants Lack Time Perception: Babies have no sense of time, especially in the first six months, making a minute of distress feel endless.[220]

Sensory Vulnerability: Brain scans have shown that infant brains look similar to adult brains on the drug LSD. Every sensory input is amplified and open, unable to filter out information without a co-regulator. With little ability to compartmentalize, they are highly susceptible to overstimulation and trauma.[221]

Intense Emotional Responses: Infants experience heightened emotional responses due to amplified sensory experiences, magnifying both joy and fear.[222]

Object Permanence: Babies lack a solid grasp of object permanence until around 7-8 months, which means they do not understand that their favorite toy continues to exist when it is out of sight. This understanding typically solidifies around 18-24 months.[223]

Maternal Fusion: Infants perceive themselves and their mothers as inseparable entities until six to nine months of age. Compared to other mammals, human babies are born prematurely—biologically unfinished—so the first three to four months outside the womb function as a kind of fourth trimester.[224] London-based psychoanalysts James and Joyce Robertson suggest that infants under the age of six months, with their lack of time perception, grieve as if their mother has died when separated from her for prolonged periods of the day. This is especially detrimental in multiple caregiver situations, such as institutional daycare.[225]

Socialization: Infants are neurologically wired for social connection. When their cues aren't met with consistent co-regulation—through eye contact, voice, and most critically in the beginning, touch—developing neural pathways in the brain may be disrupted or pruned away.[226] This can have lasting effects on behavior, stress regulation, and relationships. Additionally, despite appearances, infants engage in 'parallel play,' where they play alongside their peers rather than directly with them until around three to four years old. Early socialization without parental involvement may hinder social intelligence, and later contribute to behavioral issues.[227]

Need for Physical Touch: Babies require devoted physical touch day and night for healthy brain development.[228]

Complex Movement Requirement: Babies need complex movement to stabilize their limbic system, which governs emotion and behavior. That's why they so desperately seek rocking, swaying, or the comfort of arms—because stillness disrupts regulation. It's important to avoid confining them to baby holders, otherwise known as "buckets." Babies should not be in car seats or swings for too long. Likewise, excessive swaddling should be avoided.[229]

Emotional Processing: Infants lack the cognitive and emotional maturity to understand complex human emotions like betrayal. Even in abusive situations, children remain loyal to their caregivers. Manifestations of broken attachments typically occur in adolescence.[230]

Sleep: Babies do not need to learn how to 'sleep.' This is an innate skill they carry with them outside of the womb. Their brief sleep cycles are biologically intended to keep them alive, fed, and comforted.[231]

While American society tends to be highly affectionate toward infants, it paradoxically exhibits a casual attitude regarding their neurological fragility by leaving them for long periods or selectively deciding which cries to respond to.

This casualness seems to be manifesting in the rising incidence of psychiatric disorders, including ADHD, depression, anxiety, and aggressive behavior, in children as young as three years old. Some prominent psychologists argue that conditions like ADHD should be viewed as chronic stress responses instigated by environmental factors rather than solely neurological conditions.[232] Infant boys are particularly vulnerable to stressors and are more likely to be diagnosed with behavioral disorders or, at the very least, have more visible behavioral problems.[233] While the development of these disorders is complex and multifaceted, how parents respond to their infants' needs significantly influences their children's emotional, behavioral, and cognitive development.

After gaining a deeper understanding of the importance of proper infant care, I made several significant changes to invest more in my infants. I purposefully positioned myself in a multi-generational home where, if I couldn't attend to my crying babies, someone else would. With two under two, this arrangement was necessary for me to prevent burnout and ensure my babies had a safety net to reduce feelings of distress. In other words, even in a suburban neighborhood, I curated my own village to support me and my children. Even a family member holding my baby for a minute while I went to the bathroom changed my life as a mother; in this setting, everything felt manageable.

Responding swiftly to infants' cries acknowledges their uncompromising need for comfort and reassurance. In layman's terms, it is not possible to spoil a baby. Recognizing an infant's neurological and emotional vulnerability can empower us to provide our children the necessary care for their development.

Sleep Training Versus Traditional Practices

It's impossible to talk about how to care for infants without talking about sleep. Many Americans struggle immensely with a baby's brief sleep cycle and scoff at the phrase, "Sleep like a baby," responding, "Ha! Yeah, right!" This exasperation with infant sleep is primarily a Western phenomenon, as infant sleep does not trouble most parents in non-Western countries.

Modern sleep training, popularized in the 1980s by Dr. Richard Ferber, includes a range of contradictory methodologies.[234] The emerging 'science' of sleep training varies widely in its approach: some experts advocate for implementing good 'sleep hygiene' practices from birth, while others suggest waiting until six months.[235] The spectrum ranges from gentle techniques to more extreme measures, some resembling mild forms of food deprivation. Despite their differences, all aim to facilitate sleeping through the night, often by discouraging immediate soothing.[236][237] As discussed, a lack of responsiveness is traumatic for newborns and extremely painful for babies under a year.[238]

Sleep training advocates often assert its health and safety, but no long-term research substantiates these claims. The longest study followed children up to six years old, which cannot be considered long-term as it does not extend into adolescence or adulthood.[239] These studies also fall short in other critical aspects, such as inadequate sample size and methodology. For example, *Pediatrics* compared the behavior of twelve-month-old infants in a fade-out method group, extinction method ("cry it out") group, and control group with no intervention. The study concluded there were no behavioral differences between the three groups after a year, suggesting sleep training has no effect on behavior or attachment.[240]

This study has several limitations, including an incredibly small sample size of only 43 infants and an unreliable control group that treats Western infant sleep practices as a universal baseline. The conclusion is ultimately skewed by defining 'non-sleep training' in a vague and culturally narrow way. The study also favors sleep methods promoting infant independence, overlooking the benefits of mother-infant physical closeness. All of these factors severely undermine the conclusion. The only rational takeaway from this study, if there is one to be gained at all, is that infants do not seem to perceive a difference between gentler and harsher sleep training methods. In other words, all the children might exhibit similar behavioral delays, creating the illusion of normalcy. However, we will never know without robust research and a proper control group.

Sleep training studies require heavy scrutiny for a parent searching for answers, as many factors influence childhood development, and rigorous research is needed to account for differing variables. Many argue that gentler methods are less harmful, but we cannot conclude this hypothesis without more sound exploration. Americans rely on resources that make up their own conclusions with little to no stable research, such as the popular book *On Becoming Babywise*, which alarmingly renounces well-established attachment theory by John Bowlby in favor of its own sleep thesis.[241] Consequently, we face a flood of sleep strategies that claim to be definitive, but gravely require ongoing empirical study.

Among the studies we do have, sleep training remains problematic. Despite what many parents believe, the National Library of Medicine cites that sleep-trained infants do not sleep more than non-sleep-trained infants. Sleep-trained infants wake just as frequently but often don't cry or signal their needs. Wendy Hall, the study's author and a strong advocate for sleep training, states, "We weren't saying that the kids wouldn't wake. We were saying that they would wake, but they wouldn't have to signal their parents."[242] This may reflect a level of learned helplessness, where babies stop calling out because they have come to understand that nothing they do will elicit a response. Their quiet wakefulness may suggest unresolved discomfort or suffering that persists night after night.

This is supported by a study from Dr. Gene Anderson, which explains that when an infant cries for prolonged periods, stress cortisol levels remain in the body for at least 20 minutes.[243] If a baby cries itself to sleep, these elevated cortisol levels continue to affect brain chemistry despite what appears to be a restful slumber. Additionally, Riemann and Voderholzer found that stress and increased cortisol levels can lead to difficulties in falling asleep and maintaining sleep, as well as changes in the architecture of sleep stages.[244] Regardless of the method, no amount of training can alter an infant's basic nature; infants cannot regulate their distress independently, which can lead to chronic stress in children under a year. Despite the confidence of sleep training experts, methods that require parental separation or involve tears seem to be fundamentally at odds with an infant's biological needs.

Given these findings, sleep training should be approached with caution. Sleep training is tempting and, at times, may even seem like the only viable option, but the limited research on its long-term effects is a type of loan with uncertain risks. Particularly since factors such as genetic makeup, environmental influences, and temperament can amplify the potential consequences for some infants. As time-consuming and demanding as infants can be, we must exercise care regarding their sleep patterns to protect their vulnerable minds.

Tried and True Over a Millenium

Americans have unquestionably embraced baby cribs as the gold standard for infant sleep, with babies often expected to sleep separately from their parents, sometimes in their own rooms. Crib culture is so ingrained that parents invest significant time and money preparing beautiful nurseries. Before the 1900s, it was common for American women to sleep close to their infants, often in the same bed. Mothers sleeping next to their babies was a matter of survival. Before the advent of formula, it allowed women to establish strong nursing relationships with their babies. Over time, unfounded fears of suffocation and evolving health public recommendations encouraged separate sleeping arrangements.[245] Cribs gained widespread popularity among middle-class Americans by the early 20th century, wrongly promoted as a necessary means of preventing infant suffocation and illness.[246]

American parents are intimately aware of the exhaustion that comes from keeping a baby happy in a crib. Just picture this: It's the middle of the night, and your baby just won't settle down. You've tried everything—rocking, singing, swaddling—but nothing seems to work. They're finally asleep, so you place them back in the crib—and they're up again. You feel like you might lose your mind. You're already sleep-deprived, wondering if the adversity will ever end. What if the key to a decent night's sleep lies in two methods embraced by our ancestors for millennia?

Before air conditioning, sound machines, and baby monitors, our ancestors relied on cloth carriers and nursing to keep babies fed, happy, and restful. Breastsleeping and infant carrying are foundational practices that have stood the test of time across diverse cultures. Breastsleeping, a term coined by sleep expert James J. McKenna, refers to a mother nursing her baby while sleeping beside them. Carrying infants in slings or sacks has also been a core approach to childcare across cultures. These customs reflect biological imperatives catering to infants' immense need for closeness, comfort, and nourishment. Rather than mothers fighting to put their babies down, their babies slept soundly near them at night or while being carried during the day. These practices may seem more physically demanding, but they were the path of least resistance and still are.

First Foundations

Breastsleeping has been conspicuously missing from Western sleep literature for a long time despite it being a common practice worldwide. For our hunter-gatherer ancestors, separation from an infant, even in a side basket, could have meant imminent death from predators or harsh weather conditions. For example, in indigenous cultures like the Inuit and Yupik, mothers slept beside their babies under animal skins for temperature regulation and comfort.[247] Mothers and infants are biologically wired to sleep together, a trait shared with many other mammals. Research by Dr. McKenna has shown that intense hormonal changes in mothers prepare them to sleep next to their infants, synchronizing their sleep cycles. Observational studies have found that newborns and mothers frequently enter light and deep sleep together, maintaining a close nursing relationship. Mothers semi-arouse for 10-30 seconds before their baby needs to nurse, and then both quickly return to a deep, safe sleep until the next feeding. The hormonal and mental changes after having a baby literally forge the path for mothers to safely sleep next to their infants.

Concerns about the safety of mothers sleeping near their babies are sensationalized; incidents of a mother rolling over her baby are astronomically rare and typically involve factors like substance impairment or unintended co-sleeping due to exhaustion. According to Dr. McKenna, mothers instinctively adopt a cradled C-shape position, with their arms above the baby's head and legs cupped around, protecting the baby from accidental rolling, including by the father. Babies, seeking physical comfort and nourishment, naturally stay close to the breast and are unlikely to roll or move out of the cradled position.[248][249]

To mitigate potential risks, La Leche League International, a world-renowned breastfeeding support group, promotes the Safe Sleep Seven: no smoking, sober parents, a nursing mother, a healthy full-term baby, baby on their back, no sweating or swaddling, and a safe, unobstructed sleep surface (no extra pillows or heavy comforters, a firm mattress, packed cracks, and never cover a baby's head).[250] To uncomplicate this, imagine a mother and baby on a mattress with a single pillow and a light blanket. To further reduce the risk of suffocation, fathers, who do not have the same instinctive responses during sleep as nursing mothers, should refrain from sleeping next to newborns until the baby can proficiently roll over.[251] The mother may even decide to sleep alone with her infant for a while. Children should also refrain from sleeping with infants until they are at least a year old. It is also suggested that beds should be low to the ground or equipped with safe mesh railings to avoid injury from falling. Open side cribs or bassinets that are level with the bed can also be effective. Parents who follow these guidelines have statistically negligible suffocation incidents.

Breastsleeping helps stabilize sleep for mother and baby over time. Dr. Harvey Karp explains that newborns wake frequently despite appearing asleep.[252] In a breastsleeping scenario, a mother's continuous presence comforts her baby with each stir, naturally lengthening both their sleep cycles, which typically stabilize by eight or nine months.[253] In contrast, it's common for sleep-trained infants to experience sleep regressions—periods when a previously well-sleeping baby begins waking frequently again.

According to Dr. William Sears, a well-known American pediatrician, as babies grow and hit critical developmental stages, they become more aware and exhibit signs of separation anxiety.[254] These common regressions typically occur around 4 and 8 months but can continue beyond those stages.[255] Babies conditioned to fall asleep independently often face disrupted sleep patterns as they seek renewed comfort from their parents. While these sleep regressions are seen as normal, they occur much less frequently or not at all when infants remain close to their parents while sleeping. Safe co-sleeping offers ongoing security and sleep quality, while sleep training can break down over time as the baby ages.[256]

Mothers get more rest by breastsleeping because their limbic system is never fully awakened by standing up, and their baby is much less likely to wake up fully.[257] Additionally, according to Dr. Marc Weissbluth, babies get their deepest sleep during the first several hours of the night.[258] So, if parents go to bed around the same time as their baby, they'll get the most rest. While this isn't culturally conventional in the U.S., as parents often stay up after putting their baby to bed, this routine could allow for more rest. Couples could instead spend time together in the early morning when they feel more refreshed. Or, in more walkable cultures like Spain, it's common for a family to go to bed later together because parents are less burnt out and there is a lively evening community life.[259]

Historical practices like breastsleeping and infant carrying, observed in many modern cultures today, give us valuable insight into how humans tend to their babies without unsolicited counsel. This instinctual physical closeness is essential in promoting optimal mental health in both mothers and babies.

While breastsleeping isn't necessarily 'easy' for some mothers like myself, it is often more manageable than the alternatives: repeatedly getting up, taking night shifts, or cradling a restless baby in a rocking chair who won't settle without being held. Breastsleeping is a long-term investment that

257

avoids other types of loans. Whether a mother chooses to breastsleep, bed-share (with a formula-fed baby), room-share, or use a crib, the principles of responsive parenting remain unchanged. Parents must decide upon a sleeping arrangement that will allow them to consistently ensure their baby's comfort. Breastsleeping is simply one of the most natural forms of responsive parenting that allows mothers to immediately soothe their infants without becoming utterly sleep-deprived. Learning how to sleep safely with our infants will transform our culture and keep mother and baby together, free from fear.

The American Academy of Pediatrics

Some may question the validity of breastsleeping or bedsharing, given that many major American pediatric organizations strongly discourage the practices.[260] These guidelines are well-intentioned but misguided. The American Academy of Pediatrics (AAP) has historically promoted crib separation as a preventive measure against Sudden Infant Death Syndrome (SIDS), colloquially known as "crib death."[261] However, this isn't the first time the AAP has failed to provide credible recommendations. For instance, many American organizations, such as the National Institute of Child Health and Human Development, promoted tummy sleeping in the 1970s and 80s to prevent choking or asphyxiation. The AAP initially accepted the recommendation or, at the very least, didn't contest it, which led to a worldwide increase in SIDS deaths. With growing knowledge, the AAP promoted the "Back-to-Sleep" campaign, which urged parents to leave their babies on their backs in the 90s.[262]

The AAP has also made questionable recommendations in other aspects of infant care. In the mid-20th century, the AAP heavily promoted formula feeding over nursing, which led to a massive decline in breastfeeding despite nursing being a leading deterrent against SIDS. Today, breast milk is commonly understood as the best food source for babies; it promotes emotional and physical benefits, including specialized antibodies to fight against infection and sleep compounds like melatonin to regulate their circadian rhythm—just to name a couple. The AAP eventually realized its mistake and now endorses breastfeeding as the healthiest way to feed infants.[263]

The AAP is a Western institution with its own cultural shortcomings, and it continues to disregard essential practices from other countries that have shown better results in infant care. For example, the AAP continues to ignore evidence that bed-sharing countries often experience lower rates of SIDS. It is also concerning that the AAP has conflated SIDS with suffocation, which muddies the nuances of sleep-related deaths and how to prevent them. Its strict guidelines on keeping babies separated from their mothers may very well contribute to tragic incidents where exhausted mothers accidentally fall asleep on other surfaces in the middle of the night, like sofas, which increases the odds of suffocation by 90%.[264]

While breastsleeping or bed-sharing may be associated with a perceived risk of suffocation and SIDS, recent studies suggest that co-sleeping, when practiced safely, serves as a deterrent against SIDS. For instance, India, as well as other co-sleeping countries like Japan and Sweden, has notably lower rates of SIDS compared to nations with crib-centric sleeping practices.[265][266] India has a significantly higher infant mortality rate, primarily due to preventable causes such as diarrhea and pneumonia. However, SIDS and suffocation are statistically negligible in prominent in co-sleeping countries like India because they encourage safe practices with the belief that mom and baby benefit from being together.[267]

Ongoing research indicates that babies are much likelier to die of SIDS from separation than suffocation. Research from Heller reveals that babies need their mother's body to survive, especially as newborns. She argues that mother-baby proximity is one of the best ways to reduce the risk of SIDS. For example, a mother's breath reminds her baby to breathe, and a mother's bare skin regulates an infant's fickle body temperature.[268] The mere presence of mom keeps newborns in light sleep, helping them wake when distressed. This prevents them from slipping into a prolonged deep sleep where they may stop breathing and lack the reflex to start again, a common behavior called infant apnea. Co-sleeping manages light sleep cycles, whereas sleep training aims to get babies into deeper and longer sleep, which may contribute to SIDS.

In that same vein, the U.S. has relatively high rates of SIDS compared to other developed nations and statistically negligible rates of suffocation. In 2022, the CDC stated that of the 3,700 sleep-related infant deaths, the majority, at 61%, were attributed to SIDS and unknown causes.[269] The CDC doesn't specify whether the rest of the suffocation deaths were caused by parental suffocation in bed, and the likelihood of these deaths happening to those who deliberately bedshare safely is minuscule. Why, then, are mothers immediately warned after childbirth not to breastsleep out of fear of harming their baby when SIDS is more likely to happen to infants in a country that continually promotes leaving them alone at night?

As a parent, it's important to critically evaluate the recommendations given to us, especially when they run contrary to our natural instincts. While the AAP has done a lot of good for children and mothers, it isn't infallible. For example, it is a good practice that the AAP recommends using pacifiers as a preventative measure against SIDS. However, it's essential to recognize that before the modern binky, there was the breast. This historical context highlights the natural and protective role of breastfeeding in preventing infant mortality. At this point, it's important to hold these major organizations accountable and insist they enact a more nuanced approach to childcare.

"From Dependence Blooms Independence"

Let's examine the science of human touch. For an infant, physical touch is undeniably critical for healthy development. A study on Romanian infants in 1989 demonstrated the catastrophic effects of touch deprivation on babies. Despite receiving basic care, these orphaned infants experienced minimal affectionate touch—only 5% of the time—and suffered from 'failure to thrive.' Meaning they experienced serious health complications, including delays in physical growth and cognitive development and even early mortality.[270] Another study from the University of Illinois further illustrates the importance of physical touch where researchers looked at infant monkeys. They found that when the monkeys were deprived of physical touch—getting it less than 17% of the time—they suffered damage to their cerebellum, which is the part of the brain responsible for motor control and cognitive functions. Interestingly, this happened even though the monkeys could still see their mothers, showing that just being able to see them isn't enough for healthy development.[271] Physical touch is absolutely essential.

Though American parents tend to be highly affectionate toward their infants, Heller found that they only touch or hold their babies around 25% of the time. Exhausted American parents leave their babies for hours in cribs, swings, car seats, and loungers. This is in contrast to carrying cultures or hunter-gatherer cultures, where babies are held 70-80% of the time. Heller concluded that in many of the countries she studied, American parents often felt harassed by their own children—a condition rooted in the lack of physical touch, which made the children more needy and less independent.[272] This aligns with John Bowlby's attachment theory, which suggests that securely attached children, cared for by responsive parents, are more likely to be independent and emotionally resilient.[273] Modern expert Doctor Sam Lane Smith cites a study showing that only a third of Gen Z children are securely attached, likely influenced by cultural attitudes towards infant autonomy.[274] Essentially, children develop secure attachments and greater self-sovereignty in adulthood when their dependence is met with responsive physical touch in infancy.

What is the solution? Carrying cultures, where infants are wrapped in slings or sacks while caregivers go about their day, meet an infant's strong need for physical touch. Close proximity fosters interdependence between infants and mothers, allowing skills to be learned together—a concept at odds with America's obsession with infant independence. In these cultures, caregivers meet infants' needs promptly because leaving an infant to cry is akin to neglect. Cultures that meet an infant's dependence through early and sustained physical touch help their children become independent much earlier.

Anthropologist Sharon Heller's research further emphasizes the benefits of constant physical closeness with infants, including reducing the risk of SIDS, minimizing crying, fostering emotional attachment to the mother, gaining intimate knowledge of their needs, and providing gentle entertainment without overstimulation. Moreover, heightened physical touch through carrying connections plays a role in children's social development. Infants who are carried hear and feel their mother's voice regularly and engage in eye-to-eye contact during social interactions with adults. This early exposure to social stimuli contributes to the development of socially competent children. The takeaway? It's beneficial to carry your baby, especially your newborn, even during naps![275]

A lack of touch may result in physical and emotional delays. This can manifest in latent walking, speaking, and even social development. For example, children in other countries, like in Africa, who are carried, often walk earlier than Western infants because they consistently develop the needed core strength over time.[276]

Children who are responded to and carried also exhibit far less aggression. American toddlers are 29% more likely to present attention-seeking behavior like smacking, hitting, or seizing objects from other children. Americans view this as normal toddler behavior, but this aggression is not as prevalent in other cultures. For example, in China, mothers who closely attend to their infants and toddlers—even staying with them until they fall asleep—do not have a term for the 'terrible twos.' Even sibling rivalry is not common in indigenous cultures, where babies are constantly held by any given person at any time.[277][278][279]

Toddlers who do not receive consistent maternal touch have increased anxiety and insecurity. They may compensate for the lack of attention by becoming more clingy, restless, and tearful. As you can imagine, this conduct is exhausting and confusing to mothers. Early and constant physical touch offers an antidote to mitigate these behaviors.

Culture can also misinform us on what we believe is 'normal.' For example, Americans often attribute a child's rejection of physical affection to "stranger danger," viewing this behavior, along with clinginess—as normal for infants and toddlers. However, this behavior can be the result of insufficient touch or maternal absence, as some cultures, such as Efe toddlers of the Democratic Republic of Congo, do not experience the same level of communal anxiety.[280] Though all these generalized delays seem subtle, they impact a child's progression and ability to socialize promptly. For an infant, all is unfamiliar and somewhat chaotic. So, it's important that a mother's physical stability becomes the unchanging and nurturing environment for children to develop emotional security and resilience, rather than relying on routines or environments, which are often unstable.

Personal Thoughts

I'm not an expert, but I've observed these effects in my own experiences. While a child may be well cared for by loving and present parents, it seems that the earlier they undergo tactics enforcing physical separation, such as sleep training, the more at risk they are for certain developmental delays. There's a part of these babies that seems unsure—not quite as vigorously active, curious, or engaged as I've discerned in normal development cases. Some even exhibit flatter head shapes, likely due to prolonged time spent lying in cribs or loungers. They tend to stay closer to their mothers in public or stressful settings and are more prone to tears. Some act out on self harm when distressed. Or they limit their independent behavior, wishing to be babied into their late toddler and early preschool years. Though most of these things are subtle and be easily overlooked, I've unfortunately seen significant motor delays in the most serious cases.

I wonder if some long-term behavioral or neurological differences might arise from a complex interplay of genetics, environment, and early caregiving philosophies around independence. While we cannot argue that rigid and forced independence in infancy causes neurodivergence, it's possible that multiple factors—such as genetic predispositions, prenatal exposures, and chronic stress during early infancy—could contribute to a cascade of unwanted challenges. These observations are not conclusions but rather questions I hold as I reflect on how deeply early care shapes a child's future. The parallel rise in sleep training or infant separation practices alongside the increased recognition of neurodivergence since the 1980s continues to raise questions for me.

I have experienced the benefits of responsive touch as a mother. Unlike my firstborn, I religiously carried and held my second child around the clock for the first six months. My firstborn slept in a bassinet near me, whereas my secondborn would not sleep without me holding him, even if I sat beside him. Tending to my second child under this framework was physically exhausting, but it paid off. Miraculously, he allowed me to put him down for his daily naps at six months. He now sleeps much better than his older brother, who still wishes I stay with him during his naps. Not only did my second child learn to sleep without any force from me, but this experience reinforced how touch affects development and independence.

Parents have important decisions to make regarding their infants' early investments. Practices like babywearing and breastsleeping are good models of responsive parenting. While there is no single "right way" to parent, the principles of touch and proximity help prevent unnecessary heartache. Many parents are naturally intuitive about when and how to introduce structured sleep routines, adjusting their approach based on their child's unique temperament. Still, cultures that stress constant physical closeness between caregivers and infants tend to nurture healthier physiological and psychological outcomes. As we continue to navigate modern parenting paradigms, perhaps it's time to reconsider the enduring value of proximity and physical touch.

Better Environments for Childcare

"It felt so wrong to leave her, but everyone said it would get easier..." This is a false narrative American parents who must outsource childcare hear all too often. Our culture frequently undervalues maternal presence despite the paramount need for infants to spend significant time with their mothers. This brief period when mothers devote themselves to caring for their babies and young children should be celebrated; Americans must carve out opportunities for mothers to fully commit to this season of life. A mother's constant care is second to none; this early investment in children lays the groundwork for a healthy life. We must shift our environments to make this early connection possible and appealing for most American women.

Today, American parents spend, on average, 2-3 hours a day with their children.[281] People are galled by the rising cost of institutional childcare, viewing affordable childcare and extended maternity leave as both a right and the obvious solution to the challenges parents face. However, these measures do not align with the principles that encourage healthy and well-adjusted children. They also contribute to workplace discrimination against women. Such initiatives are potential 'loans' that harm infants and parents in the long run. So, what's to be done?

Rather than relying solely on existing mechanisms, we should create environments that actively support parents caring for their young children, especially mothers. To achieve this, we need a cultural shift and a renewed conviction that during the early, formative years of a child's life—when they are most vulnerable and reliant on maternal care—it's crucial for mothers to be present with their children. For many women, this likely entails being at home for the first few years—or mostly. Before any feminists close this book, believing I wish to 'trap women into being tradwives,' I have a much grander vision for wives and mothers. It begins with creating supportive communities and workplaces that enable mothers to balance both professional and parental responsibilities without sidelining them. I will go into greater depth about this in the next chapter.

As mentioned above, baby-carrying allows women to care for their young while managing other responsibilities, which is why we need walkable environments that actively support this practice. During my earliest postpartum moments, I was determined to carry my baby, and I was naively unaware of how difficult it was in America. Errands are only possible through a heavy and expensive car seat, which my baby hated. I wanted to keep my baby wrapped close to me while running errands, but my car-centric environment forced me to constantly take him in and out of the baby wrap. We would start to get comfortable, only for my baby to get fussy the moment he was put back in his car seat.

If I had several stops to make, walking with my baby on me wasn't an option. Round and round, I would go, endlessly transferring my frustrated baby to and from his car seat. This became too toilsome despite my resolve to carry him; I reluctantly began leaving him in his car seat when I took him places. As my baby became more aware, he would scream at our separation as I drove, which drew me to the conclusion that I'd rather not go anywhere with him and just be home. I realized that our cultural attitudes uphold suburban life by normalizing our babies' cries instead of adapting environments to meet their needs. I'm convinced this is one of the reasons why women feel their lives are 'over' after having children in America.

I spent much of that postpartum time alone in my house, with me as my baby's sole amusement for most of the day. My baby was not content to be wrapped unless we were outside or surrounded by people. Aside from walking outside for hours in the dead of winter, I had nothing fruitful to do out in the open air. I felt so lonely, tired, and stir-crazy. I began relishing the times I could return Amazon packages as a UPS store was four blocks from me. I knew I could get some sunshine, take a break, provide needed stimulation for my baby, enjoy organic exercise, and be productive all at the same time. I can only imagine the suffering some mothers go through during this time when they are alone with very demanding babies and have nowhere to go.

American car dependency disrupts the natural bond between mother and baby, resulting in feelings of isolation and exhaustion. This dependency makes it challenging for new mothers, as most errands necessitate driving, which infants often dislike and are difficult to transfer when sleeping. I have stopped many plans because I knew I could not transfer my sleeping baby from the car without waking him up. Suburban living constrains normal life by making mothers frequently feel they must follow a desperate form of rigidity to function. Take nap time, for example, a checklist of sound machines, blackout curtains, perfect temperatures, sleep sacks, swaddles, books, baths, and beds. Other cultures would find this behavior unusual because babies sleep anywhere, especially when carried! Or at least they do if a parent is living a life outside of the home.

For instance, in Nordic countries, it's common for there to be hundreds of babies sleeping in strollers outside of shops and restaurants.[282] It seems absurd, but it's true. The mother is right there, accessible at any point while enjoying her outing. She can pick up spices for dinner, all while her baby naps peacefully nearby. She gets to live a life, even after a baby!

We must replace our limited lifestyle with settings that elevate maternal presence during the formative years of infancy. Walkable settings enable baby carrying and provide the stimulation mothers and infants need for bonding. Family zoning and propinquity also provide mothers and infants with the community support they need. The initial sacrifices children require in their early years are tremendous but brief. Creating functional environments that allow mothers to invest in babyhood cultivates happier children and parents. A village setting is the key to finally meeting the needs of mothers and infants.

As we have discussed, raising an infant is an immense investment. Our view of children requires a cultural shift, recognizing infants as vulnerable beings with exceedingly tender minds and feelings. Their cries should be swiftly met with comfort, attention, and physical closeness to help preserve their emotional resilience or mental health. We can alleviate sleep deprivation and emotional burnout among American parents by debunking myths and embracing practices like carrying and breastsleeping. America can choose to pay now, securing health and affectionate attachments, or pay later with mounting interest, but the bill is always due. As we respond to our infants, we can provide the stable building blocks for a functional life. Under a new cultural framework, parents can rest assured that raising children gets easier if they invest in the first three years, particularly infancy. Though having a baby is a joy unknown, I know firsthand that always responding to an infant can be downright maddening and frequently inconvenient. However, my mantra is, "It's hard now, so it won't be harder later." We will see America flourish again with a renewed approach to children in walkable and localized spaces. Children's health is at the heart of village life, and if our infants and children come first, everything will follow suit.

20

Dear Suburbia, you've distorted motherhood.

Women are biologically designed to work within society and should not be deceived into thinking otherwise. Throughout most of human history, motherhood and work were intertwined, not separate. Take, for example, the !Kung people of southern Africa. In this hunter-gatherer society, women carried their children with them while they worked, gathering 70% of the food for the family, while men contributed the heart of the meal through hunting. Their societies were centered around women and children; both groups were well integrated into the community, working and playing side by side. [283]

In societies like those of the !Kung, the integration of work and motherhood is natural and necessary. But in today's suburban environments, this harmony has been disrupted; we've grown accustomed to the idea that mothers should either stay at home or pull away from their children to work. This black-and-white thinking is promoted by suburban environments that isolate women and children from normal society. It lacks nuance, does not consider the biological rhythms of women, and disparages mothers' natural drive to be involved members of their community. We must restore environments that affirm the importance of motherhood and allow mothers to participate fully in society without sacrificing either their children or their ambitions.

Defending motherhood and its essential role in society is not the same as idolizing the 1950s version of homemaking, commonly referred to today as the "trad wife." This caricature of the ideal wife and mother becomes perpetually more tedious, exhausting, and lonely to modern women. Especially since, ironically, most visible "trad wives" are still working women, building online empires based on their lifestyles.

The way Western culture approaches women and children is both dismissive and dehumanizing. The stigmatization against mothers and towards women as a whole is fourfold. The first problem is that Americans profoundly undervalue children. If this were untrue, the role of mothers would be tremendously revered; mothers are the primary bearers and nurturers of children in the most vulnerable points of their lives. Psychologist Dr. Erika Komisar finds that the steady presence of a mother, most prominently in the first three years, is paramount to raising mentally and emotionally resilient adults.[284] American culture ignores this fact and denies status to one of the most important and feminine of all occupations, making it seem secondary or obsolete to other pursuits.

The second issue is that our culture traps women in a 'damned if you do, damned if you don't' paradigm regarding the timeline of motherhood. Women who choose to have children in their youth, during their biological prime, are often dismissed as having 'thrown their lives away,' viewed as immature or lacking ambition. At the same time, those who delay motherhood for career or personal growth face prejudice for being 'past their prime.' The message I get from this is that if you have children at all, you've made a mistake. This was made clear to me after graduation when I ran into an old professor. Seeing my pregnant belly, he said, 'Ah—you're having a baby. Your life's over now.'

A third cultural challenge is the infrastructure that separates working women from their children, unlike local communities where work and family can better coexist. Environments should be designed to support women in balancing both roles without forcing them into a binary choice.

The fourth obstacle is the result of our failing infrastructure, which makes it so that women are not mentally, emotionally, or financially prepared to have children when they reach adulthood. The reluctance to encourage early motherhood is understandable, given how prolonged adolescence has made starting a family at a young age seem absurd. It's common today to see 19-year-olds being criticized for their decision to get married, especially young women. People cry, 'A teenage bride! She's a child!' This seems silly to me, but only because I figure she should be more than ready to take on that role at such an age. She may or may not be prepared in today's cultural climate, but if she isn't, I reckon it's because our environment has delayed her personal development. This is why I place such strong emphasis on raising children to maturity in alignment with their biological clock. With an environmental and cultural shift, women could be better supported to make motherhood a desirable choice earlier in life.

These four factors have led many women to delay motherhood. According to the American College of Obstetricians and Gynecologists, women are most fertile from their late teens to late twenties.[285] However, women are waiting until the end of this period to have children. The U.S. Census Bureau reports that the average age for working American women to have their first child is 30—nearly three years past the peak fertility window. Women go to great lengths to medically and hormonally prevent pregnancies during their healthiest years, only to deal with greater emerging health and fertility complications later on. This societal trend of delaying motherhood contributes to the rising fertility crisis in the United States, including an increased reliance on expensive IVF treatments.[286][287]

Additionally, women who postpone motherhood until their thirties put themselves in a difficult position when it comes to advancing their careers and starting a family. This delay can disrupt their professional ambitions, leading many to rely on daycare or nannies at the height of their careers. This kind of separation can weaken the mother-child bond, causing increased distress for both mother and child. At the same time, trying to manage the demands of early parenthood in corporate America can hinder career progression.

The cultural devaluation of motherhood and the expectation for women to withdraw from society once they become mothers contribute to unnecessary delays in starting a family. Women are given less than a ten-year window to be 'individuals' before being expected to sacrifice other aspects of their lives for decades. This suburban culture fails to provide the support women need, ultimately undermining their ability to balance career, family, and personal identity.

Young Mom?

Instead of following the current model of going to school, establishing a career, and postponing marriage and children until our thirties—when it becomes harder to leave a career and fertility complications are more common—we could flip the script.

As previously established, villages provide a more effective childhood education model and practical work experiences. This solid foundation encourages timely maturation, better preparing individuals for early marriage and children. Adults won't have to waste time 'finding themselves' in their twenties; they can instead establish a life with a loving partner. Under this framework, a woman could explore her career before having children, engage in supplementary work with flexible hours while her children are young, and later resume her career in full force. This is because her children are cared for by the community at large and are much more self-sufficient than they would be in current suburbia, freeing up her time.

A village, therefore, maintains a woman's career throughout the various seasons of her life. As women take advantage of their peak fertile years, early motherhood becomes a positive investment where they can complete long-term goals with their family at their side.

For instance, imagine an environment where a girl could begin training to become a nurse at 16 rather than waiting until she's 18-24. This way, she could establish her career, conceive children during her most fertile years, and return to work full or part-time when her children are ready—all within local employment opportunities. Alternatively, another girl could finish high school, get married, have children, and work toward an online degree while raising her babies. The degree would give her an engaging outlet for learning, allowing her to re-enter the workforce when the time is right. If she wishes for stronger community ties with her professors and peers, she could enroll in a program that offers both in-person and online learning.

Contrary to popular narratives, few things quite prepare or mature a woman for a career like motherhood. The absolute stamina a woman has to develop to raise a child is immense, along with the creative and problem-solving skills a woman gains in addressing her children's needs. Many studies have shown that if a woman has support during these vulnerable times, the cognitive skills used in parenting, such as multitasking and emotional intelligence, can actually enhance a woman's problem-solving abilities.[288] Having a child is a kind of 'baptism by fire,' accelerating qualities like discipline, maturity, and sacrifice—all of which contribute to stronger job performance and drive.

It's important to value motherhood at every stage, but our culture believes the thirties are the only responsible time to have children. However, under a different framework, I think most women could benefit from having children earlier. Besides it being substantially easier on the body, it can be a very empowering choice in terms of ambition. It's time to take women's needs seriously and prepare them financially and emotionally so they have the option to choose early parenthood.

If a village prepares children to become adults, women would have the education, resources, and support to raise their children in a balanced manner. They could devote time to parenting until their children are self-sufficient or ready for external care. By thriving in various seasons with flexible work environments, women really could "have it all."

Not a stay-at-home mom or a working mom, just a "mom."

The ideological warfare between stay-at-home motherhood and working motherhood is fierce. I've heard bitter critics of feminism argue that women's education has contributed to the decline of motherhood. The proposed solution is for women to stop going to college and confine themselves to a suburban home tucked quietly away to raise lots of babies. This point of view is ridiculous, as educated mothers are statistically more likely to get married and raise healthy children.[289][290]

Many women's reluctance to embrace traditional motherhood roles stems from their astute awareness of systemic flaws rather than an inherent aversion to motherhood itself. In fact, part of this vast anti-mother pedagogy has inadvertently exposed the deep flaws in the American system rather than in motherhood. This commentary on motherhood was good, notwithstanding the continual and painful persecution that dedicated mothers have had to trudge through—because, without it, we could not critically work our way out of our modern predicament.

American women constantly endure cultural campaigns that encourage the virtuous yet dim 'stay-at-home mom' versus the nefarious and bright 'working mom'—both of which lead to imbalance, guilt, or weariness. The reality of women's needs is far more complex than the binary narrative suggests. According to Pew Research, nearly half of American mothers with children under eighteen prefer working part-time as opposed to full-time or not working.[291] In a study done by the American Psychology Association, depression symptoms went down if women had some type of part-time work when their children were under preschool age.[292] This suggests that part-time jobs provide a sense of fulfillment, community, and reprieve from the demands of caregiving. We can see it's important to design places where women can be involved in wider society while raising children, whether through a job or other outlets.

When the framework is no longer corrupt, the discussion becomes more complex than simply: 'You're a good mom for staying at home versus you're a bad mom for working.' For most modern women, these two extremes don't offer the life they want. Women are going to school for 12–14 years and then being told to give up everything to raise children! Of course, this makes women feel like they have to choose one or the other. Our environment does a profound disservice to women who have spent their lives exercising their minds and talents to be told to stop or step aside.

Today, many visible career women hold positions that seem incompatible with motherhood. Many choose to remain without children and seek to make that choice appear glamorous despite having the resources to raise a family. While this is perfectly acceptable for the minority of women who are disinterested in motherhood and find great satisfaction in ambitious careers, the broader societal narrative should also recognize the desires of the majority. Most women seek a balance between family, community, and work and would not count themselves among the 1% with demanding jobs that require a 50+ hour workweek.

Throughout most of human history, before the rise of suburbia and the subsequent cultural gender war, there was simply 'mom.' An individual who is exceptionally involved in her community without being ripped from her children or enduring non-stop caretaking. Depending on the cultural context, she had many opportunities for social engagement, personal growth, and even monetary contributions. Village environments allow many more opportunities for mothers to work in a balanced manner without abandoning their children. Therefore, if America reimagines its local infrastructure to better support family life—through flexible work environments, community resources, and walkable neighborhoods—there is great hope that balance, fulfillment, and happiness can return to the average mother and her family.

Localization and flexibility

Here's an example of an ideal situation for a mother in a beautiful, peaceful, and well-designed village. It's October, and she bikes home from the bank with her children. She serendipitously encounters a friend sitting outside a local café enjoying the views. She joins her for a warm drink and has a fulfilling chat while her children play nearby. There's a courtyard with a fountain, and mini-parks have been distributed along the way. Her mixed-use city allows more visibility and safety for children. As she watches her four-year-old explore the playground set, she feels comfortable sending her oldest child home on the tram to do homework.

After catching up with her friend, she returns home to finish her other business. Her small escapade has left her feeling socially fed and productive rather than lonely and burnt out. She didn't have to intrude on her friend's time, as it was clear her friend was resting, and now both could finish their day with tasks they were interested in. She can take the reins off her older children and allow them to navigate their time and transportation. Walkability, appropriate density, and functionality reclaim freedom for the American woman.

The phrase, "It takes a village," can easily summarize the benefits of locality. However, there is value in breaking that sentiment into four main tenets. Villages

- reduce the need for mothers to micromanage their children,
- enable mothers to remain in the workforce (even if only part-time),
- ease the pressure to separate from their children and
- increase community support for childcare and socialization.

We will examine each of these reasons in further detail through some plausible scenarios.

In a community where a mother can trust that her children will safely return from school or extracurricular activities, she could enjoy a fulfilling 20-hour work week and have time for her family. A walkable setting would bring her peace about her children's safety and independence, and if she ever needed to run errands or take a break, her children would know where she was and have easy access to her. Reducing the need to constantly oversee her children would allow her more time and mental space for other activities, like earning extra money or investing in community activities. Instead, corporate America, with its strict regulations, lacks the flexibility to allow mothers to do anything but watch their children.

A village environment also helps women remain active in their careers throughout motherhood. As an illustration, a mother could become an ultrasound technician and work part-time at the local clinic without being too far from her family. I knew a woman who did exactly this. She worked a two-hour shift as an ultrasound technician on Tuesdays and Thursdays while she had young children at home. She told me, "I really needed that time to be with other people, but my children were so little that I didn't want to be gone all day. I felt like it was really good for me, and I'm grateful my work was so accommodating during that time." Village environments support part-time work, offering women a healthy balance between personal fulfillment, family care, and professional growth.

Before the 20th century, it was expected that working-class women would work with their infants in America. According to Nancy Woloch's book, *Women and the American Experience*, the culture, therefore, adapted itself to this norm in many ways, with women often working in family businesses and home businesses through craft industries.[293] This allowed mothers to better balance caregiving and provision. The switch from home-based work to factory work changed this dynamic by making rigid schedules and harsh working environments. In many cases, this created a stark separation from women and children.

Similarly, today, modern corporations' time control and liability often limit flexibility. In contrast, localized communities are capable of being more flexible and accommodating toward children in work environments. This approach allows a mother to remain close to her children without compromising her ability to contribute meaningfully to the world—or her sanity in the process.

For instance, instead of a mother leaving her baby at home, she returns to work with her baby strapped to her chest or back. It seems odd to discourage this in some work environments. My college history professor taught with her newborn for several months. Another professor of mine brought her baby to work at the beginning of her career as an elementary school teacher. The school she taught at was low-income and in desperate need of her, so they allowed her to bring her baby to class. She said, "It was such a relief to have my baby with me and help my students." Why shouldn't a woman be able to bring her baby to school? I see no reason why students could not adapt to having a baby in the classroom. Children could grow accustomed to such an environment and be cherished, protected, and loved by both students and staff. This setup is feasible in localized, community-centered schools with teaching assistants.

This flexibility isn't limited to teaching; there are many jobs where women can bring their children along. A mother could carry her child in a sling as a dance instructor if her baby's temperament allowed. She could work part-time in a jewelry store or as a landscaper. She could provide elderly care as a nurse for those needing company. The possibilities in a village are endless for enabling mothers to pursue a career without needing to be separated from their children. Keeping mothers close to their children supports healthy child development and reduces maternal stress. Women are biologically great multitaskers, and children are adaptable. The culture simply needs to adjust to women and children being together.

Finally, villages offer strong local support, making it easier for mothers to find reliable childcare from trusted individuals within the community. If a pregnant woman worked at a general store and needed a temporary replacement postpartum, she could train a teenager, perhaps even her son, to take on her role while she rested. Furthermore, villages allow families to live closer together, sharing childcare responsibilities and leaning on neighborhood friends for additional support. For instance, if two friends or sisters desire to work, they can arrange to share childcare responsibilities by alternating shifts with each other's children—one takes a morning shift while the other takes an evening shift. Similar scenarios provide plenty of cousin or friend time for the kiddos and alleviate the caretaking burden for parents. Their children are surrounded by individuals who are stable parts of their lives, rather than a nanny or daycare center. The community then becomes interdependent rather than independent, relying on each other in healthy ways and fostering unity over isolation. And might I add... much cheaper?

Additionally, these environments make women less vulnerable. Today, stay-at-home mothers may be left behind with little work experience or education to fall back on if they get divorced or widowed. However, if a woman is always working, even part-time, in her community, she is much more likely to have access to local job opportunities and support. Some cautious mothers may even save up a large nest egg over time to have financial security in case of emergencies. The main point is that if women decide to get married and have children in village environments, they don't need to be swept away by the unpredictable winds of life or completely reliant on their husband's income. This reality would add an extra level of stability and competency to the social fabric.

I've witnessed the suffering of our society pigeonholing mothers and not considering their needs—perhaps even blaming them for choosing to have children in the first place. I've felt it myself, maneuvering through environments that give me little to no support, believing that if only I could be more disciplined or have more money, my children would have what they need. Yet, even if I were perfectly disciplined and unaffected by the vices of my environment, my children and I would still need far more than what is being offered to us. At the heart of it all, we must foster walkable neighborhoods, nearby employment options, and multi-generational family communities to create ideal conditions for mothers. It's time to build communities that put mothers and their children first.

21

Dear Suburbia, we need fathers.

Our urban designs often reflect our cultural priorities. To build better communities, we must not only redesign our streets and structures, but also reimagine the roles we play within them—especially the role of fatherhood in family life. This chapter reframes one of the most contested concepts of our time: patriarchy. Today's suburban environment mirrors our current interpretation of the patriarchy: marked by isolation and rigid separation of spaces. Thus, our urbanism is rooted in control and hierarchy rather than multi-generational collaboration and care. This model weaponizes fathers as breadwinners, using financial control to enforce authority, while secluding mothers primarily to caregiving roles.

I aim to reexamine the definition of patriarchy by reorienting it toward a culture of urban design that places children above all else—cultivating values and systems that extend beyond the present moment to serve the welfare of both current and future generations.

As we've worked to overturn misconceptions about motherhood, we must also reexamine our understanding of fatherhood. In a traditional patriarchal family system, the father is seen as the head of the household, holding authority over women and children. Throughout most of human history, families have operated under this model. As women's rights and opportunities have expanded through social and technological advancements, many have begun to equate this system with oppression—and not without good reason. The patriarchy—as defined by both secular and religious institutions—deserves the pushback. Since women have achieved greater equality, people view it as an unnecessary and outdated system. Some argue that it fails not only women but also men. Society is facing destabilization as gender wars over the patriarchy intensify. This predicament largely stems from a cultural misunderstanding of a man's role as a husband and father. I argue that the patriarchy, in terms of family life, is a beneficial system for women and children when it is properly defined, understood, and practiced. Though rarely exemplified, the patriarchy, in its unadulterated form, offers a stable framework for families where parents are equal partners and everyone is properly taken care of.

Equality and the patriarchy may seem oxymoronic—and it is if the patriarchy means that men are the supreme rulers of their households and their wives must submit to their every whim. However, the patriarchy, as it is meant to be, is not a form of domination. It positions fathers as protectors of their families and leaders in areas like provision and stability to create an equal partnership with mothers. This dynamic establishes balance in what might otherwise be an unfair system, where the demands and risks of parenthood fall more heavily on women. The true purpose of the patriarchy is to complement a wife's role as a mother, not control her. A man's job as a husband and father is to use his unique powers to serve his wife and children, not to be above them. Fathers lead in ways mothers can't, just as mothers lead in ways fathers can't. This is all done in harmony for the benefit of children, the highest assets in village life.

If we truly want fathers and mothers to be equal partners, we must recognize how parenthood affects men and women differently. The process of bringing life into the world is not exactly a beacon of gender equality, and it never will be. Biology plays by its own rules. Men's contribution to the creation of children can be boiled down to a single moment of bliss, leaving women with months of physical discomfort and vulnerability. One couldn't really argue it's fairness. This imbalance, in fact, starts long before pregnancy—when a girl gets her first period and begins experiencing the physical demands of womanhood. Once a woman conceives and bears a child, it's only the start of the years of dependency required from her. The rigorous time an infant needs from their mother could never be equal in the early stages of life, even with a father's best efforts. Even though I had an extremely supportive husband, he couldn't nurse our baby, which took upwards of four hours a day. That alone is a part-time job. In general, the postpartum period is very taxing, which men can sympathize with but never truly understand. To put it simply, men do not experience the same kind of disruption to their physical state; they are never detoured in this manner.

Since men can maintain their physical capacity throughout all seasons of life, they can be steadfast anchors for their families. This continuous physical advantage, demonstrated by their high levels of testosterone and natural fortitude, is why men have historically been the primary providers and protectors. Their physical natures equip them with the ability to secure resources and combat existential threats to their wife and offspring.

With this kind of power, so to speak, there's no greater risk to women and children than malicious men. When it comes to protecting vulnerable members of society, it's often men against men. The power men possess can be used for good or evil, but make no mistake—it will never go away. Modern society may try to mitigate or even ignore sex-based differences, but until we reach some post-apocalyptic nightmare where babies are grown in labs, the biological differences in parenthood will continue to exist.

With this in mind, many women believe the only path to equality is to get on some good birth control and kiss any prospects of their future posterity goodbye. This may even come with the rejection of marriage or lifelong partners. It's true that a woman could choose this form of equality, but she risks missing out on experiences that may be very fulfilling to her. The majority of women would benefit from having the option to find balance between motherhood and their other ambitions.

Women's fear of becoming wives and mothers is a sign that our culture has corrupted the patriarchy and dismissed the value of mothers and children. The patriarchy has been a source of weaponization and abuse. Within the modern understanding of the patriarchy, people are prioritized as follows: father, mother, and children. The order acts with the father as the king, the mother as the advisor, and the children as the peasants. The shape results in a pyramid. No matter who's ever discussed this with me, it is impossible to equalize men and women in this scenario. Typically, one of three outcomes arises: 1) The father tries to use this authority to dominate his family, leading to a power struggle between him and his wife; 2) To avoid conflict or perhaps appeal to religiosity, the wife willingly submits to his dominion, subverting her identity to the family as a whole—second in command; 3) The couple, wishing for equality, simply ignores the role of the patriarchy or may even condemn it. The mental gymnastics required to justify the ordering of the father as the only authority is simply too much. Even benevolent attempts at the patriarchy usually fail in some capacity— perhaps not in practice, but most certainly in principle. Despite a husband's efforts to be good to his wife, it remains an unspoken form of oppression, as he always has the last say.

In a perfected vision of the patriarchy, the father is the head of the household, but he is not the top priority. He is not first on the list, but rather the last. The correct ordering of the patriarchy is as follows: children, mothers, and fathers. Children become the kings, and the parents' roles split as the servants, each equally and uniquely providing the very things their children need the most. It's a type of paradox in which those who know the least and need the most become the family rulers. And yet, is it not true? Is it not the parents who feed, carry, dress, bathe, and serve their children to all ends, just as we would the highest royalty? Mothers bear, nurture, and care for their children, especially in their youngest years, while fathers provide guidance, support, and physical security, serving as stable beacons for their families.

Under this definition of the patriarchy, the roles of mother and father are equal in service. The shape transforms from an insentient pyramid to a living thing, like a flower. The man embodies the stem, and the woman is the bloom, working in unity to spread their seed. Another way to think about it, is a pair of ballroom dancers. The man is the stable core, while the woman flourishes and dazzles. Together, they move in perfect unity, with their children symbolized by the graceful dance they share across the floor. In leadership, those with the most power are the greatest servants. The same is the case for mothers and fathers. With men carrying a biological mantle of strength, a father is responsible for the welfare of the entire group, overseeing it through protection, provision, and personal care.

If the patriarchy puts men first, American families and society will fail. It results in the idiom, "Throw the baby out with the bath water." The baby, nearly forgotten, is always the last to be cleaned and bathed. As a result, they receive the dirtiest water, leaving them vulnerable to illness or even death. We see this in the culture today as we build societies that dismiss the precious roles of mothers and children. A father should act as a shield, consistently protecting vulnerable members of the family unit. I imagine him with his arms wrapped around his wife and children, protecting them from the storms of life.

A father heads the family, but only in what he does best: protecting and providing for the group as a whole. He must only put his foot down when he is at risk of not being able to fulfill his role. A mother must do the same if her stewardship is jeopardized. However, if a mother and father are working in tandem as equal partners, they should never be at odds.

Villages are a perfect avenue for correcting the patriarchy in understanding and practice, as they ease the disruptions to women's lives caused by motherhood and promote balance between career and family life for both parents. They allow men to pursue provision in full force, knowing they are not inhibiting their wives' progress. While I've listed several ways this can happen in a village, I can share an example from my personal life. My husband took on the role of provider, promising to step up and deliver when I wished to be home with our children. It is only because of his stable income and his dedication to his calling as a husband and father that I have been able to write this book. With two tiny children, this book became a part-time job, with me often working 4-5 hours daily, usually during sleeping hours. Had my husband insisted I work, I could have never found the time to do the things I am passionate about, and I most certainly could not have given the time needed to fully tend to my babies.

This book may very well have taken years to write and, perhaps, never been finished. This is particularly true for other projects I was commissioned to do during this time. His foundation as a father and the head of our livelihood created a scenario where I could get the best of both worlds—fulfilling my aspirations while being present for my family. In return, my husband gets fulfillment, love, and admiration from me and his children for his consistent presence and contributions. During the many seasons of my life, his commitment to me has gifted me the flexibility I need to be both ambitious and a mother. So it's true that without him, I might have a thriving full-time career today...*maybe*, but I wouldn't have the greatest joys of my life—my children.

I wish for all men and women to receive this kind of familial stability and harmony. While suburban living stifles the lives of fathers and mothers, villages bring balance to their roles. Women are liberated in their femininity—free to create beloved, lifelong social systems while given time to exemplify their talents within their communities. Men are liberated in their masculinity—free to find true meaning in both career and family as they care for those who need and love them.

Of course, depending on the circumstance, season, or couple, these roles may shift from time to time. For instance, I view making dinner as a terrible chore, and my husband believes it to be an artistic endeavor. We share responsibilities in the household and with children, depending on our needs and personalities. There may even be moments when we switch roles completely, though I'm not sure we would like it.

In the end, our infrastructure has distorted the purpose of the patriarchy, particularly regarding the roles of fathers. Villages that place mothers and children at the center of family life offer a renewed approach to the patriarchy that benefits everyone. By putting children first, fathers and mothers can find balance in their unique roles, and every family member can once again benefit from the true essence of the patriarchy. Just as villages need children, children need fathers—present leaders committed to caring for their families alongside their wives. This renewed understanding will translate into a new era of urban design—villages and neighborhoods built to endure, where family life is supported, children are nurtured, and communities regain their balance.

Commuting

Beyond more philosophical discussions, I wish to briefly mention some troubles fathers deal with today. The modern father often suffers long, traffic-ridden commutes through barren industrial environments until he finally returns home. Beyond the suburbs, the drive is unappealing and loud, with asphalt, billboards, and fast food chains crowding every mile. He believes he is returning home to an oasis. However, as more suburbs create car-dependent communities, there will inevitably be more traffic, stripping valuable family time and sanity from him.

I knew a new father who spent over half a million dollars on a suburban home, only to discover that 1.2 million people would be added to the area, with only two roads for car exits. His commute became so arduous that he began leaving an hour earlier and staying an hour later just to avoid rush hour. He left at six am and got home at seven pm every day, giving him minimal time with his toddler, who went to bed at 7:30. This is not uncommon; many men prolong their workdays to avoid mind-numbing traffic and this can come at the detriment of their family relationships.

Beautiful, pedestrian-friendly villages or cities with walkability, mixed zoning, local businesses, and expansive public transportation allow fathers to live closer to work. At one point, my husband had a quick 7-minute bike ride as his daily commute to work. It was one of the best attributes of his job. He was often home for lunch with me and our children and was always readily available when we needed him. At the time, we rejected many job opportunities that would have given us a bigger house because they would have added a volatile commute. In contrast to the father I described previously, my children and I sometimes got three extra hours a day with him. Because I got so much time with him, I was content for him to have other hobbies like weekly intramural basketball games or boys' nights.

Fathers should not have to spend thousands of hours in a car. According to Charles Montgomery in his book *Happy City: Transforming Our Lives Through Urban Design*, a person with a one-hour commute has to earn 40% more to be as satisfied with life as someone who walks to work.[294] Also, according to a ten year study in Sweden, people who endure more than a 45-minute commute are 40% more likely to divorce.[295] In a college class I took, colloquially called "The Happiness Class," long commutes were one of the biggest dampers on life satisfaction. Men should have many more opportunities to work within their community or, at the very least, have efficient and quick public transportation. This way, they can pursue socialization, reading, music, podcasts, or work while they commute. For those who must drive, villages reduce traffic drastically, eliminating long commutes. They can take time to decompress instead of driving. Best of all, villages ensure that fathers are close to their families, allowing for more time together.

Haggard Wife

Suburbia often makes mothers and children go stir-crazy. Instead of a father coming home to peace, he may feel he is entering a war zone, where he has to comfort an emotionally haggard wife and tend to rowdy children. His wife quickly hands him their baby, disgruntled that he seems free while she is trapped at home with little to no adult interaction or help. This can cause strife between partners who are both very tired. A good father will spend time with his children and enjoy it, but childcare is still work, and nobody seems to get a break. This lack of balance could be remedied if both partners had their needs met by the right environment.

Business

Men should have many more opportunities to succeed with small businesses, particularly men who prioritize family life above all else. Some fathers function better when they can work next to their children and share their legacies with them. Localized small businesses must become a staple in American life again. It's great when a child knows where their father works and has the ability to visit him and watch him in action. It is essential for children, especially boys, to see masculine figures working in their selected trades. Additionally, it is emboldening for men to be examples to their children, providing deep connections that may otherwise be overlooked.

We have denied many American men the opportunity to share their passions and occupational pursuits with their children, thereby depriving them of the great sense of pride that comes with it. As franchises proliferate, men have fewer chances to own their businesses, work alongside their children, or find work they feel is valuable. The lack of family businesses is startling. In such a corporate and expansive world, where can men pass down their occupational and community legacies for generations? Villages can return this wonderful opportunity to them.

* * *

To protect the well-being of men, we must develop structures that allow them to succeed at work and home. We can give them the stability and support they deserve through the development of pedestrian-friendly communities with mixed zoning, local businesses, and expansive public transportation. These communities allow fathers to live closer to work, reducing commute time and increasing family time. Encouraging the growth of small, local businesses can also help fathers balance their professional and family lives, providing valuable opportunities for children to learn from and connect with their fathers. With a corrected understanding of the patriarchy that puts children first, American society can build lasting families and communities. Men will have the social and environmental framework they need to lead in meaningful ways. They will be beacons of strength and stability within their home and the rest of society.

22

Dear Suburbia, are we including the elderly and disabled?

The disabled community, or those with accessibility needs, is a group anyone could join at any moment. More obvious examples include being hit by a car and experiencing lower-body paralysis. You could also develop epilepsy as an adult, making it impossible to drive and drastically altering your independence. Or you could suffer a stroke and lose mobility on one side of your body, significantly affecting your ability to walk, drive, or perform daily tasks independently. It is cruel how ableist our society is designed, making few accommodations for independence for those who cannot drive. The question of autonomy and being able to safely get around is paramount for any civilized society; it can greatly ease caregiving burdens and improve quality of life.

For example, a man with Down Syndrome in my neighborhood, whom people affectionately call "Elvis," is often found riding his bike everywhere. He is quite independent and works at the local grocery store. However, he likely relies on his primary caretaker to chauffeur him to work because he cannot bike there safely on his own. Imagine how wonderful it would be if he could safely commute on his own. His quality of life would significantly improve, and it would make things much easier for those who care for him.

I know someone who is blind, and he would find it impossible to function independently if he didn't live in the heart of Provo, where the infrastructure accommodates walking students and allows him to lead an autonomous life. It's hard to overstate how essential it is to consider people with accessibility needs, especially since none of us are exempt from the possibility of needing such accommodations. Walkability is a solution for everyone, ensuring that, even if you find yourself with accessibility challenges, you can still lead a full and independent life.

Addressing Elderly Isolation and Lack of Connection

Restrictive laws, environments, and societal norms have isolated the elderly, leaving them to grapple with deep loneliness and a lack of connection. According to the National Institute of Medicine, many elderly individuals experience loneliness and depression due to living alone, lacking close family ties, and being disconnected from their culture of origin.[296] As a result, they aren't as socially fed as they need to be for greater longevity and life satisfaction.

Dear journal,

My aunt took her own life this summer. She had a small circle of family who loved her and knew her. I feel I should have visited her more often, but it was a long drive for me. She never married. Sometimes I wonder if she had been given the community she needed, people would have known her more... seen her. She would have had more purpose and friends. Maybe she wouldn't have been so cooped up in her home and stressed at work. Who knows?

Importance of Community for the Aging Generation

A functional community is vital for the well-being of the aging population.

A study published in *Evolution and Human Behavior* found that grandparents who spend time with their grandchildren tend to live longer lives. However, our current systems often prevent the elderly from living close to their families. Instead, the culture celebrates distinct 50+ suburbs, separating and homogenizing them.[297] This frequently shuts them away, especially in suburbs that don't have many amenities, and sends the message that we no longer wish to see them. Zoning reforms would allow for better accommodations for those wishing to remain near their families while maintaining independence.

Car-Centric World

When the elderly lose the ability to drive, they often become isolated, and their next step is typically moving to a rest home. This loss of mobility and connection leads to a sense of purposelessness, as they are cut off from opportunities to mentor the youth or pass on their wisdom to future generations. In a car-centric world, it becomes increasingly difficult for older individuals to find meaning after retirement.

Health

A lack of walkability also takes a toll on the physical health of the elderly, leading to chronic pain and early death. Villages help older individuals engage with their surroundings and participate in physical exercise that isn't too strenuous. Pedestrian hybrid societies also help prevent the isolation and loneliness experienced by many elderly individuals by fostering connections with family and community.

Redefining Work and Contribution in Later Life

One of the major issues the elderly face is the societal expectation to retire and withdraw from work entirely after a certain age. This rigid approach overlooks the valuable contributions that older individuals can continue to make to society. Instead of idealizing retirement, we should redefine work and contribution in later life, allowing individuals to remain engaged and active participants in society if they wish. This not only benefits the elderly by providing a sense of purpose but also enriches society as a whole by tapping into the wisdom and experience of older generations. What if a man works in his local village, but he wants to keep contributing, and he can? What if he wishes to pass down his business to his children, but he works 1-2 times a week? Why must he withdraw from society after a certain age? This makes no sense. Not only is it valuable to have people of all ages in the workforce, but it also deters senseless boredom and loneliness.

* * *

In conclusion, ensuring the elderly and disabled have the resources they need to maintain independence and connection requires a multifaceted approach that promotes pedestrian-friendly environments and redefines societal norms around work and retirement. Allowing older individuals and people with disabilities to remain active participants in society can create a more supportive and engaging space for everyone.

23

Dear Suburbia, marriage is okay again.

If we want to rebuild our communities around children, we must stop seeing marriage as tradition—and start seeing it as infrastructure. Our cultural values shape our urban landscapes. Marriage remains the strongest foundation for raising healthy children, which sustains the future of any village. Research consistently shows that children raised in married households fare better across a wide range of outcomes. They are more likely to thrive academically, emotionally, and socially. Marriage offers a framework of stability and support that is difficult to replicate in other arrangements.

Numerous studies, including one by the Center for Law and Social Policy, conclude that children raised in single-parent homes are statistically more likely to abuse drugs and alcohol, exhibit poor social behaviors, and commit violent crimes. Children in cohabitating relationships are also at higher risk of instability, with half of them not living with their parents by the age of five. Additionally, cohabitating relationships are statistically more likely to divorce after marriage than couples who do not cohabitate, depending on the level of initial commitment. Marriage persists as one of America's most effective institutions for reducing poverty and crime rates. When parents are married, children are more likely to enjoy a loving environment that is financially and emotionally stable.

When it comes to the support of parents and children, village infrastructure enables marriage to provide a full scope of multigenerational connections by facilitating the long-standing practice of alloparenting. Alloparenting involves parents as the primary caregivers, supported by many other hands and hearts who care for their children. This means grandma can hold the baby while the mother takes a shower, or a cousin can watch her children on Saturday mornings so she can go on a date. An uncle could take all the nieces and nephews on a forest adventure. Parents might swap children during certain working hours of the week. Because marriage strengthens familial bonds internally, it also extends out to the community at large. As more families feel supported by each other, they have the emotional reservoir to invest in their neighbors.

This creates the conditions for large, vibrant gatherings of children—many peer groups mingling, playing, and growing up together. With so many playmates close at hand, the burden of constant entertainment and supervision is measurably lifted, and a reliable social network takes its place; the kind that once characterized American neighborhoods, where bike gangs, pick-up games, and backyard forts were part of daily life. Therefore, the ultimate solution to men and women's freedom in family, work, and community lies not in promoting the isolated "nuclear" family model that emerged from suburban living but in fostering interconnected, multi-generational family communities.

The mission of this movement seeks to upend the nuclear family as the ideal and legitimately restore the American 'village.' Marriage reinforces the multi-generational living that defines village life and builds a strong web of support. Through marriage, both sides gain extra grandparents, aunts, uncles, brothers, sisters, daughters, sons, and cousins. Without marriage, these ties are more likely to be brittle or noncommittal, often not offering a strong enough sense of duty and community. Rather than a woman being referred to as just a 'girlfriend' or 'mother to my grandson,' she becomes a daughter, sister, cousin, and aunt through marriage. Likewise, her husband becomes a son, brother, cousin, and uncle. If the majority of Americans get married, even those who are not married themselves become part of a connected family.

Besides curbing loneliness, individual economic benefit, known as the "Marriage Premium," is also notable. According to a study published in the *American Economic Journal*, married individuals tend to earn higher wages than their single counterparts, with the wage premium ranging from 10-33% for men and 20-58% for women. This advantage is partly due to income pooling within households, which raises wage expectations and faster career progression, as married individuals tend to climb the job ladder more quickly.

Due to the economic benefits of legalized monogamy, married societies create a robust safety net, even in cases of divorce. I have personal experience with this phenomenon. When my mother was divorced with five children—the youngest being six months old—she was making less than $6,000 a year. However, her family and community, filled with generations of married families who had accumulated wealth and stability, provided crucial support—even offering a paid-off home to temporarily live in. My mother worked three hours a week as a caretaker for her aging grandparents, often bringing her baby with her. Thanks to the generosity of her sisters, brothers-in-law, parents, and neighbors—who frequently donated clothes, food, and money, and sometimes even covered the cost of extracurricular activities like dance or soccer leagues for us—my mother was able to stay home with her children. I didn't realize how poor we were during those years until much later, and I am still amazed at how we survived on such an income. Three years after the divorce, my mother remarried. Through the power of marriage, my stepfather became a stable father figure in our lives, providing for us children in profound ways, both emotionally and financially.

These personal benefits scale to the societal level. In Louise Perry's book

The Case Against the Sexual Revolution, both heterosexual and homosexual couples benefit immensely from legalized monogamy. This includes economic stability, mental, emotional, and physical health, added familial and community support, and shared responsibility for household errands. Cultures that uphold marriage provide their members a safety net of security and wealth, often without government intervention. Therefore, supportive infrastructure can abolish the stigma against marriage, as a form of patriarchal slavery, tied to the image of the trapped suburban housewife. Women no longer have to be vulnerable to economic destitution at any moment.

A committed marriage, coupled with children, embodies an old-school romance that can be reintegrated into our culture as we redesign our infrastructure. In doing so, we will secure a brighter future for ourselves and generations to come. Ultimately, there are no American villages without strong and healthy families, and marriage provides the essential scaffolding that holds these communities together.

* * *

We will never re-establish the American village until we shift our cultural understanding of families by rethinking how we approach raising children, supporting mothers, involving fathers, and caring for the elderly and disabled. A village is not a place as much as it is a way of life where kids get the environment they need to succeed as adults, starting from infancy and extending into adolescence. Mothers receive the infrastructure to balance work and caregiving, while fathers are fully involved in supporting their families. Villages also do a better job of including the elderly and disabled, ensuring that each individual can meaningfully participate in the community. At the heart of villages, marriage garners a close-knit network that forms the backbone of stable communities. Villagers understand how to create a society that cares for each person, from babies to grandparents and everyone in between. If we can restore a "village way of life," most Americans can once again experience the joy, growth, and vigor of happy families.

Epilogue

"This all sounds wonderful," they say—but without fail, one of the first objections I get when I talk about ending car dependency is Costco.

There are specific ideological frameworks through which suburbanites view the world—what I endearingly call *'burbs brain.'* We've discussed many of them already: the belief that children *must* have a yard to grow up healthily, that walkability means trekking five miles for groceries, that living in higher density is somehow a crime against humanity, or that the only solution to traffic is to add more lanes.

Once, while I was explaining the importance of walkability, a woman scornfully told me she'd never walk to Costco. "There are far too many things to carry home," she said. To her, the idea of an alternative to bulk shopping, let alone the possibility of not relying on a car, was inconceivable. Another friend told me, "I love Costco. I'm pretty sure my body is 90% Costco." And honestly? I get it. In a world that's traded community for consumption, free samples and cheap hot dogs feel like little luxuries.

But Costco—and warehouse-style box stores like it—aren't just enabled by car dependency. They are *built for it.* Costco is merely a symbol of the highest cultivation of suburban culture; the peak of what suburbia has to offer. Their business model depends on sprawling development that draws people from miles away to fill their trunks with bulk goods every couple of weeks. For many suburbanites, that routine isn't just normal—it's one of modern life's greatest conveniences. Against that backdrop, village life can seem like a downgrade: Costco offers the ease of one big trip—bulk savings, quality goods, member discounts, and cheap gas. Rationally, in the context of car-centric suburbia, Costco just makes *sense*.

But while box stores are celebrated as ultimate conveniences—they come with a high cost. Not all conveniences are created equal. As this book has hopefully made clear, villages provide families with different sets of conveniences. For example, children can *help* with errands. Walkable neighborhoods give capable kids autonomy and responsibility, easing the burden on exhausted parents.

In suburban infrastructure, children are sidelined for sixteen years before they can contribute to simple outside chores like grocery shopping—because commercial areas are inaccessible and unsafe without a car. While car-centric design makes parenting *harder, longer, and more expensive*, walk-ability helps children ease into adulthood—gradually and with competence. So we have to ask: which kind of convenience truly serves families—especially when one leads to a richer, more connected life?

Car-centricity cuts the heart out of community life. It isolates people in vehicles and separates homes from commerce, friendship, and daily rhythms. As great as Costco may seem within our current framework, it suffers the same pitfalls as all car-dependent box stores: it contributes to traffic congestion, undermines local businesses, erodes culture, produces enormous plastic waste, and consumes valuable land for parking. It also centralizes wealth and power—often at the expense of small-town economies.

Villages, on the other hand, offer far more than a consumer box store ever could. They support health and sustainability through strong local economies and a cleaner earth. They provide peaceful, functional communities with vibrant public spaces. They promote well-being through outdoor exploration and frequent connection. Social bonds and familial relationships flourish in walkable environments, creating multigenerational communities where design accommodates all age groups. With walkability as the foundation, villages support economies that are resilient, self-sufficient, and deeply rooted in place. Culture thrives in these conditions—grounded in tradition and shared experience—and people rediscover a sense of identity and belonging.

This isn't just about preference. Choosing between institutions like Costco and villages carries deep consequences. If we continue uplifting corporate billionaires, clinging to shallow convenience, and rejecting people-first spaces, we risk spiraling into a kind of corporate aristocracy. The American Dream is at stake. If places like Costco want to stick around, they'll need to adapt to this new vision of American life—or fade out.

It took time to retrain my own *'burbs brain.'* But as I began to look past our corrupt and unhealthy infrastructure—rooted in car-centric design—I discovered a beautiful alternative vision for American life. The choice is ours. If I have to pick between a sea of Costcos or a landscape brimming with American villages—I'll pick the village every time.

It Takes a Village

It takes a village to raise a family. Rather than lament that this concept no longer exists in the modern world, why don't we just… build villages again? Villages are the avenue for healthy families—especially healthy children. It's never been too late to make such communities a reality, and it certainly isn't now.

The suburban experiment has only been around for about seventy years, but it did most of its damage in the first decade. That tells us something: change doesn't need to take long. It's happening all around us already, at lightning speed—in the wrong direction. Every day, we wake up to find a new road, subdivision, or franchise. People often think there's not enough time for things to improve in their lifetime, but given the ingenuity of our modern world, it's not a matter of *speed*, but *direction*. We need not give up hope. We should look forward with great optimism. When Americans want something, we fight for it—and we make it happen.

Creating villages means living in peaceful, functional environments surrounded by friends and family of all ages. It's about rubbing shoulders with our fellow Americans and becoming united through beautiful spaces. It's about healing mental illness and giving purpose back to children, mothers, and fathers. It's about building places more compelling than the online world—and reclaiming control over our technological vices. It's about generating new jobs, businesses, and livelihoods. In essence, it's about allowing everyone access to water again. When we return to localization, our culture, identity, and hope for a better world will return too.

Villages mark a shift away from the consumer-driven, convenience-focused revolution of the 1950s. They guide us back to the American way of life as it was meant to be. Imagine millions of captivating villages across the United States—connecting people to places and to each other—offering us all the true freedom upon which America was built.

Let's demand change. Attend city council meetings, share new knowledge, and redirect change in a more positive direction. With many voices, we can chart a course toward a brighter present and future. The next time you look out into your neighborhood and think, *"It's enough,"* remind yourself that there is so much more. Villages amplify the great American qualities embedded at our core. We have only to reclaim the American Dream— not one characterized by quiet, lonely suburbia, but by spirited and lively villages where children roam, parents are supported, and communities are knit together by strong multigenerational families.

Notes

PROLOGUE

1   *Newsies*. Directed by Kenny Ortega. Burbank, CA: Walt Disney Pictures, 1992.

2   Bassuk, Ellen, and Deborah Franklin. "Understanding Urban Inequality." *New England Journal of Public Policy* 32, no. 4 (2018): 45-67,72. Accessed August 10, 2024. https://scholarworks.umb.edu/cgi/viewcontent.cgi?article=1538&context=nejpp.

3   Nasaw, D. (1985). *Children of the city: At work and at play*. Oxford University Press.

4   James Truslow Adams, *The Epic of America* (Boston: Little, Brown, and Company, 1931), 214.

5   Pew Research Center. "Americans are more pessimistic than optimistic about many aspects of the country's future." *Pew Research Center*, September 18, 2023. https://www.pewresearch.org/short-reads/2023/09/18/americans-are-more-pessimistic-than-optimistic-about-many-aspects-of-the-countrys-future/.

6   Pew Research Center. "A 42% Increase in Desire for Suburban Living Since 2018." *Pew Research Center*, 2018. https://www.pewsocialtrends.org/wp-content/uploads/sites/3/2018/05/Pew-Research-Center-Community-Type-Full-Report-FINAL.pdf.

7   New York Intelligencer. "What's Not to Like? Plenty, as It Turns Out. The Mood in America Is Arguably as Dark as It Has Ever Been in the Modern Era…" *New York Magazine*, 2008. Accessed June 3, 2024. https://nymag.com/intelligencer/2018/08/frank-rich-2008-financial-crisis-end-of-american-dream.html.

8   Public Religion Research Institute. "American Values Survey: 2014." Public Religion Research Institute, September 2014. https://www.prri.org/wp-content/uploads/2014/09/PRRI-AVS-with-Transparancy-Edits.pdf.

9   Not Just Bikes. "Why We Won't Raise Our Kids in Suburbia." YouTube video, 10:34. August 10, 2021. https://www.youtube.com/watch?v=oHlpmxLTxpw&t=96s.

DEAR SUBURBIA, IT WASN'T SUPPOSED TO BE THIS WAY.

10   Buettner, Dan. *The Blue Zones: Lessons for Living Longer From the People Who've Lived the Longest*. Washington, DC: National Geographic Society, 2008.

11   PragerU. "The War on Cars." Prager University. Accessed June 3, 2024. https://www.prageru.com/video/the-war-on-cars.

12   Vanderbilt, Tom. "When Pedestrians Ruled the Streets." Smithsonian Magazine, June

2019. Accessed June 3, 2024. https://www.smithsonianmag.com/innovation/when-pedestrians-ruled-streets-180953396/.

13   Norton, Peter D. "When Cities Treated Cars as Dangerous Intruders." The MIT Press Reader, June 3, 2020. Accessed June 3, 2024. https://thereader.mitpress.mit.edu/when-cities-treated-cars-as-dangerous-intruders/.

14   Norton, Peter D. *Fighting Traffic: The Dawn of the Motor Age in the American City.* Cambridge, MA: MIT Press, 2008.

15   Buchanan v. Warley, 245 U.S. 60 (1917).

16   Tugwell, Rexford G. "My idea is to go just outside centers of population, pick up cheap land, build a whole community, and entice people into it. Then go back into the cities and tear down whole slums and make parks for them." Quoted in Buder, Stanley. Visionaries and Planners: The Garden City Movement and the Modern Community. New York: Oxford University Press, 1990, 176.

17   United States v. National City Lines, 186 F.2d 562 (7th Cir. 1951).

18   United States Public Roads Administration. Give Yourself the Green Light. 1954. Film.

19   Congress Approves the Federal-Aid Highway Act." U.S. Senate, June 26, 1956. Accessed June 3, 2024. https://www.senate.gov/artandhistory/history/minute/Federal_Highway_Act.htm.

20   Cortright, Joe. "How a Freeway Destroyed a Neighborhood, and May Again." City Observatory, February 5, 2020. Accessed June 3, 2024. https://cityobservatory.org/how-a-freeway-destroyed-a-neighborhood-and-may-again/.

21   Jacobs, Jane. *The Death and Life of Great American Cities.* New York: Random House, 1961.

DEAR SUBURBIA, IT'S NOT SAFE ANYMORE.

22   National Safety Council. "Motor Vehicle Deaths Again Reach an Estimated 46,000 in 2022." 2023. Accessed August 8, 2024. https://www.nsc.org/newsroom/motor-vehicle-deaths-reach-estimated-46,000.

23   Marohn, Charles L. 2012. "Roads, Streets, Stroads, and Park Roads." Strong Towns. August 20, 2012. https://www.strongtowns.org/journal/2012/8/20/roads-streets-stroads-and-park-roads.html.

24   Marohn, Charles L. 2012. "Roads, Streets, Stroads, and Park Roads." Strong Towns. August 20, 2012. https://www.strongtowns.org/journal/2012/8/20/roads-streets-stroads-and-park-roads.html.

25   Marohn, Charles L. 2018. "What's a Stroad and Why Does It Matter?" Strong Towns. March 1, 2018. https://www.strongtowns.org/journal/2018/3/1/whats-a-stroad-and-why-does-it-matter.

26   Marohn, C. L. (2021). *Confessions of a Recovering Engineer: Transportation for a Strong Town*. Wiley, chap 7.

27   Marohn, C. L. (2021). *Confessions of a Recovering Engineer: Transportation for a Strong Town*. Wiley, chap 2.

28   Governors Highway Safety Association. *Pedestrian Traffic Fatalities by State: 2022 Preliminary Data*. 2023. https://www.ghsa.org/resources/Pedestrians23.

DEAR SUBURBIA, I'M TIRED OF WAITING IN TRAFFIC.

29   Diane Alisa. "There's No Escape." End Car Dependency Blog, July 2023. https://blog.en dcardependency.org/2023/07/theres-no-escape.html.

30   City Observatory. "Reducing Congestion: Katy Didn't." City Observatory. Last modified December 22, 2014. https://cityobservatory.org/reducing-congestion-katy-didnt/.

DEAR SUBURBIA, I DON'T WANT TO BE UNDER CORPORATE CONTROL.

31   Robinson-Patman Act, 15 U.S.C. § 13 (1936).

32   Jacobs, Jane. *The Death and Life of Great American Cities*. New York: Random House, 1961.

33   Brooker's Founding Flavors Ice Cream. "Our Story." Accessed August 9, 2024. https://br ookersicecream.com/our-story/.

34   Quednau, Rachel. "Why Walkability." Strong Towns. February 22, 2016. Accessed June 3, 2024. https://www.strongtowns.org/journal/2016/2/22/why-walkability.

35   Mitchell, S. (2016). Big-Box Swindle: The True Cost of Mega-Retailers and the Fight for America's Independent Businesses. Beacon Press.

36   Klinenberg, Eric. *Palaces for the People: How Social Infrastructure Can Help Fight Inequality, Polarization, and the Decline of Civic Life*. New York: Crown, 2018.

37   Goldman, David. "Target Loses $10B Following Boycott Calls over LGBTQ-Friendly Clothing." New York Post, May 28, 2023. Accessed August 9, 2024. https://nypost.com/2023/05/28/target-loses-10b-following-boycott-calls-over-lgbtq-friendly-clothing/.

38   Feuer, William. "Chick-fil-A Drops Donations to Christian Charities after LGBT Protests." CNBC, November 18, 2019. https://www.cnbc.com/2019/11/18/chick-fil-a-drops-donations-to-christian-charities-after-lgbt-protests.html.

39   Lewis Mumford, *The City in History: Its Origins, Its Transformations, and Its Prospects* (New York: Harcourt, Brace & World, 1961), 252.

DEAR SUBURBIA, AMERICA LOOKS... DIFFERENT.

40   Leyden, Kevin M., Abraham Goldberg, and Philip Michelbach. "Understanding the Pursuit of Happiness in Ten Major Cities." *Urban Affairs Review* 47, no. 6 (2011): 861–888. Accessed June 3, 2024. https://ifp.nyu.edu/2011/journal-article-abstracts/understandi ng-the-pursuit-of-happiness-in-ten-major-cities/.

41   Aesthetic City. "This Town Did the Impossible." YouTube video, 11:45. February 22, 2016. https://www.youtube.com/watch?v=XfonhlM6I7w&t=24s.

42 McIntosh, Sophie. "The History of the New York City Brownstone." CitySignal, August 2, 2022. https://www.citysignal.com/nyc-brownstone-history/.

43 "Lee's Discount Liquor Billboard." Las Vegas Billboards. Accessed June 5, 2024. https://lasvegassun.com/news/2013/jun/15/no-laughing-matter-liquor-store-chain-removing-con/.

44 Deseret News. "State Street Tarnishes Orem's Luster." Deseret News, September 30, 1991. https://www.deseret.com/1991/9/30/18943736/state-street-tarnishes-orem-s-luster/.

45 Hess, Alan. Googie Redux: Ultramodern Roadside Architecture. San Francisco: Chronicle Books, 2004. Accessed June 5, 2024. https://oms.library.okstate.edu/s/oklahoma-built/item/27636.

46 The Hill. https://thehill.com/changing-america/resilience/smart-cities/4162455-paved-paradise-maps-show-how-much-of-us-cities-are-parking-lots/.

47 LotGuard USA. "Common Parking Lot Crimes." Accessed June 5, 2024. https://www.lotguard.com/the-role-of-surveillance-cameras-in-parking-lot-security/.

48 Marohn, Charles L. *Confessions of a Recovering Engineer: Transportation for a Strong Town*. Wiley, 2021.

49 Yuen, Belinda. "The Role of Beauty in Sustainable Urban Development." *Journal of Urban Design*, vol. 10, no. 2, 2005, pp. 191-206.

50 Montgomery, Charles. *Happy City: Transforming Our Lives Through Urban Design*. Farrar, Straus and Giroux, 2013.

51 "Zermatt is Car-Free." Zermatt. Accessed June 5, 2024. https://www.zermatt.ch/en/arrival.

52 "Amsterdam's Canals." Amsterdam.info. Accessed June 5, 2024. https://www.amsterdam.info/canals/.

DEAR SUBURBIA, I REALLY WANT A HOME.

53 Hayden, D. (2003). *Building Suburbia: Green Fields and Urban Growth, 1820-2000*. Vintage Books.

54 Urban Sprawl | Definition, Examples, Problems, Causes, & Alternatives," Britannica, accessed June 5, 2024, https://www.britannica.com/topic/urban-sprawl.

55 Duany, A., Plater-Zyberk, E., & Speck, J. (2000). *Suburban Nation: The Rise of Sprawl and the Decline of the American Dream*. North Point Press.

56 Hall, P. (2002). *Cities of Tomorrow: An Intellectual History of Urban Planning and Design in the Twentieth Century*. Blackwell Publishing.

57 Egan, Ladd. "Utah's $20K First-time Homebuyer Assistance Program Starts in July." KSL.com, May 7, 2023. Accessed June 6, 2024. https://www.ksl.com/article/50645604/utahs-20k-first-time-homebuyer-assistance-program-starts-in-july.

58 Henwood, Benjamin F., Suzanne L. Wenzel, Eric Rice, Hailey Dent Doran, and Andrew R. Finnerty. "Permanent Supportive Housing: Addressing Homelessness and Health

Disparities?" *Psychiatric Services* 64, no. 3 (2013): 237-239. https://psychiatryonline.org/doi/10.1176/appi.ps.201200515.

59   Governor of California. "California Clears More Than 1,250 Homeless Encampments in 12 Months." Accessed June 6, 2024. https://www.gov.ca.gov/2022/08/26/california-clears-more-than-1250-homeless-encampments-in-12-months/.

60   "Sit-lie ordinance." Wikipedia. Last modified March 30, 2024. https://en.wikipedia.org/wiki/Sit-lie_ordinance.

61   Christopher, Ben. "California Homelessness: Where Are the State's Billions Going? Here's the New, Best Answer." Jefferson Public Radio, February 19, 2023. https://www.ijpr.org/poverty-and-homelessness/2023-02-19/california-homelessness-where-are-the-states-billions-going-heres-the-new-best-answer.

62   Los Angeles Homeless Services Authority. "Change in LA: Homelessness Down in City of L.A. for First Time in Years Following Urgent Action Taken by Mayor Bass." Mayor Karen Bass, City of Los Angeles, June 28, 2024. Accessed August 5, 2024. https://mayor.lacity.gov/news/change-la-homelessness-down-city-la-first-time-years-following-urgent-action-taken-mayor-bass.

63   Florida, Richard. *The New Urban Crisis: How Our Cities Are Increasing Inequality, Deepening Segregation, and Failing the Middle Class—and What We Can Do About It.* New York: Basic Books, 2017.

64   Mayer, Nathaniel Lee. "House Prices Have Doubled in the Past Decade—Here's Why." Newsweek, September 28, 2022. https://www.newsweek.com/house-prices-double-ten-years-1745297.

65   CNBC. "The Housing Market Explained in 6 Charts." CNBC, July 13, 2024. https://www.cnbc.com/2024/07/13/the-housing-market-explained-in-6-charts.html.

DEAR SUBURBIA, I DON'T FEEL SO GOOD.

66   Centers for Disease Control and Prevention. "Heart Disease Facts." Last reviewed May 15, 2024. https://www.cdc.gov/heart-disease/data-research/facts-stats/index.html

67   Mental Health America. "2022 Mental Health America Adult Data." *Mental Health America.* Accessed August 7, 2024. https://mhanational.org/issues/2022/mental-health-america-adult-data.

68   Better Health Channel. "The Dangers of Sitting." Last modified January 2019. https://www.betterhealth.vic.gov.au/health/healthyliving/the-dangers-of-sitting.

69   American Heart Association. "AHA Recommendations for Physical Activity in Adults." *Heart.org.* Accessed August 9, 2024. https://www.heart.org/en/healthy-living/fitness/fitness-basics/aha-recs-for-physical-activity-in-adults.

70   The Copenhagen Post. "Danes Do More Exercise Than Other EU Nations." Updated April 11, 2017. https://cphpost.dk/2017-04-11/news/danes-do-more-exercise-than-other-eu-nations/.

71   Centers for Disease Control and Prevention. "Fast Food Consumption Among Adults in the United States, 2013–2016." National Center for Health Statistics Data Brief, No. 322, October 2018. https://www.cdc.gov/nchs/products/databriefs/db322.htm.

72   Hari, Vani. "Here Are the 55 Ingredients in a Chick-fil-A Sandwich—Should You Eat Them?" Food Babe, March 12, 2014. https://foodbabe.com/here-are-the-55-ingredient s-in-a-chick-fil-a-sandwich-should-you-eat-them/.

73   Tsakiris, Thrasivoulos, Theodora-Niki Tolia, Nikolaos Katsaros, Charilaos B. Giannoulis, Panagiota Ragos, and Kyriakos Anastassopoulos. "Evaluating the Role of Tartrazine in Cancer." Anticancer Research 35, no. 3 (2015): 1465-1484. Accessed June 7, 2024. https://ar.iiarjournals.org/content/35/3/1465.

74   Martinez Steele, Euridice, Larissa Gomes Machado, Renata Levy, Jean-Claude Moubarac, Dariush Mozaffarian, and Carlos A. Monteiro. "Ultra-processed Foods and Added Sugars in the US Diet: Evidence from a Nationally Representative Cross-sectional Study." *American Journal of Clinical Nutrition*, May 6, 2015. Accessed June 7, 2024. https://web.archive.org/web/20180128170910/http://ajcn.nutrition.org:80/content/ early/2015/05/06/ajcn.114.100925.abstract.

75   Moss, Michael. *Hooked: Food, Free Will, and How the Food Giants Exploit Our Addictions.* New York: Random House, 2021.

76   Johnson, Paul M., and Paul J. Kenny. "Dopamine D2 Receptors in Addiction-Like Reward Dysfunction and Compulsive Eating in Obese Rats." *Nature Neuroscience* 13, no. 5 (May 2010): 635-641. https://www.ncbi.nlm.nih.gov/pmc/articles/PMC2947358/. Erratum in Nature Neuroscience 13, no. 8 (August 2010): 1033.

77   Jacka, Felice N. "Nutritional Psychiatry: Where to Next?" *EBioMedicine* 17 (March 2017): 24-29. https://www.ncbi.nlm.nih.gov/pmc/articles/PMC5360575/.

78   Centers for Disease Control and Prevention. "Prevalence of Childhood Obesity in the United States." Accessed June 11, 2024. https://www.cdc.gov/obesity/php/data-researc h/childhood-obesity-facts.html?CDC_AAref_Val=https://www.cdc.gov/obesity/data/c hildhood.html.

79   "Kids In Finland Ride Their Bicycles To School In -17°C Weather." Unofficial Networks, November 20, 2019. https://unofficialnetworks.com/2019/11/20/kids-in-finland-ride- their-bicycles-to-school-in-17c-weather/.

80   Buettner, Dan. *The Blue Zones: Lessons for Living Longer from the People Who've Lived the Longest.* Washington, DC: National Geographic Society, 2008.

81   Hubs.Life. "Interactive 3D Spaces for Learning." TikTok video, May 30, 2023. https://w ww.tiktok.com/@hubs.life/video/7239153448313294126.

DEAR SUBURBIA, MOTHER EARTH NEEDS YOU.

82   Aria Bendix. "Paper, Bamboo Straws Contain PFAS 'Forever Chemicals'." NBC News, August 25, 2023. https://www.nbcnews.com/health/health-news/paper-bamboo-straw

s-contain-pfas-forever-chemicals-rcna101614.

83   "83 Billion Metric Tons of Plastic and Counting." University of California, July 19, 2017. https://www.universityofcalifornia.edu/news/83-billion-metric-tons-plastic-and-coun ting.

84   Earth Day Network. "Fact Sheet: Single Use Plastics." Earth Day. https://www.earthday. org/fact-sheet-single-use-plastics/.

85   Ritchie, Hannah, and Max Roser. "Plastic Pollution." Our World in Data, September 2018. https://ourworldindata.org/plastic-pollution.

86   Scrub Daddy. "About Scrub Daddy." Accessed June 22, 2024. https://scrubdaddy.com/a bout/.

87   "Human Consumption of Microplastics." Environmental Science & Technology 53, no. 12 (2019). https://doi.org/10.1021/acs.est.9b01517.

88   Chelin Jamie Hu, Marcus A Garcia, Alexander Nihart, Rui Liu, Lei Yin, Natalie Adolphi, Daniel F Gallego, Huining Kang, Matthew J Campen, Xiaozhong Yu, Microplastic presence in dog and human testis and its potential association with sperm count and weights of testis and epididymis, Toxicological Sciences, 2024;, kfae060, https://doi.org/ 10.1093/toxsci/kfae060.

89   Wright, S.L., & Kelly, F.J. (2017). Plastic and Human Health: A Micro Issue? Environ- mental Science & Technology, 51(12), 6634-6647.

90   Mendelson, Anne. Milk: The Surprising Story of Milk Through the Ages. New York: Knopf, 2008.

91   Strasser, Susan. Waste and Want: A Social History of Trash. New York: Henry Holt and Company, 1999.

92   PR Newswire. "Disposable Diapers Add Millions of Tons of Waste to Landfills Each Year, According to EPA Report." PR Newswire, January 11, 2017. https://www.prnewswi re.com/news-releases/disposable-diapers-add-millions-of-tons-of-waste-to-landfills- each-year-according-to-epa-report-300384344.html.

93   Becker, Joshua. Clutterfree with Kids. Tucson, AZ: Becoming Minimalist, 2014.

94   Yale Environment Review. "Most Materials Are Recyclable. So Why Can't Children's Toys Be Sustainable?" Yale University, February 23, 2021. https://environment-review.y ale.edu/most-materials-are-recyclable-so-why-cant-childrens-toys-be-sustainable.

95   IQAir. "Salt Lake City Air Quality Index (AQI) and Utah Air Pollution." Accessed June 22, 2024. https://www.iqair.com/us/usa/utah/salt-lake-city.

96   Sivertsen, Bjarne, Martin G. Solberg, Jarle Aasestad, Mariann Moltu, and Torleiv A. Tønnesen. "Plume-Based Analysis of Vehicle Fleet Air Pollutant Emissions and the Contribution from High Emitters." Atmospheric Measurement Techniques Discussions 8, no. 3 (2015): 2881-2909. Accessed August 9, 2024. https://amt.copernicus.org/prepri nts/8/2881/2015/amtd-8-2881-2015.pdf.

97   Sunyer, J., Esnaola, M., Alvarez-Pedrerol, M., Forns, J., Rivas, I., López-Vicente, M., Suades-González, E., Foraster, M., Garcia-Esteban, R., Basagaña, X., Viana, M., Cirach, M., Moreno, T., Alastuey, A., Sebastian-Galles, N., Nieuwenhuijsen, M., & Querol, X. (2015). Association between traffic-related air pollution in schools and cognitive development in primary school children: a prospective cohort study. *PLoS medicine, 12*(3), e1001792. https://doi.org/10.1371/journal.pmed.1001792

DEAR SUBURBIA, WHY ARE YOU SO EXPENSIVE?

98   AAA. "Annual New Car Ownership Costs Boil Over $12K." Accessed June 22, 2024. AAA Newsroom. https://newsroom.aaa.com/2023/08/annual-new-car-ownership-costs-boil-over-12k/.

99   Policygenius. "Car Ownership Statistics by State (Updated 2023)." Accessed June 22, 2024. Policygenius.https://www.policygenius.com/auto-insurance/car-ownership-statistics-in-the-united-states/.

100   Statista. "U.S. Average Monthly Passes in Transit Mode of Transport 2017-2019." Statista, 2019. Accessed August 9, 2024. https://www.statista.com/statistics/990891/us-average-monthly-passes-in-transit-mode-transport/.

101   The Aesthetic City. "Elfreth's Alley: The Oldest Residential Street in America." YouTube video, 9:25. November 22, 2023. Accessed August 9, 2024. https://www.youtube.com/watch?v=iv9fWEekFUM&t=200s.

102   Houston Public Media. "Katy Freeway Commuters Finally Get Relief." October 28, 2008. Accessed June 22, 2024. https://www.houstonpublicmedia.org/articles/news/2008/10/28/12510/katy-freeway-commuters-finally-get-relief/.

103   Marohn, Charles L., Jr. *Strong Towns: A Bottom-Up Revolution to Rebuild American Prosperity*. Hoboken, NJ: Wiley, 2019.

104   Marohn, Charles L. "The Real Reason Your City Has No Money." Strong Towns, January 9, 2017. Accessed June 22, 2024. https://www.strongtowns.org/journal/2017/1/9/the-real-reason-your-city-has-no-money.

105   Bloomberg. "Quantifying the Cost of Sprawl." Bloomberg, May 21, 2013. https://www.bloomberg.com/news/articles/2013-05-21/quantifying-the-cost-of-sprawl.

106   Utah Highway Safety Office. 2022 Crash Facts. March 2024. Accessed June 22, 2024. https://highwaysafety.utah.gov/wp-content/uploads/sites/22/2024/03/2022-Crash-Facts_Utah-HSO-1.pdf.

107   European Commission. *Road Safety Country Overview: Switzerland 2024*, 4. Accessed June 22, 2024. https://road-safety.transport.ec.europa.eu/document/download/3b0603e9-07ed-4854-85a3-3373d37f4b57_en?filename=erso-country-overview-2024-switzerland.pdf.

108   Global Wellness Institute. "US Leads Overall Spend in $828 Billion Physical Activity Market." Press release, October 2020. Accessed June 22, 2024. https://globalwellnessins

titute.org/press-room/press-releases/us-leads-overall-spend-in-828-billion-physical-a
ctivity-market/.

109 PR Newswire. "2019 US Mental Health Spending Topped $225 Billion, with Per Capita
Spending Ranging from $37 in Florida to $375 in Maine: OPEN MINDS Releases New
Analysis." May 6, 2020. Accessed June 22, 2024. https://www.prnewswire.com/news-re
leases/2019-us-mental-health-spending-topped-225-billion-with-per-capita-spending-
ranging-from-37-in-florida-to-375-in-maine—open-minds-releases-new-analysis-301
058381.html.

110 Evans, David Mickey, director. *The Sandlot*. 20th Century Fox, 1993.

DEAR SUBURBIA, YOU'VE TURNED US AGAINST EACH OTHER.

111 Pew Research Center. "The Generation Gap in American Politics." March 1, 2018.
Accessed June 22, 2024. https://www.pewresearch.org/politics/2018/03/01/the-genera
tion-gap-in-american-politics/.

112 FamilySearch. "The Greatest Generation: Characteristics and History." FamilySearch,
May 12, 2023. https://www.familysearch.org/en/blog/greatest-generation-years-chara
cteristics.

113 Encyclopaedia Britannica, s.v. "Silent Generation," accessed August 9, 2024, https://ww
w.britannica.com/topic/Silent-Generation.

114 Bureau of Labor Statistics. "History of Child Labor in the United States—Part 1: Little
Children Working." Monthly Labor Review. January 2017. Accessed June 22, 2024.
https://www.bls.gov/opub/mlr/2017/article/history-of-child-labor-in-the-united-sta
tes-part-1.htm

115 Miller, Laura J. "Family Togetherness and the Suburban Ideal." Sociological Forum 10,
no. 3 (1995): 393–418. http://www.jstor.org/stable/684782.

116 Popenoe, David. *Life Without Father*. New York: The Free Press, 1996.

117 Nardi, Peter M. *Men's Friendships*. Newbury Park, CA: Sage Publications, 1992.

118 Cohen, Lizabeth. *A Consumer's Republic: The Politics of Mass Consumption in Postwar
America*. New York: Knopf, 2003.

119 Jackson, Kenneth T. Crabgrass Frontier: *The Suburbanization of the United States*. Oxford
University Press, 1985.

120 Putnam, Robert D. Bowling Alone: The Collapse and Revival of American Community.
Simon & Schuster, 2000.

121 Friedman, Betty. *The Feminine Mystique*. W. W. Norton & Company, 1963.

122 Schulman, Bruce J. The Seventies: *The Great Shift in American Culture, Society, and Politics*.
Da Capo Press, 2001.

123 Fry, Richard. "Americans Are Moving at Historically Low Rates, in Part Because
Millennials Are Staying Put." Pew Research Center, February 13, 2017. Accessed June

22, 2024. https://www.pewresearch.org/short-reads/2017/02/13/americans-are-movi
ng-at-historically-low-rates-in-part-because-millennials-are-staying-put/.

124 Twenge, Jean M. Generations: *The Real Differences between Gen Z, Millennials, Gen X,
Boomers, and Silents—and What They Mean for America's Future.* New York: Atria Books,
2023.

125 "Generation X." *Encyclopedia Britannica.* Accessed June 22, 2024. https://www.britannic
a.com/topic/Generation-X.

126 "Generation X: Characteristics & History," *FamilySearch*, accessed July 10, 2024, https://w
ww.familysearch.org/en/blog/generation-x-characteristics-history.

127 Putnam, Robert D. *Bowling Alone: The Collapse and Revival of American Community.* New
York: Simon & Schuster, 2000.

128 Kantor, Keith. "The Health State of Generation X (Born 1965-1981)." Dr. Keith Kantor.
Accessed June 22, 2024. https://www.drkeithkantor.com/the-health-state-of-generatio
n-x-born-1965-1981/.

129 PBS NewsHour. "Why the Pandemic Is Forcing Millennials to Move Back Home with
Their Parents." *PBS*, August 4, 2020. Accessed June 22, 2024. https://www.pbs.org/news
hour/show/why-the-pandemic-is-forcing-millennials-to-move-back-home-with-their-
parents.

130 Ax, Joseph. "Kidnapped Children Make Headlines, but Abduction Is Rare in U.S." *Reuters*,
January 11, 2019. Accessed June 22, 2024. https://www.reuters.com/article/us-wiscons
in-missinggirl-data/kidnapped-children-make-headlines-but-abduction-is-rare-in-u-s-
idUSKCN1P52BJ.

131 Meckler, Laura. "U.S. Education Reform and National Policy: The Troubling Failure
of Education Reform in America." *Time*, February 6, 2020. Accessed June 22, 2024.
https://time.com/5775795/education-reform-failed-america/.

132 "Millennial." *Encyclopedia Britannica.* Accessed June 22, 2024. https://www.britannica.c
om/topic/millennial.

133 Twenge, Jean M. Generations: *The Real Differences between Gen Z, Millennials, Gen X,
Boomers, and Silents—and What They Mean for America's Future.* New York: Atria Books,
2023.

134 Feldman, Jack. "Religion Declining in Importance for Many Americans, Especially for
Millennials." *Religion News Service*, December 10, 2018. https://religionnews.com/2018/
12/10/religion-declining-in-importance-for-many-americans-especially-for-millennial
s/.

135 Children's Health Council. "Lonely, Burned Out, and Depressed: The State of Millennials'
Mental Health Entering the 2020s." Accessed June 22, 2024. https://www.chconline.org
/resourcelibrary/lonely-burned-out-and-depressed-the-state-of-millennials-mental-he
alth-entering-the-2020s/.

136 Cassandra, L. (2020/03//). Eating disorders in 'Millennials': Risk factors and treatment strategies in the digital age. *Clinical Social Work Journal*, 48(1), 46-53. doi:https://doi.org /10.1007/s10615-019-00733-z.

137 Romano, Aja. "OK Boomer: How a Meme Triumphed Over Generational Divides." *Vox*, November 19, 2019. Accessed June 22, 2024. https://www.vox.com/2019/11/19/20963 757/what-is-ok-boomer-meme-about-meaning-gen-z-millennials.

138 Pew Research Center. "A Generational Gap in American Patriotism." *Pew Research Center*, July 3, 2013. Accessed June 22, 2024. https://www.pewresearch.org/short-reads/2013/ 07/03/a-generational-gap-in-american-patriotism/.

139 Ueda, P., C.H. Mercer, C. Ghaznavi, and D. Herbenick. "Trends in Frequency of Sexual Activity and Number of Sexual Partners Among Adults Aged 18 to 44 Years in the US, 2000-2018." JAMA Network Open 3, no. 6 (June 2020): e203833. https://www.ncbi.nl m.nih.gov/pmc/articles/PMC7293001/.

140 Wang, Wendy, and Laurie DeRose. "How Much of Gen Z Will Be Unmarried at 40?" Institute for Family Studies, October 6, 2020. https://ifstudies.org/blog/how-much-of-gen-z-will-be-unmarried-at-40.

141 CNBC. "Recession Fears Tank Gen Z Dating and Plans for Marriage, Pets, Kids." Last modified October 18, 2022. https://www.cnbc.com/2022/10/18/recession-fears-tank-gen-z-dating-and-plans-for-marriage-pets-kids.html.

DEAR SUBURBIA, YOU'VE STOLEN OUR CULTURE AND IDENTITY.

142 Middle Georgia State University. "What is the Great Resignation?" Accessed June 22, 2024. https://www.mga.edu/news/2022/04/what-is-the-great-resignation.php.

143 Wilcox, W. Bradford, and Christopher G. Ellison, eds. *Religion, Families, and Health: Population-Based Research in the United States.* New Brunswick, NJ: Rutgers University Press, 2010.

144 Lowe, Zara. "Experts Explain Why You Don't Feel Christmassy." *Metro*, December 20, 2018. Accessed June 22, 2024. https://metro.co.uk/2018/12/20/experts-explain-dont-f eel-christmassy-8269500/.

145 Brower, Beth. *The Unselected Journals of Emma M. Lion.* Salt Lake City: Ploughshares, 2016.

146 Sowell, Thomas. *White Guilt: How Blacks and Whites Together Destroyed the Promise of the Civil Rights Era.* New York: HarperCollins, 2006.

147 "Most Marriages Due to Dancing." *The New York Times.* 9 May 1907, http://query.nytim es.com/gst/abstract.hgtml?res=9C06E2DC133EE033A2575AC1A9639C46697D6CF.

148 Stanford University. "Online Dating Popular Way U.S. Couples Meet." *Stanford News*, August 21, 2019. Accessed August 10, 2024. https://news.stanford.edu/stories/2019/08 /online-dating-popular-way-u-s-couples-meet.

149 Giordano, Ralph G. Social Dancing in America: *A History and Reference Volume Two, Lindy Hop to Hip Hop, 1901-2000.* Westport, CT: Greenwood Press, 2007.

150 Giordano, Ralph G. Social Dancing in America: *A History and Reference Volume Two, Lindy Hop to Hip Hop, 1901-2000.* Westport, CT: Greenwood Press, 2007.

DEAR SUBURBIA, IT'S ALL UP TO YOU.

151 Urban Land Institute. *Mixed-Use Development Handbook.* Urban Land Institute, 2003.

152 University of California Agriculture and Natural Resources (UCANR). "Water Use of Turfgrass and Landscape Plant Materials." UC *Agriculture and Natural Resources.* Accessed July 13, 2024. https://ucanr.edu/sites/UrbanHort/Water_Use_of_Turfgrass_and_Landscape_Plant_Materials/.

153 Vance, J. D. Hillbilly Elegy: *A Memoir of a Family and Culture in Crisis.* New York: Harper, 2016.

154 Bureau of Justice Statistics. Drugs and Crime Facts: Drug Use and Crime. Accessed July 13, 2024. https://bjs.ojp.gov/drugs-and-crime-facts/drug-use-and-crime#drug-related.

155 Centre for Economic Policy Research. "Why Education Reduces Crime." *VoxEU.* Accessed July 13, 2024. https://cepr.org/voxeu/columns/why-education-reduces-crime.

156 Rodríguez-Pose, A., & von Berlepsch, V. (2018). Does population diversity matter for economic development in the very long term? Historic migration, diversity and county wealth in the US. *European Journal of Population,* 34(5), 843–873. https://doi.org/10.1007/s10680-018-9507-z.

157 Federal Reserve Bank of St. Louis. (2020). Worker diversity and wage growth since 1940. *Review,* 102(1), 1–20. https://doi.org/10.20955/r.102.1-20.

158 Rowling, J.K. *Harry Potter and the Sorcerer's Stone.* Scholastic, 1998.

159 Jacobs, Jane. *The Death and Life of Great American Cities.* New York: Random House, 1961.

160 Milgram, S. (1977). The familiar stranger: An aspect of urban anonymity. Urban Life, 6(1), 3-24.

161 Gehl, Jan. 2010. *Cities for People.* Island Press, p. 47.

162 City of Hood River. "Short-Term Rentals." Accessed July 13, 2024. https://cityofhoodriver.gov/planning/short-term-rentals/.

163 Statista. "Share of Population Who Own a Home in Spain from 2006 to 2022." Last modified May 2023. Accessed August 23, 2024. https://www.statista.com/statistics/543390/house-owners-among-population-spain/.

164 "The 'Burbs." Directed by Joe Dante, performances by Tom Hanks, Bruce Dern, Carrie Fisher, Rick Ducommun, and Corey Feldman, *Imagine Entertainment,* 1989.

165 CNBC. 2023. "In some states, it's 'nearly impossible' to buy a home that isn't part of a homeowners association, expert says." October 31. Accessed July 16, 2024. https://www

.cnbc.com/2023/10/31/what-the-rise-of-homeowners-associations-means-for-americ
ans.html

166 Rothstein, Richard. *The Color of Law: A Forgotten History of How Our Government Segregated America.* New York: Liveright Publishing Corporation, 2017.

167 Getlen, Larry. "Corporations Are Buying Houses, Robbing Families of American Dream." *New York Post,* July 18, 2020. Accessed July 16, 2024. https://nypost.com/2020/07/18/c orporations-are-buying-houses-robbing-families-of-american-dream/.

168 ABC News. "The 15-minute city conspiracy." ABC News Australia, February 27, 2023. Accessed July 16, 2024. https://www.abc.net.au/news/2023-02-27/the-15-minute-city-conspiracy/102015446.

DEAR SUBURBIA, HERE'S HOW TO IMPLEMENT WALKABILITY AND VILLAGE INFRASTRUCTURE.

169 Alexander, B. K. (2018). *Rat Park: How a rat paradise changed the narrative of addiction.* ResearchGate. https://www.researchgate.net/publication/ 328563723_Rat_Park_How _a_rat_paradise_changed_the_narrative_of_addiction.

170 "Seattle Department of Transportation. (2024, July 8). Sidewalks update: 250 new blocks. SDOT Blog. https://sdotblog.seattle.gov/2024/07/08/sidewalks-update-250-new-bloc ks/"

171 Federal Highway Administration, "Raised Pedestrian Crossings," accessed July 10, 2024, http://www.pedbikesafe.org/pedsafe/countermeasures_detail.cfm?CM_NUM=7.

172 "Advisory bike lines increase risk of cyclist casualties," Road.cc, last modified October 2, 2020, https://road.cc/content/news/advisory-bike-lines-increase-risk-cyclist-casualtie s-279553.

173 Institute for Transportation and Development Policy (ITDP), "Pedestrian Bridges Make Cities Less Walkable: Why Do Cities Keep Building Them?," February 29, 2024, https://i tdp.org/2024/02/29/pedestrian-bridges-make-cities-less-walkable-why-do-cities-keep -building-them/.

174 "Skinny Roads Save Lives, According to a Study on the Width of Traffic Lanes," NPR, November 13, 2023, https://www.npr.org/2023/11/13/1212589284/skinny-roads-sav e-lives-according-to-a-study-on-the-width-of-traffic-lanes.

175 "Why the Dutch Wait Less at Traffic Lights," YouTube video, 10:34, posted by "Not Just Bikes," July 10, 2024, https://www.youtube.com/watch?v=knbVWXzL4-4.

DEAR SUBURBIA, MANY TRANSPORTATION OPTIONS ARE GOOD.

176 "Salt Lake City Streetcar System Map, 1940." *TransitMap.net.* Accessed July 24, 2024. https://transitmap.net/salt-lake-1940/.

177 Mims, Christopher. "This 300 MPH Bullet Train Will Take You From DC to New York in Just an Hour." *Fast Company,* November 7, 2013. https://ww2w.fastcompany.com/3021 224/this-300-mph-bullet-train-will-take-you-from-dc-to-new-york-in-just-an-hour.

178 *Smithsonian Magazine*. "Trains Running Three Minutes Behind Anger Swiss People." May 8, 2014. https://www.smithsonianmag.com/smart-news/trains-running-three-minutes-behind-anger-swiss-people-180949334/.

179 Bureau of Transportation Statistics. "Transportation Fatalities by Mode." U.S. Department of Transportation. Accessed August 29, 2024. https://www.bts.gov/content/transportation-fatalities-mode.

180 Bay Area Transportation Authority. "Economic Impact of Public Transportation." Accessed August 29, 2024. https://www.bata.net/how-to-ride/economic-impact-of-public-transportation.html.

DEAR SUBURBIA, VILLAGES NEED CHILDREN.

181 Salsberg, Barry Neild. "Patrica, Italy: Town Selling One-Euro Homes Struggles to Survive." *CNN*, August 8, 2023. https://www.cnn.com/travel/patrica-italy-town-one-euro-homes-struggle/index.html.

182 *Birthgap: Childless World*. Directed by Stephen J. Shaw. 2023. Worldwide Films. Accessed August 27, 2024. YouTube video, 1:30:45. https://www.youtube.com/watch?v=12345abcde.

183 King, Martin Luther Jr. "I Have a Dream." Speech, March on Washington for Jobs and Freedom, Washington, D.C., August 28, 1963.

DEAR SUBURBIA, YOU'RE DISEMPOWERING OUR CHILDREN.

184 Smedley, Tadd. "Kids and Cars: Today's Teens in No Rush to Start Driving." *USA Today*, August 4, 2021. https://www.usatoday.com/story/sports/nascar/2021/08/04/kids-and-cars-todays-teens-in-no-rush-to-start-driving/48148523/.

185 Smith, Betty. *A Tree Grows in Brooklyn*. New York: Harper & Brothers, 1943.

186 Haidt, Jonathan, and Greg Lukianoff. *The Coddling of the American Mind: How Good Intentions and Bad Ideas Are Setting Up a Generation for Failure.* New York: Penguin Press, 2018.

187 Office of the U.S. Surgeon General. "Protecting Youth Mental Health: The U.S. Surgeon General's Advisory." U.S. Department of Health and Human Services, 2021. https://www.hhs.gov/sites/default/files/surgeon-general-youth-mental-health-advisory.pdf.

188 National Recreation and Park Association. *Children in Nature: Improving Health by Reconnecting Youth with the Outdoors.* Ashburn, VA: National Recreation and Park Association, 2013. https://www.nrpa.org/uploadedFiles/nrpa.org/Advocacy/Children-in-Nature.pdf.

189 Louv, Richard. Last Child in the Woods: Saving Our Children from Nature-Deficit Disorder. Chapel Hill, NC: Algonquin Books, 2005.

190 Hanscom, Angela J. *Balanced and Barefoot: How Unrestricted Outdoor Play Makes for Strong, Confident, and Capable Children.* New Harbinger Publications, 2016.

191 Dunn, John Wright. *A Natural History of the Hedgerow: And Ditches, Dikes, and Dry Stone Walls*. New York: The Overlook Press, 2016.

192 Gray, Peter. Free to Learn: Why Unleashing the Instinct to Play Will Make Our Children Happier, More Self-Reliant, and Better Students for Life. New York: *Basic Books*, 2013.

193 Drug Abuse Statistics. "Teen Drug Use." *Drug Abuse Statistics*. Accessed August 29, 2024. https://drugabusestatistics.org/teen-drug-use/.

194 Doucleff, Michaeleen. *Hunt, Gather, Parent: What Ancient Cultures Can Teach Us About the Lost Art of Raising Happy, Helpful Little Humans*. New York: Avid Reader Press / Simon & Schuster, 2021.

195 Committee on Improving the Health, Safety, and Well-Being of Young Adults; Board on Children, Youth, and Families; Institute of Medicine; National Research Council. *Investing in the Health and Well-Being of Young Adults*. Edited by RJ Bonnie, C Stroud, and H Breiner. Washington, DC: National Academies Press, 2015. https://www.ncbi.nlm.nih.gov/books/NBK284782/.

196 CBS News. "Uneven Playing Field: Middle Class and Poor Kids Are Ditching Youth Sports." *CBS News*. Last modified August 8, 2019. https://www.cbsnews.com/news/uneven-playing-field-middle-class-and-poor-kids-are-ditching-youth-sports/.

197 Heller, Sharon. *The Vital Touch: How Intimate Contact with Your Baby Leads to Happier, Healthier Development*. New York: Henry Holt & Co., 1997.

198 Jacobs, Jane. *The Death and Life of Great American Cities*. New York: Random House, 1961.

199 Devlin Peck. "Teacher Burnout Statistics." *Devlin Peck*. Accessed September 4, 2024. https://www.devlinpeck.com/content/teacher-burnout-statistics.

200 Neufeld, Gordon, and Gabor Maté. Hold On to Your Kids: Why Parents Need to Matter More Than Peers. New York: Ballantine Books, 2006.

201 Cross, Jennifer F., M.D. "What Does Too Much Screen Time Do to Children's Brains?" *Health Matters*. NewYork-Presbyterian, October 10, 2019. https://healthmatters.nyp.org/what-does-too-much-screen-time-do-to-childrens-brains/.

202 Age of First Exposure to Pornography Shapes Men's Attitudes Toward Women." *American Psychological Association*. August 3, 2017. https://www.apa.org/news/press/releases/2017/08/pornography-exposure.

203 Shekar, Malli B., Sita R. Vanka, Susheela L. Marukala, and Lakshmi V. Rudrapati. "Determinants of Parent–Child Relationship Satisfaction and Its Impact on Parents' Well-Being and the Quality of Life of Children with Intellectual Disabilities." *Journal of Child and Family Studies* 32, no. 8 (2023): 2011-2023. https://doi.org/10.1007/s10826-023-02562-y.

204 Paolucci, Elizabeth Oddone, Mark Genuis, and Claudio Violato. *A Meta-Analysis of the Published Research on the Effects of Pornography*. Calgary, Alberta: National Foundation

for Family Research and Education; *University of Calgary.* https://citeseerx.ist.psu.edu/d ocument?repid=rep1&type=pdf&doi=e7692a0c4e0a8c307117c6edf5712a2f07bbf855.

205 Fung, Katherine. "Pornhub Officially Blocks Users in Another State." *Newsweek.* May 18, 2023. https://www.newsweek.com/pornhub-officially-blocks-users-another-state-1921173.

206 Twenge, Jean M. Generations: The Real Differences Between Gen Z, Millennials, Gen X, Boomers, and Silents—and What They Mean for America's Future. New York: Atria Books, 2023.

DEAR SUBURBIA, INFANTS ARE WORTH THE INVESTMENT.

207 Agency for Healthcare Research and Quality (US). *2022 National Healthcare Quality and Disparities Report.* Rockville, MD: Agency for Healthcare Research and Quality (US), October 2022. https://www.ncbi.nlm.nih.gov/books/NBK587174/.

208 BBC. "Every Moment of Their Life Is Play: How Babies Learn Through Everyday Activities." *Tiny Happy People.* Accessed September 7, 2024. https://www.bbc.co.uk/tiny-happy-people/articles/zbjm7nb#:~:text=Every%20moment%20of%20their%20life,a%20plastic%20purpose%2Dmade%20toy.

209 Whiting, Beatrice Blyth, and Carolyn Pope Edwards. *Children of Different Worlds: The Formation of Social Behavior.* Cambridge, MA: Harvard University Press, 1988.

210 Holt, Luther Emmett. *The Care and Feeding of Children: A Catechism for the Use of Mothers and Children's Nurses.* 1894. New York: D. Appleton and Company.

211 Watson, John B. *Psychological Care of Infant and Child.* New York: W.W. Norton & Company, 1928.

212 Spock, Benjamin. *The Common Sense Book of Baby and Child Care.* New York: Duell, Sloan and Pearce, 1946.

213 John Bowlby, *Attachment and Loss:* Volume I, Attachment (New York: Basic Books, 1969).

214 Margaret S. Mahler, Fred Pine, and Anni Bergman, *The Psychological Birth of the Human Infant: Symbiosis and Individuation* (New York: Basic Books, 1975).

215 James J. McKenna, Sleeping with Your Baby: A Parent's Guide to Cosleeping (Washington, DC: Platypus Media, 2007).

216 Ludington, Susan, Xiaomei Cong, and Fariba Hashemi. "Infant Crying: Nature, Physiologic Consequences, and Select Interventions." *Neonatal Network* 21, no. 2 (April 2002): 29–36. https://doi.org/10.1891/0730-0832.21.2.29.

217 "Understanding the Stress Response," Harvard Health Publications, updated March 18, 2016, health.harvard.edu/staying-healthy/understanding-the-stress-response.

218 Michael Randall, "The Physiology of Stress: Cortisol and the Hypothalamic-Pituitary-Adrenal Axis," Dartmouth Undergraduate Journal of Science, February 3, 2011, dujs.dart mouth.edu/2011/02/the-physiology-of-stress-cortisol-and-the-hypothalmic-pituitary-adrenal-axis.

219   St. Petersburg-USA Orphanage Research Team. "The Effects of Early Social-Emotional and Relationship Experience on the Development of Young Orphanage Children." *Monographs of the Society for Research in Child Development* 73, no. 3 (2008): vii-viii, 1-262, 294-5. https://doi.org/10.1111/j.1540-5834.2008.00483.x.

220   Piaget, Jean. *The Origins of Intelligence in Children*. New York: International Universities Press, 1952.

221   Hamilton, Jon. "Your Brain on LSD Looks a Lot Like a Baby's." *NPR*, April 17, 2016. https://www.npr.org/2016/04/17/474569125/your-brain-on-lsd-looks-a-lot-like-a-babys.

222   LoBue, V., & Ogren, M. (2022). How the Emotional Environment Shapes the Emotional Life of the Child. *Policy insights from the behavioral and brain sciences*, 9(1), 137–144. https://doi.org/10.1177/23727322211067264.

223   Piaget, Jean. *The Origins of Intelligence in Children*. New York: International Universities Press, 1952.

224   Karp, Harvey. "'The Fourth Trimester.'" *Contemporary Pediatrics*, vol. 21, no. 2, 2004, pp. 94–104.

225   James Robertson and Joyce Robertson, "Young Children in Brief Separation: A Fresh Look," *Psychoanalytic Study of the Child* 26 (1971):264-315.

226   McLaughlin, Katie A., et al. "Neglect as a Violation of Species-Expectant Experience: Neurodevelopmental Consequences." Biological Psychiatry, vol. 82, no. 7, 2017, pp. 462–471.

227   Parten, Mildred B. "Social Participation Among Preschool Children." The Journal of Abnormal and Social Psychology 27, no. 3 (1933): 243–269. https://doi.org/10.1037/h0073939.

228   Heller, Sharon. Vital Touch: How Intimate Contact with Your Baby Leads to Happier, Healthier Development. New York: Holt Paperbacks, 1997.

229   A. Ambrose, *Stimulation in Early Infancy* (New York: Academic Press, 1969).

230   Bowlby, John. *Attachment and Loss*. Vol. 1, *Attachment*. New York: Basic Books, 1969.

231   Heller, S. (1997). *The vital touch: How intimate contact with your baby leads to happier, healthier development*. Henry Holt and Company.

232   Saccaro, L. F., Schilliger, Z., Perroud, N., & Piguet, C. (2021). Inflammation, Anxiety, and Stress in Attention-Deficit/Hyperactivity Disorder. *Biomedicines*, 9(10), 1313. https://doi.org/10.3390/biomedicines9101313.

233   Narvaez, Darcia. "Be Worried About Boys, Especially Baby Boys." *Psychology Today*, January 13, 2017. https://www.psychologytoday.com/us/blog/moral-landscapes/201701/be-worried-about-boys-especially-baby-boys.

234   Ferber, Richard. *Solve Your Child's Sleep Problems*. New York: Simon & Schuster, 1985.

235 "What You Need to Know About Sleep Training Your Baby." *What to Expect,* February 10, 2021. https://www.whattoexpect.com/first-year/sleep/sleep-training-baby/.

236 "Taking Cara Babies." *Taking Cara Babies.* Accessed September 8, 2024. https://takingcarababies.com/.

237 Jassey, Lewis, and Jonathan Jassey. *The Newborn Sleep Book: A Simple, Proven Method for Training Your New Baby to Sleep Through the Night.* New York: Perigee, 2014.

238 Bowlby, John. *Attachment and Loss*: Volume I: Attachment. 2nd ed. New York: Basic Books, 1982.

239 Korownyk, C., & Lindblad, A. J. (2018). Infant sleep training: rest easy?. *Canadian family physician Medecin de famille canadien, 64*(1), 41.https://www.ncbi.nlm.nih.gov/pmc/articles/PMC5962992/.

240 Meltzer, Lisa J., and Beth A. Mindell. "Behavioral Interventions for Infant Sleep Problems: A Review." *Pediatrics* 137, no. 6 (2016): e20151486. https://doi.org/10.1542/peds.2015-1486.

241 Ezzo, Gary, and Robert Bucknam. *On Becoming Babywise: Giving Your Infant the Gift of Nighttime Sleep.* 5th ed. Colorado Springs: Multnomah Books, 2012.

242 Walker, Katherine. "How Sleep Training Affects Babies." *BBC Future,* March 23, 2022. https://www.bbc.com/future/article/20220322-how-sleep-training-affects-babies.

243 Gene C. Anderson, "Risk in mother-infant separation postbirth," *Image: Journal of Nursing Scholarship* 21 (Winter 1989), 196-99.

244 Feng, Y. Z., Chen, J. T., Hu, Z. Y., Liu, G. X., Zhou, Y. S., Zhang, P., Su, A. X., Yang, S., Zhang, Y. M., Wei, R. M., & Chen, G. H. (2023). Effects of Sleep Reactivity on Sleep Macro-Structure, Orderliness, and Cortisol After Stress: A Preliminary Study in Healthy Young Adults. *Nature and science of sleep, 15,* 533–546. https://doi.org/10.2147/NSS.S415464

245 McKenna, James J. *Safe Infant Sleep: Expert Answers to Your Cosleeping Questions.* Platypus Media, 2020.

246 Smithsonian Magazine. "A History of Cribs and Other Brilliant and Bizarre Inventions for Getting Babies to Sleep." *Smithsonian Magazine.* Accessed September 8, 2024. https://www.smithsonianmag.com/history/history-cribs-and-bizarre-inventions-getting-babies-sleep:contentReference{index=2}.

247 McKenna, James J. *Safe Infant Sleep: Expert Answers to Your Cosleeping Questions.* Platypus Media, 2020.

248 Heller, S. (1997). The Vital Touch: How intimate contact with your baby leads to happier, healthier development. Henry Holt and Company.

249 McKenna, James J. *Safe Infant Sleep: Expert Answers to Your Cosleeping Questions.*

250 La Leche League International. "The Safe Sleep Seven." *La Leche League International,* accessed September 8, 2024. https://llli.org/news/the-safe-sleep-seven/.

251 La Leche League International. "The Safe Sleep Seven." *La Leche League International*, accessed September 8, 2024. https://llli.org/news/the-safe-sleep-seven/.

252 Karp, Harvey. *The Happiest Baby on the Block: The New Way to Calm Crying and Help Your Newborn Baby Sleep Longer.* New York: Bantam Books, 2003.

253 *Heller, S. (1997). The Vital Touch: How intimate contact with your baby leads to happier, healthier development. Henry Holt and Company.*

254 Sears, William, Robert Sears, James Sears, and Martha Sears. *The Baby Sleep Book: The Complete Guide to a Good Night's Rest for the Whole Family.* New York: Little, Brown and Company, 2005.

255 Taking Cara Babies. "Sleep Regressions: Everything You Need to Know." Accessed September 25, 2024. https://takingcarababies.com/sleep-regressions.

256 Small, Meredith F. *Our Babies, Ourselves: How Biology and Culture Shape the Way We Parent.* New York: Anchor Books, 1998.

257 Heller, S. (1997). The Vital Touch: How intimate contact with your baby leads to happier, healthier development. Henry Holt and Company.

258 Weissbluth, Marc. *Healthy Sleep Habits, Happy Child: A Step-by-Step Program for a Good Night's Sleep.* 4th ed. New York: Ballantine Books, 2015.

259 Serrano-Martínez, Maria. *Mediterranean Diet and the Spanish Lifestyle: Cultural and Nutritional Aspects.* Madrid: Editorial Mediterránea, 2018.

260 Cribs for Kids. "AAP Recommendations 2022." *Cribs for Kids.* Accessed September 25, 2024. https://cribsforkids.org/aap-recommendations-2022/.

261 Children's Hospital of Philadelphia. "Sudden Infant Death Syndrome (SIDS)." *Children's Hospital of Philadelphia.* Accessed September 25, 2024. https://www.chop.edu/conditions-diseases/sudden-infant-death-syndrome-sids.

262 Eunice Kennedy Shriver National Institute of Child Health and Human Development. "Safe to Sleep®: Campaign History." *Safe to Sleep.* Accessed September 25, 2024. https://safetosleep.nichd.nih.gov/campaign/history.

263 Baumslag, Naomi, and Dia L. Michels. *Milk, Money, and Madness: The Culture and Politics of Breastfeeding.* Westport, CT: Bergin & Garvey, 1995.

264 Rechtman, L. R., Colvin, J. D., Blair, P. S., & Moon, R. Y. (2014). Sofas and infant mortality. *Pediatrics, 134*(5), e1293–e1300. https://doi.org/10.1542/peds.2014-1543.

265 Welles-Nystrom B. (2005). Co-sleeping as a window into Swedish culture: considerations of gender and health care. *Scandinavian journal of caring sciences, 19*(4), 354–360. https://doi.org/10.1111/j.1471-6712.2005.00358.x.

266 McKenna, James J. "Cosleeping Around the World: How Cultures Practice Safe Infant Sleep." *The Natural Child Project.* Accessed October 10, 2024. https://www.naturalchild.org/articles/james_mckenna/cosleeping_world.html.

267 Million Death Study Collaborators, Bassani, D. G., Kumar, R., Awasthi, S., Morris, S. K., Paul, V. K., Shet, A., Ram, U., Gaffey, M. F., Black, R. E., & Jha, P. (2010). Causes of neonatal and child mortality in India: a nationally representative mortality survey. *Lancet (London, England), 376*(9755), 1853–1860. https://doi.org/10.1016/S0140-6736(10)61461-4

268 Heller, S. (1997). The Vital Touch: How intimate contact with your baby leads to happier, healthier development. Henry Holt and Company.

269 Centers for Disease Control and Prevention. *"About SUID and SIDS." Last modified September 17, 2024.* https://www.cdc.gov/sudden-infant-death/about/index.html.

270 Nelson, Charles A., Nathan A. Fox, Charles H. Zeanah, Peter J. Marshall, Anna T. Smyke, and Dana Guthrie. "Cognitive Recovery in Socially Deprived Young Children: The Bucharest Early Intervention Project." Science 318, no. 5858 (2007): 1937–40. https://doi.org/10.1126/science.1143921.

271 Mary Kay Floeter and William Greenough, "Cerebellar plasticity: modification of Purkinje cell structure by differential rearing in monkeys," *Science 206* (1979):227-29.

272 Heller, S. (1997). The Vital Touch: How intimate contact with your baby leads to happier, healthier development. Henry Holt and Company.

273 Bowlby, John. Attachment and Loss. Basic Books, 1969.

274 Smith, Adam Lane. *Slaying Your Fear: A Guide for People Who Grapple with Insecurity.* Independently published, 2019.

275 Heller, S. (1997). The Vital Touch: How intimate contact with your baby leads to happier, healthier development. Henry Holt and Company.

276 M. Gerber, "The psychomotor development of African children in the first year and the influence of maternal behavior," *Journal of Social Psychology* 47 (1958) 185-95.

277 Heller, S. (1997). The Vital Touch: How intimate contact with your baby leads to happier, healthier development. Henry Holt and Company.

278 Vidal S. Clay, " The effect of culture on mother-child tactile communication" Ph.D diss. Teacher College, Columbia University, 1966.

279 B. B. Whiting and C. P. Edwards, *Children of Different Worlds* (Cambridge Harvard University Press, 1988).

280 Tronick, Edward Z., Gilda A. Morelli, and Paula K. Ivey. 1992. "The Efe Experience: Infants and Toddlers in an African Hunter-Gatherer Culture." In *Child Development in Cultural Context*, edited by Joan B. Lancaster, Jane Bequaert Holmes, and Alice Schlegel, 37–55. New York: Oxford University Press.

281 U.S. Bureau of Labor Statistics. "Average Hours per Day Parents Spent Caring for and Helping Household Children by Employment Status and Sex." Last modified July 2021. https://www.bls.gov/charts/american-time-use/activity-by-parent.htm.

282 Medium. "Why Scandinavians Leave Their Babies to Nap Outside All Year Round." *Modern Parent*, last modified May 19, 2020. https://medium.com/modern-parent/why-scandinavians-leave-their-babies-to-nap-outside-all-year-round-ceee0f00faef.

DEAR SUBURBIA, YOU'VE DISTORTED MOTHERHOOD.

283 Encyclopaedia Britannica. "Forest Dwellings." African Architecture. *Encyclopaedia Britannica*, 12 June 2023. https://www.britannica.com/art/African-architecture/Forest-dwellings.

284 Komisar, Erika. *Being There: Why Prioritizing Motherhood in the First Three Years Matters.* New York: Penguin Random House, 2017.

285 American College of Obstetricians and Gynecologists. "Having a Baby After Age 35: How Aging Affects Fertility and Pregnancy." ACOG, https://www.acog.org/womens-health/faqs/having-a-baby-after-age-35-how-aging-affects-fertility-and-pregnancy. Accessed October 10, 2024.

286 United States Census Bureau. "Fertility Rates Declined for Younger Women, Increased for Older Women." Census Bureau, https://www.census.gov/library/stories/2022/04/fertility-rates-declined-for-younger-women-increased-for-older-women.html. Accessed October 10, 2024.

287 Gordon, S. (2023, August 8). As infertility rates rise, data shows much of the U.S. lives in a fertility desert. WWNO. https://www.wwno.org/public-health/2023-08-08/as-infertility-rates-rise-data-shows-much-of-the-us-lives-in-a-fertility-desert.

288 Kim P. (2016). Human Maternal Brain Plasticity: Adaptation to Parenting. New directions for child and adolescent development, 2016(153), 47–58. https://doi.org/10.1002/cad.20168.

289 Reeves, R. V., & Sawhill, I. V. (2017, May 31). The most educated women are the most likely to be married. *Brookings.* https://www.brookings.edu/articles/the-most-educated-women-are-the-most-likely-to-be-married/.

290 Mineo, L. (2022, January 6). Turns out smarter kids are made, not born. *Harvard Gazette.* Retrieved from https://news.harvard.edu/gazette/story/2022/01/turns-out-smarter-kids-are-made-not-born/.

291 Pew Research Center. "Mothers and Work: What's Ideal?" *Pew Research Center*, August 19, 2013. https://www.pewresearch.org/short-reads/2013/08/19/mothers-and-work-whats-ideal/.

292 American Psychological Association. (2011, December 12). Part-time work helps moms' mental health. APA. https://www.apa.org/news/press/releases/2011/12/working-moms.

293 Woloch, Nancy. *Women and the American Experience.* New York: McGraw-Hill, 2010.

DEAR SUBURBIA, WE NEED FATHERS.

294 Montgomery, Charles. *Happy City: Transforming Our Lives Through Urban Design.* Farrar, Straus and Giroux, 2013.

295 Sandow, E. (2014). Til Work Do Us Part: The Social Fallacy of Long-distance Commuting. *Urban Studies*, 51(3), 526-543. https://doi.org/10.1177/0042098013498280.

296 Singh, A., & Misra, N. (2009). Loneliness, depression and sociability in old age. *Industrial Psychiatry Journal*, 18(1), 51–55. https://doi.org/10.4103/0972-6748.57861.

297 Study: Grandparents Who Babysit Live Longer." CBS News. August 7, 2024. https://www.cbsnews.com/chicago/news/study-grandparents-babysit-live-longer/.

About the Author

Diane Alisa lives in Utah with her husband and two sons. She graduated in theater at Brigham Young University, where she honed her skills and passion for performance. Over the years, she has brought her love for the arts to life through professional and community theater productions, as well as singing, dancing, writing, and playing the piano.

A devoted advocate for mothers, children, and faith in God, Diane is passionate about fostering, joy and a renewed sense of community. Diane looks forward to continuing her work as a storyteller and performer, using her talents to inspire and uplift others in more cohesive communities.

You can connect with me on:

🌐 https://endcardependency.org

🔗 https://instagram.com/diane_alisa

www.ingramcontent.com/pod-product-compliance
Lightning Source LLC
Chambersburg PA
CBHW060125130626
46556CB00006B/2236